Global Political Justice

Edited by
Terry Macdonald and Miriam Ronzoni

Routledge
Taylor & Francis Group
LONDON AND NEW YORK

First published 2014
by Routledge
2 Park Square, Milton Park, Abingdon, Oxon, OX14 4RN

Simultaneously published in the USA and Canada
by Routledge
711 Third Avenue, New York, NY 10017

Routledge is an imprint of the Taylor & Francis Group, an informa business

This book is a reproduction of *Critical Review of International Social and Political Philosophy*, volume 15, issue 5.

British Library Cataloguing in Publication Data
A catalogue record for this book is available from the British Library

ISBN13: 978-0-415-53122-1

Typeset in Times New Roman
by Taylor & Francis Books

Publisher's Note
The publisher accepts responsibility for any inconsistencies that may have arisen during the conversion of this book from journal articles to book chapters, namely the possible inclusion of journal terminology.

Contents

Citation Information

The chapters in this book were originally published in the *Critical Review of International Social and Political Philosophy*, volume 15, issue 5 (November 2012). When citing this material, please use the original page numbering for each article, as follows:

Chapter 1
Introduction: the idea of global political justice
Terry Macdonald and Miriam Ronzoni
Critical Review of International Social and Political Philosophy, volume 15, issue 5 (November 2012) pp. 521–534

Chapter 2
Global actors and public power
Barbara Buckinx
Critical Review of International Social and Political Philosophy, volume 15, issue 5 (November 2012) pp. 535–552

Chapter 3
Global public power: the subject *of principles of global political legitimacy*
Andrew Hurrell and Terry Macdonald
Critical Review of International Social and Political Philosophy, volume 15, issue 5 (November 2012) pp. 553–572

Chapter 4
Two conceptions of state sovereignty and their implications for global institutional design
Miriam Ronzoni
Critical Review of International Social and Political Philosophy, volume 15, issue 5 (November 2012) pp. 573–592

Chapter 5
Assessing the global order: justice, legitimacy, or political justice?
Laura Valentini

Critical Review of International Social and Political Philosophy, volume 15, issue 5 (November 2012) pp. 593–612

Chapter 6
Creating cosmopolitans
Patti Tamara Lenard
Critical Review of International Social and Political Philosophy, volume 15, issue 5 (November 2012) pp. 613–630

Chapter 7
The injustice of territoriality
Paul Muldoon
Critical Review of International Social and Political Philosophy, volume 15, issue 5 (November 2012) pp. 631–648

Chapter 8
Cosmopolitan justice and the league of democracies
Avia Pasternak
Critical Review of International Social and Political Philosophy, volume 15, issue 5 (November 2012) pp. 649–666

Chapter 9
On the concept of climate debt: its moral and political value
Jonathan Pickering and Christian Barry
Critical Review of International Social and Political Philosophy, volume 15, issue 5 (November 2012) pp. 667–685

Please direct any queries you may have about the citations to
clsuk.permissions@cengage.com

Introduction: the idea of global political justice

Terry Macdonald[a] and Miriam Ronzoni[b]

[a]*School of Social and Political Sciences, University of Melbourne, Australia*
[b]*Centre for Advanced Studies 'Justitia Amplificata', University of Frankfurt, Germany*

Introduction

The past 30 years have witnessed the flourishing of normative international political theory as a new field of research with its own agenda, debates, and methodological disputes. While there is increasing acceptance of the idea that global institutions require justification just as much as domestic ones, there is still wide disagreement about whether the specific normative standards for building and justifying institutions should be identical, or even roughly equivalent, in these two political domains. Developing a better understanding of what is distinctive about the problems raised by the global political order, and which conceptual and methodological approaches are best suited to address them, thus represents one of the most pressing challenges in this theoretical field.

Much discussion on these topics has been framed as debate about appropriate standards of 'global justice' – reflecting the wider dominance of the concept of 'justice' as a lens for normative political theorizing since Rawls. Moreover, the global justice literature has been overwhelmingly focused to date on questions about the *distributive* aspects of justice, such as: what is a just global distribution of the world's resources? Is inequality as significant a normative problem globally as it is domestically? Less attention has been given to questions about how the global political order (through which the production and distribution of goods is institutionalized) is itself to be constituted – most fundamentally, how *power and conflict* are to be managed and institutionally channelled in securing the background conditions for particular social and economic relationships and distributions, and how *cooperative arrangements for collective decision-making and action* should be structured to facilitate this process. Given that practical dilemmas concerning the institutional management of power, conflict and political cooperation have played a central role in shaping both the history of international politics over the last century, and intellectual agendas of international relations scholarship during that period, it is perhaps surprising that they have not achieved comparable prominence in normative debates about global politics.

The aim of this collection is to take some steps towards remedying this neglect. Some aspects of these questions have been tackled already within literatures on global democracy, and this work has contributed a rich set of theoretical ideas that can help to direct the analyses developed in this collection. However, we believe that tackling these questions exclusively through the conceptual lens of democracy – beginning with some normative ideal of this, and asking how it can best be realized in the global domain – circumscribes too narrowly the range of normative questions about the global political order that are opened to critical scrutiny. It assumes from the outset too much of what we believe needs to be investigated – namely what range of institutional arrangements might be justifiable, and what methods of justification will be most appropriate, in the global context.

For our purposes here, we therefore adopt the more general concept of *global justice* as a starting point for our analysis, and we label the narrower bundle of political questions and challenges we wish to focus on as constituting the topic of *global political justice*. Whether and how democratic institutions should play a role in the realization of global political justice then remains an open question for our contributors to explore. We also note that the concept of 'justice' itself is not beyond critical interrogation, and we accordingly adopt the concept of global political justice more as a common point of departure from the focus on distributive issues than as a fixed analytical framework; as such, our contributors are invited to consider, where appropriate, whether the concept of 'justice' – as distinct from, say, 'legitimacy' – does in fact provide the most suitable lens for normative analysis of the institutional management of power, conflict and political cooperation within the global political order. Finally, the contours of the value of legitimacy itself are controversial – should we conceive of it as a weaker moral standard than justice, or as a value with its own distinct normative content? Our contributors were invited to address this conceptual issue, as well.

In applying the label of *global political justice* to our topic, we mean to contrast 'political' justice mainly with 'distributive' justice, but we recognize that the line separating these categories is far from clear. Since our primary aim in this collection is to make progress in thinking about substantive problems of global political justice – that is, questions about the justice of specific political practices and institutions, and the normative standards by which they are regulated – we must provide at least a preliminary account (a working agenda, as it were) of which practices, institutions, and normative standards we regard as characteristically *political*. In this introduction, we attempt to demarcate more precisely what we take to be *political* about global political justice, and to clarify the relationship between our topic and a set of related methodological and normative debates (on global 'democracy', political 'realism', and 'non-ideal theory'), which in different ways draw political problems about power, conflict and cooperation into theoretical analysis of global justice. In the course of doing so, we also hope to highlight some reasons for viewing the topic of global political justice as one of great significance, and deserving of greater attention than it has so far received.

Why do we need a more *political* theory of global justice?

At first glance it might seem puzzling for us to suggest that the global justice literature is not now sufficiently 'political' in focus, given that recent debates on global distributive justice have mushroomed to a large extent *as a response to* the observation that we are now in what can be called the global 'circumstances of politics' (Bohman 2004, Laborde 2010). As Cécile Laborde (2010, p. 50) characterizes these political circumstances, they involve 'complex new forms of unchecked arbitrary power exercised across national borders: more and more people are vulnerable to decisions made from afar, anonymously, and over which they have little control'. Much literature on global distributive justice recognizes that distributive duties across borders arise largely because global inequality is produced through institutionalized forms of power that are problematic and therefore call for justification. In other words, the fact that global justice has become such a prominent topic of investigation to begin with reflects a widespread acceptance of some underlying assumptions about the political character of the existing global order.

The claim that the current global order constitutes a political sphere in the relevant sense is closely associated with (one or both of) two more specific observations. On the one hand, the kinds of social conflicts typically in need of institutional 'taming', and the kinds of shared social problems typically solved through collective political decision-making institutions, now occur beyond sovereign territorial boundaries; consequently, we confront the problem of how to overcome these social conflicts and challenges through *the development of new* political institutions at the transnational and at the global level. On the other hand, many problematic forms of power are *already* being exercised at those levels. As in domestic contexts, these forms of power, from a normative perspective, call for justification and control, so as to make them capable of gaining widespread acceptability among those subject to and called upon to support them (linked to what some call 'legitimacy') and/or capable of achieving fuller moral justifiability (what many call 'justice').

Such claims about the political character of the global order have become very prominent in recent debates about global justice because of the implications they may have for our thinking about the scope and content of duties of distributive justice across borders. But these claims raise another important question that has so far received less theoretical attention: to the extent that we agree we are in the 'global circumstances of politics' and confront a global political order in need of justification, why do we not investigate the normative credentials of this underlying political order *directly* (rather than merely making assumptions or assertions about these matters as a preamble to normative theorizing about our duties of global socio-economic justice)? We believe that we should do so: there is a need to investigate more directly and systematically which features of the global order call for distinctively political forms of normative critique and institutional response, and to consider what should follow from this for our practical attitudes and decision-making in relation to these.

To some readers it may not yet be entirely clear how we take these questions of global political justice to be problematically sidelined from mainstream distributive theories of global justice. After all, this body of work has deep roots in a theoretical literature on justice originating with Rawls, who himself claimed his account of justice to be fundamentally political in a certain sense. So it may help for us to explain further how the *theory of political justice* we are concerned with here is distinct from the *political theory of justice* for which Rawls is so well known. Much has been written about the sense in which Rawls's theory of justice can best be understood as political in character – by Rawls himself in his *Political Liberalism* (1996), and by two decades of subsequent commentators. We cannot attempt to survey or add substantially to this vast literature here; instead we want to highlight one quite general feature of Rawls's political theory of justice which helps to illuminate the distinction between the kinds of political problems central to Rawls's analysis, on the one hand, and the kinds of political problems we wish to bundle under the heading of political justice, on the other.

At a very general level, we can say that Rawls's theory of justice is political in the sense that it takes a particular kind of political society, or political order (in the case of his *Political Liberalism*, a democratic society operating within the institutional framework of a liberal state) as the starting point for the theoretical enterprise. The liberal-democratic political order provides a starting-point for Rawls's theory in two fundamental senses. First, the liberal-democratic political order is assumed as a background condition in identifying the *practical political problems* that the theory of justice is tasked with solving: the fundamental institutions constitutive of the liberal-democratic political order are called the 'basic structure of society', and the practical focus is placed on the problem of how socio-economic burdens and benefits should be distributed within and through this institutional structure. Second, the liberal-democratic political order, and the fundamental political values that underpin it (the 'public political culture', in Rawls's terms), are taken as building blocks for the *method of normative justification* itself that identifies and validates a particular conception of justice (as the ideals of public reason and overlapping consensus, and more generally the idea of a 'political, not metaphysical' conception of justice, suggest).

A significant consequence of this kind of approach to the theory of justice is that *the fundamental constitutive features of the political order itself* – the set of practices and processes that constitute its basic institutions and social fabric, and the relationships of power that sustain them – is placed beyond the critical jurisdiction of the theory. For if the basic institutional and social features of the political order are to serve as firm foundations for the theory of distributive justice (as part of the 'public political culture' of liberal-democratic states which constitutes Rawls's methodological starting point in *Political Liberalism*), then they must be taken in some sense as fixed, and not themselves presented as primary targets for critical normative interrogation in the theory. As a result, proceeding with a theory of justice that is political in the Rawlsian sense (a theory of justice that is 'political' as distinct from 'metaphysical', as Rawls puts it) turns out to discourage systematic theorizing about justice that is political in the different sense of *investigating the justice or injustice of an underlying political order* – its constitutive institutions, and underlying social norms and relationships of power.

It is this latter kind of political theory of justice – theory that investigates the justice or injustice of an underlying political order, rather than the distributive patterns within it – that we are here calling theorizing about of political justice. This kind of theory is not (necessarily or only) political in its theoretical foundations (though it might be that too), but rather is political in *the practical target of its normative investigation* – that is, in the nature of the subject it is aiming to regulate with its substantive normative principles of justice.

At the present time, questions about political justice, understood in these terms, arise with greater urgency at the level of global politics than in domestic contexts – for the simple reason that the fundamental constitutive features of the political order are much less stable and more deeply contested in the global case. In the case of domestic theories of justice focused on the problem of how to distribute social burdens and benefits among citizens of a settled liberal-democratic political order, members of this group generally accept the overarching liberal-democratic political order as legitimate or justified, and this acceptance is relatively stable. At the very least, this stable political acceptance of the political order ensures that a theory of justice taking elements of this order as foundational axioms will have a certain pragmatic value in facilitating a workable political consensus on normative principles to regulate the common political life of this group of citizens. In the *global* case, however, there is not a political order in place with a comparable level of political stability and wide acceptance among participants, which could be invoked in an equivalent fashion to provide foundations for an analogously political theory of global justice.

Disanalogies between domestic and global political orders arise at three levels in particular. First, normative inquiry and justification cannot begin in the global case with the assumption of consensus about the boundaries or definitive features of the *political community or demos* – as Rawls begins with the assumption of a settled 'closed society' in his domestically-focused *Theory of Justice* (1999) – since the criteria for delineating political communities of different kinds, and according them special forms of political recognition and normative status, is itself a matter of significant controversy. Second, we cannot begin in the global case with an assumption of consensus about the appropriate *political subject of principles of justice* (as Rawls begins in his *Theory of Justice* with the stipulation of the 'basic structure of society' as subject) since there is very little clarity as to what range of institutional forms should count as part of this structure in the global case, in the absence of *both*: 1) a strong and stable world state, or constitutional equivalent that could supply a firm institutional core; and 2) a clear account of which forms of transnational power should be bound by institutional regulation to begin with. Third, we cannot even begin with the assumption of a shared commitment to the liberal-democratic norms of individual liberty and equality (as Rawls does in his *Political Liberalism*), because these basic political values do not attract anything close to the same degree of endorsement on a global scale as they do within stable liberal-democratic states, and – more fundamentally – because it is not yet clear that democratic institutionalization is what the global order *requires* (this is one substantive question that a theory of global political justice should investigate).

An important implication of this is that a theory of justice focused on the global domain cannot take a settled underlying political order for granted – as a political foundation for the theory – to the same extent as this seems to be appropriate in many domestic contexts. This means that questions about the structure of the underlying political order must themselves be subject to direct normative scrutiny, as a starting point for a theory of global justice. As part of this, the theory of global political justice needs to confront questions about the implications of *disagreement* on these fundamental matters – that is, about the just scope and character of political community, the just structure of fundamental political institutions, and the justification of fundamental political values. Disagreement on these matters is likely to have particular significance for normative thinking about the justification of global arrangements for practical decision-making about the control and channelling of power, and the management of collective decision-making processes, since conventional normative and institutional solutions to these problems (such as various democratic models) sometimes presuppose agreement on, or at least stable solutions to, these matters as a starting-point for their justification and design, and it is not altogether clear how these should fare where such agreement or stability has not been established.

The claim that political questions of this kind should be at the forefront of debates about global justice can be augmented by considering how central such questions have been to the real-world political dilemmas, conflicts, and projects that have shaped international history over the last century, and to the themes central to the work of the empirical scholars of international relations who study this political domain. The normative ideas that have driven both institution-building projects in international political practice, and intellectual agendas in international relations scholarship, have been most centrally preoccupied with the political problems of achieving international order and cooperation in the face of significant moral disagreement, conflicts of material interests, and the abuse of political power (particularly in relations among states, but also increasingly in the decision-making structures and activities of powerful international organizations and non-state actors). It is this shared set of political preoccupations that unifies otherwise divergent 'Realist' literatures on the stabilizing and disciplining effects of an international 'balance of power', 'Liberal Internationalist' literatures on the conditions for international cooperation and the rational design of institutions, and 'Constructivist' and 'English School' literatures focused on understanding the sociological and historical processes through which particular international orders are created, transformed, and legitimated.

Much international relations scholarship focused on these political problems is social-scientific or historical in approach, and does not attempt to undertake directly *normative* analysis. Nonetheless, these international relations research programmes – and the real international problems and projects to which they have responded – have been strongly shaped by normative commitments to particular visions of global political order, insofar as the questions they have posed and answered have been geared towards the goal of finding solutions of particular kinds (as members of decision-making communities and collectives) to the practical problems of global power, order, and cooperation that we have been discussing. The problem, however, is that many fundamental elements of the normative visions and ideals driving these political elements of international practice and scholarship remain (relatively) critically uninspected and under-theorized – relative, that is, to the level of critical scrutiny and analysis theorists have focused on the normative ideals and principles guiding the distribution of social goods. A theory of political justice, then, is intended to serve as a corrective to this existing theoretical deficiency, and develop more rigorous and systematic normative frameworks for guiding practical political deliberation and decision-making about the most justified institutional responses to problems of global power and order, conflict and cooperation, stability and transformation.

How can we begin to build better theories of global political justice?

So far we have given a brief account of the range of political problems upon which we wish to focus through the concept of global political justice; but while we have indicated how these have received less attention than they deserve within the mainstream global justice literature, it is of course not true that these sorts of political problems have been neglected entirely across the wider field of normative political theory. There are a number of theoretical literatures that do highlight problems of power, conflict, and order in important and relevant ways – most notably those framed as discussions of 'global democracy', 'political realism', and 'non-ideal' theory. It is helpful to consider what insights these established literatures might bring to bear upon the problems at hand, as well as the limitations of these literatures for our purposes.

First, the literature on 'cosmopolitan' or 'global' *democracy* offers a range of institutional models designed to solve the problems of controlling political power and fostering stable and justified processes for collective decision-making at a global level – which are important aspects of the topic of global political justice as we have characterized it. But there are some compelling reasons for thinking that the wider range of political problems and dilemmas that we have set out above cannot be adequately addressed through exclusively democratic theoretical lenses.

One reason for this is that many proposed blueprints for democratic global orders incorporate insufficient analysis of whether the democratic institutional forms that deliver political justice within nation-states can achieve the same result when dealing with the very different forms of power and collective political agency that structure the global political domain. The problems we wish to highlight here are associated with familiar challenges to the project of global democracy posed by critics who claim that global democracy is unviable because we lack the kind of demos that provides a foundation for democracy within nation-states, and relatedly that we cannot have global democracy without a world state (or functional equivalent, in the form of a constitutionalized framework of global law) to provide the focal-point for democratic control and accountability, and to facilitate processes of collective democratic decision-making.

To some extent these challenges can be confronted from within the democratic tradition, through creative thinking about how to adapt democratic principles and institutional designs more carefully to the different sociological background conditions prevailing in the global political domain. But the challenges cannot be fully overcome via such strategies because it is wrong to think that these problems – about the character of the demos and the institutional framework for collective decision-making and agency at a global level – are merely technical or instrumental in character. Rather, these challenges present normative as well as technical problems for the global democratic project; they have implications for the justifiability or legitimacy of democratic institutions in the global context, not only its feasibility or most functionally effective institutional form.

These challenges press us to address some deeper normative questions – for instance those regarding the constitutive criteria for political communities with justified claims to democratic self-determination, the relationships between these criteria and the sociological or institutional preconditions for meaningful collective agency (of democratic or non-democratic kinds), the normative character of political order and its relationship to other political values such as justice and democracy, and so on. In the context of such debates, the question of whether the forms of global institutionalization that we need to solve problems of global political justice are of a democratic kind remains open. If the issue at stake is how to bind and control problematic forms of global public power, then only a better investigation of the particular characteristics of these forms of power and the specific problems they raise can tell us whether the best way to bind them is through democratic control, through arbitration, through thicker international juridification (via international courts), or through yet another institutional strategy.

Tackling these large normative questions requires us to revisit some of the foundational questions in social and political thought that preoccupied many of the classical thinkers in the modern Western tradition, whose ideas helped shape the development of nation-state-based political orders in domestic political life. In so doing, we may have much to learn from the growing body of theoretical work sometimes labelled as 'political realism', which attempts to integrate insights from classical political thinkers, such as Hobbes among others, back into the contemporary field of political theory so heavily influenced in recent times by Rawlsian theories of justice. One potentially very useful idea emanating from this contemporary 'realist' literature, but with deep roots in a longer theoretical tradition, has been raised by Bernard Williams in his short but evocative essay on 'Realism and Moralism in Political Theory' (2005). This is the idea that the most fundamental normative quality for a political order to possess is not justice or democracy but rather *legitimacy* – a normative quality that will under some historical and sociological conditions create normative demand for democracy and other liberal institutions, but is more basic than and not reducible to them. While highly suggestive, Williams's normative account of legitimacy is not a fully-developed theory, and moreover its Hobbesian influence gives it a very state-centric flavour, making its implications for normative thinking about the global political order somewhat opaque. But it is nonetheless helpful in pressing us to reflect more systematically on the deeper normative commitments that shape the validity and stability of underlying political orders – upon the foundations of which just democratic institutional schemes can sometimes be built – and to evaluate the deeper historical and sociological preconditions for our normative commitment to the justice of democratic institutions in this light.

Another important reason why we cannot expect the theory of global democracy to resolve all the issues of global political justice we have identified is that we believe that the *methodology* employed in much mainstream literature on global democracy leaves it poorly-equipped to offer practical guidance on many of these political problems. This is a function of certain methodological features that mainstream democratic theory shares in common with what Rawls called 'ideal-theoretical' approaches to the theory of distributive justice. More specifically, both frame the normative problem they seek to address in terms of specifying the content of some kind of ideal social or political *end-state*: a perfectly justified system of social holdings in the case of global distributive justice, and an equally perfectly justified system of participatory rights in the case of global democracy. While theories (of distributive justice and democracy) that aim to specify the content of such ideal social states-of-affairs or systems are commonly understood to be instances of ideal theory, the methodological alternative to ideal theory is seen to be what Rawls called 'non-ideal theory' – namely the theory of what we should do when full justice cannot be achieved due to the non-compliance of some social actors with principles of justice (or, on some accounts of non-ideal theory, contextually-specific constraints or obstacles of other kinds).

The problem with these methodological strategies is that they do not equip us with tools for tackling questions that are concerned *neither* with specifying the content of ideal end-states, *nor* with figuring out what to do when these ideal end-states cannot be achieved in the here and now, but rather with a third kind of problem – namely, how to manage conflict and organize collective decision-making when *we do not know (or cannot agree) on what should count as an ideal end-state*, specified in terms of an ideal set of holdings or in terms of an ideal set of participatory rights and political procedures. The kind of uncertainty or disagreement we have in mind here extends beyond 'reasonable disagreement' on specific matters relating to public policy or personal conduct of the kind that is permitted within a pluralist liberal society on a Rawlsian model of justice; we are talking here instead about uncertainty or disagreement in relation to the much more fundamental political matters concerning the basic features of a justified political order, of the kind we discussed above.

The problem of how to manage political conflict and collective decision-making in the face of this kind of disagreement and uncertainty cannot be dealt with within the framework of so-called ideal theory – at least not as this is characterized on the Rawlsian account – since there agreement on these fundamental matters is required as a foundation for the justification of particular ideal end-states. But nor can theoretical responses to this problem be characterized as a form of non-ideal theory, since the very concept of the non-ideal presupposes knowledge or agreement about the content of the ideal, and this is often precisely what is lacking when problems of political justice arise. In the scenarios dealt with by conventional non-ideal theory, the ideal political destination is known, but we lack the motivational resources (or other basic favourable conditions) necessary to reach it, and our task is to consider how to get ourselves as close as possible to this destination (by determining what counts as 'as close as possible', and what is the fairest and most justified way of getting there). In contrast, the scenarios to be dealt with by the theory of global political justice, as we have characterized it, take a different form: they are scenarios in which we understand what kind of trouble we want to get out of, but not what ultimate end-point we want to reach. In this case we need a method of theory-building that offers us a roadmap out of our present impasse, without demanding that this map will also mark a route towards a final destination. This is neither ideal nor non-ideal theory as they are conventionally characterized, and to understand how to build a theory of this kind it is therefore likely to be necessary to revisit some of our underlying methodological ideas, concerned with the nature and most suitable strategies of political justification.

The contributions of the papers in this collection to the theory of global political justice

The papers in this collection approach the fundamental problems of global political justice, as we have characterized these here, from a number of perspectives, and contribute insights on a range of conceptual, methodological, and substantive dimensions of these problems.

First, these authors make different use of the concepts of *justice*, *political justice*, and *legitimacy*, in conceptualizing and grappling with the problems of power, conflict, and collective action underlying the constitutive structures of the global order that are the focus of our interest here. Two of the papers – by Valentini, and by Hurrell and Macdonald – tackle the conceptual question of how the problems of political *justice* are related to the problem of political *legitimacy*, which is sometimes identified as distinct from certain normative ideas of justice and justification. Four of the papers – by Ronzoni, Valentini, Lenard, and Pickering and Barry – also develop arguments that grapple with and shed some light upon the complex interface between *distributive* and *political* dimensions of the problem of global justice. In particular, some focus on motivations and capacity for political action (Lenard, and Pickering and Barry), whereas others focus on the *priority* of political problems (understood as problems of power regulation and decision-making mechanisms) over distributive ones (Ronzoni and Valentini).

All contributions to this collection engage with several of the fundamental *substantive* normative questions that we have identified as central to the problem of global political justice. First, we have three papers dealing with what are essentially boundary questions with respect to the constitutive elements of the global political order: Hurrell and Macdonald, and Buckinx, set out different though related accounts of global *public power* as a basis for understanding the character of the *subject* of our regulative political principles for global life, while Muldoon tackles the question of how the global political community itself should be constituted, and the limits of our capacity to answer this fundamental question in properly normative terms. Two papers – by Ronzoni and Pasternak – address the critically important question of the role that states should play in the pursuit of collective interests and the regulation of conflict and the abuse of power within the global domain. Ronzoni argues that the main political injustice in the current configuration of the global system might well be the threat it poses to the effective problem-solving capacity of states and that global institutional design should aim at removing the gravest obstacles to 'positive' sovereignty. Pasternak considers what special capacities and responsibilities might lie with *democratic* states, specifically, in advancing the aims of global political justice. Finally, Lenard, and Pickering and Barry, focus on the role of non-institutional political practices – practices of collective identification and imagination (Lenard) and practices of political rhetoric and conceptual 'framing' (Pickering and Barry) – in shaping and sustaining political commitments to certain duties of global justice.

Finally, some of the papers also address *methodological* questions concerning how we should approach the task of designing and justifying global institutions. Valentini connects her conceptual argument about the relationship between norms of justice and political legitimacy to a methodological distinction between ideal and non-ideal theory. Hurrell and Macdonald connect the value of political legitimacy to a form of political justification that begins with existing forms of political agency and identity and uses these as the basis for justification of the institutions that these existing agents create to manage conflicts and abuses of power that emerge among them, and to facilitate collective action in pursuit of their shared goals. Resonating with some aspects of this argument, Muldoon questions the capacity of justificatory arguments to extend their reach down to the constitution of political societies themselves, suggesting that political justification itself may only be possible within a political order in which a certain sociological status of citizenship has already been achieved.

Acknowledgements

This collection developed from a workshop on 'Global Political Justice' held at the Monash University Prato Centre, in Prato, Italy, 2008. In addition to the authors of these papers we thank the following participants in this workshop for their intellectual contributions to the project: Charles Beitz, Jennifer Rubenstein, Cristina Lafont, Kate Macdonald, Mathias Koenig-Archibugi, Luis Cabrera, Zofia Stemplowska, AJ Julius, Eszter Kollar, Raffaele Marchetti, and Daniele Archibugi.

Notes on contributors

Terry Macdonald is a Senior Lecturer in Politics and International Relations at the University of Melbourne, having previously held positions as Junior Research Fellow and Lecturer at Merton College, Oxford University, Research Fellow at the Centre for Applied Philosophy and Public Ethics at the ANU, and Lecturer in Politics at Monash University. Her previous publications include *Global Stakeholder Democracy* (Oxford University Press, 2008).

Miriam Ronzoni is a Research Fellow at the Centre for Advanced Studies 'Justitia Amplificata', in Frankfurt. Her work mainly focuses on issues of global justice and constructivism. Her publications include *Social Justice, Global Dynamics: Theoretical and Empirical Perspectives* (Routledge, 2011, co-edited with Ayelet Banai and Christian Schemmel) well as research articles appeared in journals such as *Philosophy and Public Affairs*, *Politics, Philosophy, and Economics*, and *Review of International Studies*.

References

Bohman, J., 2004. Republican cosmopolitanism. *The journal of political philosophy*, 12 (3), 336–352.

Laborde, C., 2010. Republicanism and global justice. a sketch. *European journal of political theory*, 9 (1), 48–69.

Rawls, J., 1996. *Political liberalism*. New York: Columbia University Press.

Rawls, J., 1999. *A theory of justice*. Rev. ed. Oxford: Oxford University Press.

Williams, B., 2005. Realism and moralism in political theory. *In:* Geoffrey Hawthorn, ed. *In the beginning was the deed: realism and moralism in political argument*. Princeton, NJ: Princeton University Press, 1–17.

Global actors and public power

Barbara Buckinx

Institute of Advanced Studies in the Humanities, Goethe University Frankfurt, Germany

Prominent recent scholarship in global political justice has focused on creating conceptual space for international NGOs – and sometimes also corporations and states – as fully-fledged participants in global governance. While acknowledging the achievements of international non-state actors, I argue that core global governance tasks – of global distribution, regulation or administration – should not be assigned to them. Drawing from neo-republican theory, I contend that such actors fall short of the formal criteria that are necessary for constituting a global public actor, because they do not have a global function and orientation. The distinction between public and private actors matters, since it conditions our expectations for them: both categories of actors are asked to avoid dominating individuals, but public actors must, in addition, protect individuals from third-party domination.

In domestic republican theory, individual liberty is protected in and by the state. As the public actor that is responsible for matters of governance, the state takes on the task of ensuring that individuals are shielded from the dominating power of other individuals, corporations, and organizations in civil society. In the absence of a world state, it is not clear what actor ought to assume the role of 'public power' globally. Scholars such as Archibugi (2008), Dryzek (2006, 2008), Kaldor (2003), Kuper (2004), and Macdonald (2008) have emphasized the role of global civil society organizations in (democratizing) global governance. I take a critical look at the global political role of non-state actors, including international value-driven organizations such as non-governmental organizations (NGOs), churches, and unions and for-profit organizations such as transnational corporations (TNCs). The increased participation in global governance of value-driven organizations, in particular, has been perceived as beneficial. However, while I agree that certain international non-state actors might have a salutary effect on practices of global governance, I will argue that core global governance tasks connected to the protection of liberty – global distribution, regulation or administration – should not be assigned to them. Instead, we ought to expect only those global actors that are more properly speaking public in nature – such as the global institutions of the United Nations (UN) system – to dedicate themselves to protecting individual liberty, and I suggest that we redouble our efforts to help them improve the way that they do so.

I.

One way to answer the question of who should govern the world is to evaluate particular global actors, and to ask of those actors that already do the most 'good' – according to a particular standard, say, of freedom or fairness – that they take on tasks of governance. However, this is not my approach. First, in the current world order, *all* global actors – value-driven organizations, states, global institutions, and TNCs – frequently have pernicious influence. At times, TNCs pollute the local environment (e.g. Kurzman 1987), global institutions impose programs for development that reduce rather than increase economic growth (e.g. Vreeland 2003), international NGOs offer humanitarian aid that is ill-advised or ineffective (e.g. Maren 1997), and states[1] conduct wars of aggression (e.g. Karsch 2002, de Waal 2003) – each doing so at will, without regard to the wishes of the affected populations. Global actors *of all kinds* are frequently oppressive ones, and individuals around the world suffer when they interact with them. Of course, some global actors are more oppressive than others. International NGOs may be among the most effective and benign global actors, but, as I see it, their superior performance need not imply that they must be at the forefront of global governance.

Indeed, I leave aside the question of the various actors' shortcomings or relative superiority, and I ask instead what it means to ask a particular kind of actor to take on global governance tasks. To put it differently, I ask whether it is *appropriate* to expect of actors such as international NGOs that they adopt as a core function the (improved) governance of the world. Relying on republican theory, I will argue that actors such as international NGOs and corporations fall short of the formal criteria that are necessary for constituting a global public actor. The distinction between public and private actors matters greatly, since it conditions our expectations for them: both categories of actors are asked to avoid dominating individuals, but public actors must, in addition, also protect individuals from third-party domination.

In domestic republican theory, the domestic actor that is responsible for tasks of governance is the *state*, and it has this role by virtue of its *public* nature (e.g. Pettit 1997, Skinner 1998, 2008, pp. 83–101, Honohan 2002, Maynor 2003 pp. 13–30). Generally, the term 'public', as an adjective, refers to that which concerns the people as a whole, within the boundaries of the republic. It presumes the existence of a public, as a noun, since, as Richardson (2002, pp. 180–181) argues, only if there is a public does it make sense to 'set about drawing lines between what properly concerns it (and hence is "public" in one sense) and what does not (and hence is by contrast "private") or between what is addressed to it (and hence "public" in another sense) and what is not'. The public life of the polity is 'the life of the community as that is based in matters of common knowledge or belief' (Pettit 1997, p. 165), with individuals knowing that something is the case but also knowing that it is commonly known that it is the case, and so forth.

The state consists of a set of formal 'public' institutions, which have a set of administrative functions of both a regulatory and distributive nature. Such institutions ensure that certain goods are made available to the community as a whole, without (non-reasoned) restrictions; so-called 'public goods' (e.g. Miller 1999, p. 10). They also adjudicate claims among actors within the boundaries of the state, and they regulate the behavior of domestic actors. They view themselves self-consciously as public agents, that is, as agents primarily responsible for matters related to the polity as a whole (cf. Dewey 1954). The state is a *public* power within domestic boundaries insofar as it imposes an institutional structure and rules and regulations on the citizenry.

In other words, a state is public because its function is co-extensive with the polity and it includes among its primary tasks duties of administration and regulation, and the distribution of public goods. It also conceives of itself as a public actor, fulfilling a public function. Crucially, as a public actor, the state must reduce the vulnerability of its citizens to domination by others – such private citizens, factions, or corporations – in society. In republican theory, domination is akin to subjection or servitude: a person is dominated when she is not effectively shielded from the ability of other actors to interfere on an arbitrary basis in her decision-making. An intervention is arbitrary when it is carried out on an arbitrary basis: what matters is the procedure by which the decision is made, rather than the extent to which the outcome of the decision happens to accord with the wishes of the affected (Pettit 1997, Maynor 2003, Bohman 2007).

The state must ensure that private actors in society are unable to interfere arbitrarily in the lives of its citizens, and it pursues this task in various ways. It regulates the economic and other activity of powerful individuals and groups within society, so that no individual or collective actor in society can dominate any other. A constitutional regime of law can tackle the problem of private domination by affirming the equal status of all citizens irrespective of their power and status, and by allowing citizens and government officials to use the (criminal) justice system to address instances of domination by private actors. The state also distributes goods, such as medical care and education, so that individuals have the necessary means to resist submission to the power of others. Finally, it administers these and other programs that are deemed to be in the public interest. We might call this wide-ranging task that of ‘freedom protection’. By virtue of its character as a public actor, and by way of its governance practices of administration, regulation and distribution, the state aims to protect individuals from private sources of domination. In addition, if it is to avoid becoming a *dominating* public actor, the state has to be controlled by the citizenry in how it interferes. We might call this straightforward ‘domination avoidance’.

In addition to the state, there are private actors such as corporations, NGOs, religious organizations, political factions, and the like. Private actors behave, and are expected to behave – and be constituted – very differently from public actors. They do not tend to take on tasks of a public nature; they do not administer public programs or regulate the behavior of other actors in society. Moreover, we usually are, and ought to be, reluctant to ask them to take on such tasks. Since their scope is usually not co-extensive with that of the polity, they cannot be relied upon to serve, speak for, or represent the citizenry as a whole. Instead of acting on behalf of the polity, they act, and are expected to act, on behalf of the special interests that they represent. Relatedly, they do not expose themselves to the kind of scrutiny that we subject the state to. It would be difficult to hold such actors democratically accountable, and even more difficult to exert control over their rule. In this context, any declaration on their part of an intention to govern the polity would rightly be met with suspicion. This is not to deny that private actors are of great value. They tend to enrich the lives of their members greatly, and they may indirectly invigorate public life more generally. However, they cannot and should not be asked to take on tasks of governance and protect individuals from domination. In the case of private actors, the relevant standard of non-domination is that of ‘domination avoidance’; they ought not to dominate others.

Private and public actors are thus held to different standards. The former can certainly be required to refrain from dominating individuals, but only the latter must serve as public power, restraining the power of the aforementioned private actors without becoming sources of domination themselves. Both categories of actors must avoid dominating individuals, but public actors must, in addition, also take on the task of securing the non-domination of individuals.

II.

Let me now explore whether it might be possible to define what it means for a global actor to be ‘public’ in an analogous fashion. If this works, we could then determine whether international NGOs should be expected to perform functions of global governance – and whether they should merely avoid dominating individuals or also protect individuals from third-party domination – by asking whether they are *public* or *private*.

Since there is no world state, no actor exists which, in the global sphere, resembles the state in its domestic role. In light of this disanalogy, it might be advisable to depart from neo-republican theory, and instead expect *all* global actors to meet the exact same standard of non-domination: say, that of 'domination avoidance'. Like Macdonald's (2008) recent cosmopolitan-democratic account of global governance, I could define as 'public' those global actors which affect the lives of individuals in some relevant way, and such actors could be equally responsible for helping to bring about a state of affairs in which the values that our respective approaches espouse – democracy and autonomy, and non-domination – are maximized. However, I believe that the distinction can be drawn differently. In what follows, I suggest that certain global actors are more properly 'state-like' or public than others, and that their designation of public or private need not depend on the extent of their impact on individuals' lives.

Before I continue, however, let me first explain my taxonomy[2] of global actors in a bit more detail. By global actors, I mean actors that operate beyond the domestic realm, in the domain of the world order. They may be 'international', 'transnational', or truly 'global' (cf. Mann 1997, p. 475). The most salient category of global actors are for-profit actors, primarily TNCs, which are headquartered in one country but have offices, manufacturing plants and/or affiliates in multiple parts of the world. The second category of global actors is that of value-driven actors such as international NGOs, churches, or trade unions. Humanitarian aid organizations such as Mercy Corps have significant economic clout and fund an array of projects, from microloans to reproductive health education, in countries around the world.[3] Third, we have global institutions, such as those in the UN system, which facilitate cooperation, integration and harmonization across states, and in a range of policy and issue areas, from climate change to peace and security. Some are formal, treaty-based regional or international institutions, but there are also less formal transnational networks, which involve informal cooperation among states, and institutions that allow for both governmental and non-governmental participation. Finally, there is the state. Neo-republican theory tends to focus more on the state's role as a domestic actor, but it is undeniably the case that states also act in global politics. Some of their interactions with other actors are non-dominating, while others include arbitrary interference on their part, or take place against the background of their capacity to interfere in such a way. States are engaged in a wide range of global activity; they cooperate with other states, establish international institutions, and exert influence over the global actions of for-profit and value-based organizations. Many states also have the military capability to invade other countries.

Having enumerated the four categories of global actors, the question remains whether any of these actors represent something akin to 'public global power'. It is not immediately clear which global actor, if any, sufficiently resembles the state: most importantly, there is no unified global public, and no single global public sphere.[4] Nevertheless, it is possible to determine whether a global actor is *somewhat* public in the relevant respects. Like their domestic counterpart, the public character of global actors may be ascertained by the scope and character of their *function*, and by their *orientation*. Accordingly, an actor is properly public in the global sense if it meets the following criteria:

(1) Its primary function is co-extensive with the human world and it includes among its primary tasks duties of public governance, such as the administration and regulation of global affairs, and the distribution of global public goods.
(2) It conceives of itself as a global public actor, fulfilling a global public function, akin to how the state understands its domestic role.

In the absence of a global state or global public, it is unlikely that this standard can be met fully. Nevertheless, I suggest that some global actors come considerably closer to meeting these criteria than others.

The first criterion stipulates that the purpose of public global actors must be to serve the world population, rather than to a particular group or state, and that it must focus on duties of governance. Since human beings are not bound together as citizens in a global state or as participants in a global public sphere, it is not clear what it would mean for an actor to have a fully *global* public function. With the possible exception of the United Nations General Assembly, most global actors have tasks whose scope is less than fully co-extensive with the entire human community. At the domestic level, we feel justified in calling an agency *public* when it falls under the rubric of the state, the boundaries of which correspond with the boundaries of the people. Thus, the juvenile justice system or local government agencies are domestic public actors even though they deal with subsections – demographic, geographic, or other – of the domestic population. The same context does not exist at the global level, and it may therefore be difficult to determine whether international NGOs that focus on earthquake victims or on the needs of children, for instance, perform a global public function. Similarly, it may not be clear whether the Catholic Church forfeits its global public status because it is more active in sub-Saharan Africa and South America than, say, in the Middle East.

However, since even the institutions of the domestic state might fail to meet the scope criterion if they were assessed in separation from one another, I suggest we loosen this criterion in the global setting. Instead, we should ensure that we mirror, as fully as possible, the unified character of the domestic political domain, and ask whether global actors meet this standard (of global public scope) in conjunction with others – provided of course that they understand themselves as being part of this larger web of actors.

Irrespective of whether they do so well, states proclaim to be public actors because they advance *public* or common *interests*. It may be in the interest of the community to have the state provide public goods, for instance, or adjudicate disputes between private actors. We should consider to what extent global actors perform the same duties in the global domain. In order to examine what could count as a 'public interest' where there is no public, I will refer to Andrew Kuper's helpful distinctions between five ways of understanding the public good. Only two of these interpretations must be ruled out for my purposes: the concept of the common good, which, as Kuper (2004, p. 88) also argues, relies on claims about the 'way of life of a group', and the idea that a good is public when it is 'good for the scheme of social cooperation'. These interpretations are unworkable at the global level, since there is no global scheme of social cooperation, and no global public. However, it is possible to determine whether a particular good concerns or addresses more or fewer individuals. A public good at the global level could mean one of three things: first, that which is 'good for all', that is, 'shared or shareable by all constituents'; second, that which is 'good in the aggregate'; or third, that which is 'good for a majority of individuals', with the stipulation that the majority is a fluid one, and shifts from issue to issue (Kuper 2004, pp. 87–88).

While Kuper opts for the last interpretation to the exclusion of the others, this is, in my view, not the correct choice. Any of the three interpretations make possible a discussion about what is truly public at the global level, and any can thus be admissible in a global conversation about such issues. Nevertheless, the 'good of all' indicates global publicness in a stronger sense than the 'good for a fluid majority', and this in turn gives us more certainty about an actor's publicness than the 'aggregate good'. I will discuss this in turn.

Kuper presumes that there will be little agreement on that which is 'good for all', but I disagree. The prevention of disastrous climate change, for instance, benefits 'all', since the survival of the planet is good for all but the most suicidal of human beings.[5] A global corporation whose primary products provide 'green' energy, for instance, can thus be said to be a public actor because the good it provides is 'good for all'. Similarly, global security also concerns the human community as a whole. This is not to say that a global actor cannot be public if it performs a function that relates to the 'good of the majority'. For instance, a global institution that helps settle trade disputes between states may be a public actor, because it provides a service for the citizens of the 'winner' as well as for the citizens of the states that are not involved. The latter presumably benefit from a well-functioning system of international trade, after all. Even the citizens of the 'loser' are beneficiaries of such a system – as long as the rules are such that, if they lose on issue after issue, some provision is made to accommodate them. It is thus possible to make the argument that this global institution is a public actor, and it is only slightly more difficult than in the case of the corporation whose work benefits all.

A global actor may also have a public function when it provides a 'good in the aggregate'. The publicness of an NGO that provides primary education to children in a range of poor countries can be justified in this way. After all, the education of those children will benefit individuals around the world in the aggregate, even if it does not benefit certain individuals at all. By comparison, in the domestic setting, primary education may be considered to be in the 'common good' of the community. However, given the absence of a global public, such a justification is not accessible at the level of global politics. In the example, the NGO could even stand accused of providing a private good – one that advances the interests of certain individuals, rather than the public interests of a 'global community' more broadly. Since individuals may deny the existence of a human community of this sort, this third interpretation of the 'public interest' is the least promising one for global publicness.

Because there is no global public, the publicness of global actors will often have to be imputed rather than confirmed at the global level. The overlapping judgments of different domestic publics – as well as, perhaps, a distributive public such as the EU (see Bohman 2007, pp. 84–92) – may provide a partial substitute. Nevertheless, global actors will often only be partially public.

Of course, we must first ascertain whether the global actor meets the second criterion, which concerns the actor's orientation. As I will suggest below, certain actors, which meet the first criterion of publicness, in relation to their scope and function, may not identify as global public actors. Irrespective of whether they have a global public function, global actors cannot meaningfully be said to represent global public power when they do not exercise this power willingly, and self-consciously. Instead, global public actors should be expected to declare their power as such. The domestic state presents itself as the agent that is responsible, more than any other, for matters that concern the community in its entirety. With the exception of the claim of exclusivity, perhaps, the same ought to be demanded from public actors at the global level. In the next section, I consider which of the four categories of global actors best meets the standard of publicness.

III.

I will discuss the four agents – the state, the for-profit organization, the value-driven organization, and the global institution – in turn. Given its domestic public role, the *state* may appear to be the best candidate for public power at the global level as well. When states act globally, they regularly perform governance-related functions, and, on occasion, they also view their global function as an extension of their domestic, public one. However, the state's global function is never *primarily* that of global administration or regulation, or the global distribution of goods. Unlike the domestic state's relationship with the domestic public, the globally-acting state does not impose a basic structure, coercively, on the world population. Crucially, this is also not how the state envisions its own role in the global order. Their stated justifications for foreign aid or humanitarian interventions notwithstanding, states principally aim to represent domestic interests abroad, advocating on their citizens' behalf – or, if they are not republics, on the behalf of whoever has captured the state. While there may be some overlap between domestic and global interests, this is unlikely to be the case at all times, and across all issues. Indeed, the allocation of foreign aid, in particular, is often driven by domestic interests that are unrelated to (foreign) human need (Miller 2010, pp. 143–144). After all, the state is by its very nature the state of *some* rather than of all or of others, and – when it undertakes action at the global level – it is one private actor among others.

Let me now turn to the category of *for-profit organizations*. Recall that a global actor is public when its primary function is co-extensive with the human world and when it includes among its primary tasks duties of public governance, such as the administration and regulation of global affairs, and the distribution of global public goods. It must also conceive of itself as a global public actor. For-profit organizations fail to meet this standard. For-profit organizations such as corporations meet the first criterion of publicness – of scope and character – to the extent that they are capable of addressing needs that are common, in one of the three senses described above, to the entire global population. Like states, however, they do not primarily perform global governance tasks, nor do they believe that this is what they do. Instead, they identify as profit-oriented organizations, operating in the non-public sphere of the market. Many for-profit organizations pursue charity projects, but these are, as their name suggests, peripheral to the aim of maximizing profit.

If neither states nor for-profit organizations approximate the public character of the domestic state, perhaps we ought to turn to *value-driven organizations* such as NGOs. This third category, of value-driven organizations, is a diverse one. Mary Kaldor (2003, p. 79) uses the umbrella term 'global civil society actors', and lists among its members social movements, NGOs, think tanks, and transnational civic networks. Like for-profit organizations, value-drive organizations are important actors in the global order. According to estimates from 2001, there are approximately 40,000 international NGOs,[6] and the number has undoubtedly increased since then. Value-driven private organizations enter partnerships with governments and corporations, and they are often incorporated in public global institutions.

Because of their peculiar nature – they pursue particular values or causes rather than profit – they have often been a benign presence in global politics. It is not surprising, then, that scholars have been overwhelmingly supportive of their role in global governance.

The question, however, is whether they should be expected to take on tasks of global governance, and whether they should prevent domination by third parties in addition to avoiding domination themselves. While this is a closer case, it seems that most value-driven organizations would fail to meet the requisite standard of publicness, which, we recall, posits that a global actor is public to the extent that, first, it has a global scope and character, and second, it declares itself to the world as a public actor. Value-driven organizations meet this first criterion better than states or their for-profit counterparts do. Value-driven organizations perform an array of public functions, seeking to shape regional or global governance, as well as the politics of foreign states, and helping to distribute global public goods (see e.g. Scholte 2002, pp. 145–165). However, on the whole, they may fail to meet the second criterion, because they view themselves in an important respect as critical outsiders. Practically speaking, they may be as much 'inside' global governance as other actors, but conceptually, they often place themselves in opposition to other – public and private – forms of power (Kaldor 2003, pp. 80–81). They may declare, for instance, that they perform governance functions that others neglect to perform, or that they serve as the world's conscience in the face of the failure of states and others to act against injustice (Kaldor 2003, e.g. p. 209).

Their performance of governance functions may in and of itself imply a critique of (individual or concerted) state inaction. After all, domestic NGOs do not tend to (partially) govern domestic societies in the West; presumably, this is the case not because they are forcibly prevented from doing so by the government, but because there is simply less need for them to do so. Perhaps we may deduce from this that they are reluctant to function as a substitute government. International NGOs often operate in countries that are poor and/or suffering from war or natural disasters, and that are thus relatively weak. As a result, international NGOs may take on governance duties even when their domestic counterparts do not. The organizations may be well placed, practically speaking, to at least temporarily take over governance tasks, such as the distribution of vital resources. However, value-driven organizations tend self-consciously to occupy a place as a *surrogate* for state-like power, not as its instantiation. The International Committee of the Red Cross, for instance, can perform its function precisely because it is *not* itself a state actor or associated with one.

Finally, there is the category of *global institutions*. Ranging from formal treaty-based organizations to informal networks, this is another very diverse category. More so than the other three categories of actors, the functions of global institutions are governance-related and focused on the world population as a whole, and they more clearly conceive of themselves as fulfilling a global function akin to that of the domestic state. In the recent decades, they have become important contributors to global governance, capable of facilitating cooperation, integration and harmonization across states. Global institutions are often but not always statist, treaty-based organizations, and they sometimes – though not always – assume and exercise power that previously belonged to the sovereign state. While there are formal international organizations, established by treaty, there are also less formal transnational networks, which involve informal cooperation among states. At the end of the spectrum are ostensibly private bodies such as the International Standardization Organization (ISO) (Kingsbury, Krisch and Stewart 2005). Although the ISO is unconnected to government in any way, it fulfills the public, regulatory function of adopting standards that harmonize products across borders (Kingsbury, Krisch and Stewart 2005, p. 20). The ISO is perhaps the most interesting example of how a completely non-governmental organization can nevertheless be public by virtue of its orientation.

I do not mean to suggest that global institutions represent *non-dominating* public global power. Their lack of accountability to states or their citizens suggests that they may be *dominating* ones, but they are nevertheless *public* global institutions rather than private ones. Crucially, what sets them apart from an organization like Amnesty International or Mercy Corps is that they are *formally* subject to public scrutiny. In addition, their agenda is subject to change in a way that an NGO's mission statement is not, and they are, or might at some point be, subsumed under a wider competency area of the UN or another global umbrella organization. Even though the public nature of global institutions cannot be equated with that of the domestic state – since domestic public actors are made more so because they are in the service of a unified public – they nevertheless meet the standard of publicness better than the other global actors.

IV.

At this stage, it is possible for the reader to question why I place such weight on the distinction between public global institutions, on the one hand, and the various private global actors, on the other. After all, I have acknowledged the diversity that exists within the categories, and I have also admitted that public global institutions frequently prevent individuals from exercising control over the institutions' interference in their lives. If the existing global institutions such as those associated with the UN are unlikely to protect individuals from domination, the reader may wonder why I nevertheless ask that they – and only they – take on this role, and why I avoid relying on international NGOs. Instead, I could require more generally that all global actors promote the freedom of individuals worldwide to the best of their ability, and that all global actors subject themselves to the control of individuals or groups worldwide to the extent that they impact their freedom.

This is indeed an implication for my argument that could be drawn from Onora O'Neill's 'Agents of Justice'. Writing about distributive justice rather than global governance, O'Neill (2001, p. 194) argues that the distinction between 'primary' and 'secondary' agents of justice cannot be sustained in the context of the state ineffectiveness and oppression, and that justice must instead 'be built by a diversity of agents and agencies that possess and lack varying ranges of capabilities'. In particular, she argues that it is inappropriate to accord the state the status of 'primary' agent of justice to the exclusion of others, and to presume, in light of their for-profit nature, that corporations can contribute only barely or not at all. Attempts to deny certain classes of actors a constructive role are likely based on a 'highly ideologized' rather than a realistic understanding of their nature and motivation (O'Neill 2001). While I have attempted to acknowledge fairly the 'public' functions of private global actors – including for-profit and value-driven organizations – my distinction between their privateness and the publicness of the public global institutions hinges to a large extent on the actors' orientation. It is possible that the global actors that I call private are more willing to identify as public actors than I think, and I should ask that they take on the task of global public power to the best of their ability (see also Wettstein 2009).

Unlike O'Neill, who argues that global actors should be assessed by their capacity for good, Terry Macdonald focuses on their capacity for harm. Instead of defining publicness by reference to an actor's scope, function, and orientation, as I do, she argues that the relevant criterion for publicness is the impact of its activities on autonomy. No global actor is singled out as essentially different in character; instead, all global actors 'should be subject to *direct democratic control in accordance with their impact on the capacities of populations to lead autonomous lives*' (Macdonald 2008, p. 23, her emphasis). Her liberal conception of public power locates it in the relationships between actors, with NGOs, corporations, states, and international organizations all capable of exercising 'public power' over others. While Macdonald focuses primarily on NGOs, her argument applies broadly to all global actors, including transnational corporations and international organizations.[7]

While there is much to admire about her project, I believe that her understanding of what counts as public in a global setting may come with a few disadvantages. First, her account may not be sufficiently demanding. Macdonald risks letting certain actors – public global actors, in my understanding of that term – off too easily. Her standard of democratic accountability to stakeholders falls short of what I would demand of global institutions by virtue of not just their function but also their orientation. In particular, I would ask that they be accountable to populations beyond those whose capacity for autonomy they impact (to use Macdonald's terminology). As I see it, it does not seem excessive to ask that they also concern themselves with violations against autonomy (or freedom as non-domination) by third parties. Macdonald, on the other hand, does not seem to demand more from global institutions than she does from other actors.

To be fair, Macdonald does reserve space for the role of what I call public actors. She suggests that new institutions must be established to hold the various global actors – in my terms, for-profit organizations, value-driven organizations, states, and public global institutions – to account (Macdonald 2008, e.g. p. 32, pp. 224–227). However, her standard for democratic control may still not be sufficiently demanding in its scope. As I see it, public institutions must be accountable not to the populations whose capacities for autonomous lives they impact but to *the community by reference to which they function as a public actor*. At the global level, this is the global human community.

Second, Macdonald's account may be excessively demanding with regard to the role of private global actors. She asks that all private global actors – in the way that I understand this term – are brought under the 'direct democratic control' of the populations whose capacity for autonomy they impact. I agree that private institutions must be accountable to the relevant individuals, but it seems unwise to require that they be 'directly' accountable. At the domestic level, such actors are regulated by public institutions, and they are often not directly accountable to stakeholder communities. Instead, they may be accountable to such communities only indirectly, by way of their accountability to the polity as a whole – assuming for a moment that the polity as a whole is not a stakeholder in a relevant sense. While corporations, NGOs, and other global actors must be prevented from dominating individuals, this can often be achieved when they are successfully restrained by public global institutions. A focus on accountability is not always necessary or optimal.

Finally, I hope to also have a satisfactory response to O'Neill's challenge, or rather, her challenge as it applies to global governance. I agree with O'Neill that it is wrong to presume that certain actors are categorically incapable of performing certain public functions. However, some actors self-consciously view their primary role to be a public one, and others do not. Corporations, by definition, do not. They may perform 'public' tasks, but they do not think of themselves as public actors in all that this entails. They should of course contribute to global governance to the best of their ability – by refraining from arbitrarily interfering in the lives of individuals, or by submitting to global regulation, for instance. As O'Neill suggests, we may even ask of them that they perform duties of global governance when the existing public global actors fall short. However, in my view, public global actors must have the global promotion of freedom as non-domination as a primary goal, and it seems incongruous to expect this of organizations that define themselves as profit-seeking.

It is possible to retort that, like public global actors, private global actors must also be asked to prevent domination by third parties when they are capable of doing so. It is true that private actors are often able to step in where public actors are failing, and it would be unfortunate to discourage this altogether. However, we have reason to be suspicious when a global actor that is not public – in other words, that does not have a global scope, or global public function and orientation – takes on the task of preventing domination by third parties. It is reasonable, for instance, to suspect that a corporation, in promoting global non-domination, will also or even primarily aim to advance its own, profit-oriented interests. After all, the pursuit of profit is its raison-d'être. More importantly, even a well-intentioned private global actor such as an international NGO cannot properly perform the task of promoting non-domination without refashioning itself as a public actor. International NGOs generally aim to be responsive and accountable to their board members, their donors, and selected recipients, rather than to the global population more generally. They are also keen to retain the privilege of taking initiative in determining which causes to support, rather than opening up that question to input by the global population. As a result, they risk promoting non-domination in a paternalistic manner, *for the benefit* of individuals worldwide rather than *on their behalves*.

Finally, ostensibly private organizations that perform global governance tasks and work to prevent domination by third parties, and that do so as a substitute for state action rather than as a second-best alternative to it, are in fact public actors, and should be reconceived as such. Crucially, however, not all private actors should be encouraged to undergo such a transformation. Private global actors perform important functions – they create wealth, for instance, and provide space for individuals to express themselves separately from, and possibly in opposition to, the state and other public actors. It is imperative that we acknowledge their role(s), and allow them to retain their private character. Unless we wish to abolish private actors altogether, we should accept that it is appropriate to hold them to a different standard.

V.

Much of the most interesting recent scholarship in global governance has focused on creating conceptual space for international NGOs – and sometimes also TNCs and states – as fully-fledged participants in global governance. Some, though of course not all, of this work is motivated by the glaring shortcomings of global institutions such as those associated with the UN. As a corrective, I suggest that we direct a bit more of our attention towards improving the way that public global institutions perform their function, rather than towards perfecting the way that private international NGOs substitute for them.

The problem that remains is that of global institutional change. Private global actors such as NGOs and corporations may not be the optimal 'global governors', but the global actors that *are* public often fail to perform this function well and/or effectively. Public global institutions undeniably already serve various important public functions, such as the administration of global politics or the regulation of the global economy. They have increased the efficiency of global governance by, for instance, encouraging the harmonization of standards across states, and they may redistribute resources. They have also integrated states into the world economy, and they are sources of authority which may be relied upon to support collective action in times of an international crisis. Finally, they have engaged in law-making and norm-building. However, many global public institutions are ineffective and/or oppressive in nature. The question that we are left with is therefore how they could be transformed into effective, non-dominating global governance institutions. I acknowledge that this is a serious challenge, but I maintain that it would not serve us well to avoid the challenge altogether by continuing to rely largely on non-state actors such as international NGOs.

Acknowledgements

Earlier versions of this paper were presented at Princeton University, the Association for Political Theory conference, and the annual meeting of the American Political Science Association. I would like to thank the participants as well as Richard Beardsworth, Tamara Jugov, Terry Macdonald, Miriam Ronzoni, and Amy Shuster for their very helpful comments and suggestions.

Notes

1. When they are democratic, states may be benign actors *domestically*, but I am considering them here in their capacity as *global* actors.
2. I recognize that my taxonomy is somewhat coarse, and that it does not fully take into account the many differences that exist among actors in the four categories. While I believe that my taxonomy fits the purposes of this paper, I refer the reader to the following edited volume for a more complete overview of the (functions of) various actors in global politics: Higgott, Underhill and Bieler (2000).
3. In 2005, the resources of Mercy Corps totaled nearly $185 million, which enabled the organization to sustain projects in 42 countries, helping 10 million people. From 2000 to 2006, Mercy Corps spent nearly $40 million in Eritrea, which has a total yearly budget of $409 million, of which more goes to the military than to health and education programs combined. See http://www.mercycorps.org and https://www.cia.gov/library/publications/the-world-factbook/.
4. James Bohman argues that there are in fact multiple, overlapping publics. See Bohman (2007, ch. 2).

5. There may be disagreement, of course, about the credibility or severity of the threat to the survival of the planet, but once it has been established that there is a problem, it is not just in the interest of 'the majority' but in the interest of 'all' to seek a solution.
6. United Nations Development Program, *Human Development Report 2000*, http://hdr.undp.org/en/media/HDR_2000_EN.pdf Approximately 3000 NGOs are in consultative status at the UN. See http://www.un.org/esa/coordination/ngo/pdf/INF_List.pdf
7. Her book is concerned primarily with the public power of NGOs. She has recently published a book chapter, however, which focuses on corporations: see Macdonald (2010).

Note on contributor

Barbara Buckinx is a Kassel Foundation postdoctoral fellow at the Goethe University Frankfurt. She received her PhD in Politics from Princeton University in 2010 and has held fellowships at Frankfurt's Center for Advanced Studies 'Justitia Amplificata' and the Political Theory Project at Brown University. She has published on topics in global political theory in *Global Governance, Global Government* (SUNY Press), *Ethics and International Affairs*, and *Global Justice: Theory Practice Rhetoric*.

References

Archibugi, D., 2008. *The global commonwealth of citizens: toward cosmopolitan democracy*. Princeton, NJ: Princeton University Press.

Bohman, J., 2007. *Democracy across borders: from Dêmos to Dêmoi*. Cambridge, MA: MIT Press.

de Waal, T., 2003. *Black garden: Armenia and Azerbaijan through peace and war*. New York: New York University Press.

Dewey, J., 1954. *The public and its problems*. Athens, OH: Swallow Press.

Dryzek, J.S., 2006. *Deliberative global politics: discourse and democracy in a divided world*. Cambridge: Polity Press.

Dryzek, J.S., 2008. Two paths to global democracy. *Ethical perspectives*, 15 (4), 469–486.

Higgott, R.A., Underhill, G.R.D., and Bieler, A., eds., 2000. *Non-state actors and authority in the global system*. London: Routledge.

Honohan, I., 2002. *Civic republicanism*. New York, NY: Routledge.

Kaldor, M., 2003. *Global civil society: an answer to war*. Cambridge: Polity Press.

Karsch, E., 2002. *The Iran–Iraq War, 1980–1988*. Oxford: Oxford University Press.

Kingsbury, B., Krisch, N., and Stewart, R.B., 2005. The emergence of global administrative law. *Law and contemporary problems*, 68 (3&4), 15–61.

Kuper, A., 2004. *Democracy beyond borders: justice and representation in global institution*. Oxford: Oxford University Press.

Kurzman, D., 1987. *A killing wind: inside Union Carbide and the Bhopal catastrophe*. New York: McGraw-Hill.

Macdonald, T., 2008. *Global stakeholder democracy: power and representation beyond liberal states*. Oxford: Oxford University Press.

Macdonald, T., 2010. Corporations and global justice. rethinking 'public' and 'private' responsibilities. *In*: K. Macdonald and S. Marshall, eds. *Fair trade, corporate accountability and beyond: experiments in globalising justice.* Aldershot: Ashgate, 137–148.
Mann, M., 1997. Has globalization ended the rise and rise of the nation-state? *Review of international political economy*, 4 (3), 472–496.
Maren, M., 1997. *The road to hell: the ravaging effects of foreign aid and international charity.* New York: Free Press.
Maynor, J.W., 2003. *Republicanism in the modern world.* Cambridge: Polity Press.
Miller, D., 1999. *Principles of social justice.* Cambridge, MA: Harvard University Press.
Miller, R.W., 2010. *Globalizing justice: the ethics of poverty and power.* New York: Oxford University Press.
O'Neill, O., 2001. Agents of justice. *Metaphilosophy*, 32 (1&2), 180–195.
Pettit, P., 1997. *Republicanism: a theory of freedom and government.* Oxford: Oxford University Press.
Richardson, H.S., 2002. *Democratic autonomy: public reasoning about the ends of policy.* Oxford: Oxford University Press.
Scholte, J.A., 2002. Civil society and governance in the global polity. *In*: M. Ougaard and R. Higgott, eds. *Towards a global polity.* London: Routledge, 145–165.
Warwick University/ESRC Centre for the Study of Globalisation and Regionalisation Working Papers, 130 (4), 1–51.
Skinner, Q., 1998. *Liberty before liberalism.* Cambridge: Cambridge University Press.
Skinner, Q., 2008. Freedom as the absence of arbitrary power. *In*: C. Laborde and J. Maynor, eds. *Republicanism and political theory.* Oxford: Blackwell Publishing, 83–101.
Vreeland, J.R., 2003. *The IMF and economic development.* Cambridge: Cambridge University Press.
Wettstein, F., 2009. *Multinational corporations and global justice. human rights obligations of a quasi-governmental institution.* Stanford, CA: Stanford University Press.

Global public power: the *subject* of principles of global political legitimacy

Andrew Hurrell[a] and Terry Macdonald[b]

[a]*Department of Politics and International Relations, Oxford University, UK;*
[b]*School of Social and Political Sciences University of Melbourne, Australia*

This paper elaborates the concept of *global public power* as the subject of principles of political legitimacy in global politics, and defends it through a critical comparison with other concepts widely employed to depict this regulative subject: states, global basic structure, and global governance. The goal underlying this argument is to bring some greater unity and integration to conceptual understandings of the subject of principles of political legitimacy within analyses of global politics, and in doing so to frame a broader research agenda for locating in practice the concrete political agencies and institutions that are appropriate targets for demands of political legitimation under the prevailing empirical conditions of global *pluralism*.

Introduction

We currently confront a pressing demand for greater legitimacy in the exercise of political power within the global domain. The uncontrolled exercise of power by a range of actors – including states, international organizations (IOs), non-governmental organizations (NGOs), transnational corporations (TNCs), and hybrid institutional actors of various kinds – is widely documented and subject to routine critique. This criticism is associated with vociferous demands for building greater participation, accountability, transparency, democracy, and similar (often broadly liberal) institutions for political control. The viability of this reformist agenda is significantly undermined, however, by deep ambivalence about the appropriate *subject* of standards of political legitimacy such as these.

Here, there is much uncertainty and disagreement surrounding questions of the following kind. Ought only states be subject to control via application of such regulatory political principles? Can IOs achieve legitimacy through delegation of their powers by states, or must they be directly subject to legitimate political control? Ought corporations and/or NGOs be directly subject to these regulatory principles, as many of their critics claim and these organizations themselves increasingly acknowledge? Do we need to build new political agencies to generate political legitimacy, or is it a matter only of establishing effective controls for the existing ones? In more general terms, which political actors and institutions ought to be subject to political critique and control in global politics, through application of normative standards of political legitimacy? These questions comprise the challenge posed by the political *pluralism* of the global order to our settled understandings about political legitimacy and its regulative subject: by pluralism, we mean an order in which important forms of political power are exercised somewhat independently by myriad state, intergovernmental, and non-state actors operating at multiple and overlapping jurisdictional levels, rather than unified through any one supreme global political authority or hierarchy of constitutional principles (Cerny 1999, 2006, Macdonald 2008, Macdonald and Macdonald 2010, Krisch 2011).

Answering these questions is a task of crucial importance, since it is impossible to formulate coherently or pursue politically any set of principles for strengthening global political legitimacy until we understand what it is precisely that these principles are supposed to regulate. John Rawls (1999, p. 25) has famously observed that 'the correct regulative principle for a thing depends on the nature of that thing'. Insofar as there is agreement that widely-endorsed standards of global political legitimacy (such as accountability, transparency, and so on) entail the 'correct regulative principles' for global political life, progress in the pursuit of such legitimacy thus depends upon answering the converse question: what is the 'nature of the thing' that these are the correct regulative principles *for*?

Despite the importance of this question, there is a surprising lack of convergence within existing analyses of global political legitimacy on any clear concept of the subject of these principles. Three very different concepts of this regulative subject, in particular, are frequently invoked in different sub-fields of the literature. First, the idea that *states* are subjects of these principles is commonplace within traditions of political and legal philosophy that link the concept of political legitimacy either to the justification of coercive state power, or to the authority of a state's legal norms and directives. Second, the idea that principles of global political legitimacy should regulate a global *basic structure* or *institutional scheme* is sometimes encountered within post-Rawlsian theoretical literatures on global 'justice', in which the question of the subject of principles of *political legitimacy* is not clearly distinguished from the question of the subject of *distributive principles of justice*, such that the same regulative subject – global basic structure – is (sometimes implicitly) ascribed to both. Third, literatures on institutional legitimacy that spring from the discipline of international relations commonly adopt a more empirically-grounded notion of global *governance* – or sometimes disaggregated 'global governance institutions' – as the subject(s) of principles of political legitimacy.

The differences between these conceptual understandings of this regulative subject are striking in several dimensions, as we will proceed later here to discuss in more depth. But these differences are rarely brought into clear focus or direct confrontation through any systematic conceptual analysis – perhaps because they predominate within different political sub-disciplines from which the problem of global political legitimacy can be approached. It is our contention here, however, that our precise concept of the subject of principles of global political legitimacy is in fact a matter of great theoretical importance, since this is what frames our thinking about where and how in global political life our substantive principles of political legitimacy should be *applied*; more specifically, our concept of this subject will have enormous implications for how we go about the task of identifying the concrete institutions or actors that ought to be targeted and regulated as means of strengthening political legitimacy at the global level.

It is our aim in this paper to bring some greater unity and integration to conceptual understandings of the subject of principles of political legitimacy within analyses of global politics, and in doing so to frame a broader research agenda for locating in practice the concrete political agencies and institutions that are appropriate targets for demands of political legitimation under the prevailing empirical conditions of global *pluralism*. We begin by setting out some fundamental assumptions about the normative character and purpose of principles of political legitimacy, and explain where the problem of political legitimacy is situated within the broader domain of what we are calling, in this collection, 'global political justice'. Drawing on this analysis we identify some simple desiderata for a theoretical concept of the subject of principles of global political legitimacy to operate under conditions of political pluralism. Next, we draw on these desiderata to highlight the limitations of the standard concepts of this regulative subject – states, basic structure, and governance – and in doing so we clear the theoretical ground for a new conceptual framework. We then present the idea of *global public power* as a more promising concept through which to frame further investigation of the concrete political scope of this subject, and sketch in conclusion some specific normative and empirical questions that would need to be answered as part of a broader research programme focused on mapping the concrete agents and institutions of global public power in contemporary world politics.

Principles of global political legitimacy and the problem of their subject

The best place to start in tackling the question of what kind of subjects should be regulated by principles of political legitimacy is to consider in more depth: *what kind of normative principles are principles of political legitimacy*, and what are they *for*? Grasping the relationship between normative principles of political legitimacy and other kinds of normative principles (such as moral principles of 'distributive justice', or principles of 'morality' more broadly speaking) is not a straightforward matter, and there are many different views about the relationships between these types of normative principles.

It is often thought that principles of political legitimacy can be understood as a category of principles of applied morality, concerned with the moral justification of some *special political subject* – such as the state, or some more specific feature of the state, such as its coercive power, or its 'moral power' to impose obligations on its subjects to comply with the law through the function of political 'authority' (Wellman 1996, Copp 1999, Simmons 1999, Buchanan 2002). We agree it is true that principles of political legitimacy can be distinguished from other moral principles in part by their special political subject. However, since the *character* of this subject is precisely the question we are placing at issue here, we cannot begin our analysis with an overarching concept of political legitimacy that *itself* incorporates statist assumptions about the subject – as the concepts of political legitimacy as the right to coercive rule, on the one hand, or as the moral power to impose obligations to comply with law, on the other, both do – since this would generate a circular argument.

Fortunately, we take the view that principles of political legitimacy are distinguished from other kinds of normative principles not only by their special subject, but *additionally* through being grounded in forms of justification that bear a far from straightforward relationship to moral justification; this is fortunate, since this other independent conceptual dimension of legitimacy supplies us with a starting-point for conceptual reflection on the subject of principles of legitimacy that can yield a *non*-circular argument about the question of subject. It is beyond the scope of this paper to present a fully developed account of 'political normativity', and the relationship between 'moral' and 'political' justification in general terms, of the kind that would be required to explain fully and vindicate our view about this second conceptual dimension of political legitimacy. But it is nonetheless important for the present purposes at least to state clearly what we take to be some key features of the justificatory practices that underpin principles of political legitimacy, so that our assumptions on this matter – and the ways in which our desiderata for a concept of the subject of principles of political legitimacy depend on them – are at least transparent.

One view, with which ours resonates in some key dimensions, holds that principles of political legitimacy are distinguished from certain other moral principles by their special function of embodying something akin to 'non-ideal' standards of justice. On this view, principles of legitimacy set out the conditions under which political institutions will be worthy of compliance and support in the here and now as the best that we can (right now) achieve, as distinct from articulating ideal standards for orienting institutional evaluation and longer-term reformist aspiration (Rawls 1996, Valentini 2012).

Although we do not make use here of the categories of 'ideal' and 'non-ideal', this view of political legitimacy embodies one important insight that we wish to endorse, by highlighting the way in which principles of political legitimacy – such as 'transparency', 'accountability', 'participation', etc. – are constituted in part by *strategic* goals, of a kind that can be pursued only with the right kind of responsiveness to a very full range of empirical facts. It is of course true that these principles are justified in part through reference to moral values (such as individual autonomy and equality, for instance). But the content of the principles is also determined with responsiveness to the strategic goal of restraining political power, and ensuring some compliance by the powerful with the fundamental moral norms of the social order. Whereas ideal theories of justice deliberately disregard problems of moral non-compliance – seeking only institutions that could attract stable support if actors were motivated by moral reasons (Rawls 1996), not institutions that can attract stable support given actors' actual, and often less morally pure, motivations – it is precisely the possibility and pervasive reality of such (non-compliant) abuses of power that *real* political institutions (and their associated principles of political legitimacy) must be formulated to regulate. The importance of developing principles of political legitimacy that are responsive to such political realities is of particular weight in the context of global politics, given the huge scale of inequalities (of power, status, and social and economic condition) at this level, and the temptations for predation and abuse that these inequalities routinely create.

We can elaborate and refine this very general claim with the following statement about the justificatory practices underpinning principles of political legitimacy: they are characterized by a central preoccupation with solving *the problem of political order*, and building political institutions that can achieve *real political acceptability* among their participants as a central instrument for doing so. What we are here calling political *order* is connected to the institutionalized pursuit of certain fundamental *common interests*, which – in significant part at least – constitutes a group as a political society (Bull 1977, Hurrell 2007). By political *acceptability* we mean the justifiability of political institutions in terms of reasons that are articulated and widely supported within certain wider social practices – of political claim-making, recognition, and mutual justification – in which the institutions in question are historically and sociologically embedded, and in which those subject to the power of the institutions are participants.[1] These two features of political justification are emphasized also by some recent proponents of so-called 'realist' approaches to normative political theory

– most notably by Bernard Williams (2005) in his sketch of a realist political theory with the idea of legitimacy at its centre.[2]

With this understanding of political legitimacy in mind, we are in a position to clarify how it relates to the concept of 'political justice', as that has been characterized in this collection. Briefly, we can say that the question of political legitimacy falls within the scope of the question of political justice, but is more narrowly circumscribed than it in the following sense. The more ambitiously drawn question of political justice seeks to determine not only the principles by which the agents and institutions within political societies should politically *regulate* one another, but also how these fundamental sociological entities should be politically *constituted* in the first place – that is, what their basic institutional structures and social identities ought to be. The question of political legitimacy, in contrast, brackets these deeper constitutive questions from the normative analysis, as the content of the shared interests and the character of the institutions established to advance them (which together shape the political 'order'), as well as the social identities of the political actors that seek recognition and make and justify claims in relation to these institutions, are taken as historical and sociological givens at the outset of the normative analysis.

Identifying these features of the practices of political justification that are associated with principles of political legitimacy falls a long way short of articulating a full normative theory of political legitimacy. There is enough in what we have sketched, however, to enable us to draw out some very basic *desiderata* for a concept of the subject of principles of political legitimacy, which we can subsequently employ in a critical assessment of common concepts of this subject in established literatures. Here we identify five desiderata – four of which impose direct *conceptual* requirements on our concept of subject, and one of which attaches it to fulfilment of a *substantive empirical* criterion. As we shall indicate as we proceed, these desiderata are derived from a conjunction of the following: the very general normative account of the purpose and character of principles of political legitimacy that we have just set out; an empirical picture of the current global political order that casts it as 'pluralist', as earlier characterized; and the logical demands of the substantive practical questions about global political regulation we are ultimately interested in settling, and the investigation of which our concept of the subject of these principles will be utilized to frame.

The first desideratum (D1) is the straightforward conceptual requirement that our concept of the subject of principles of political legitimacy must be *sociologically non-stipulative* – that is, non-question-begging, or at least somewhat conceptually *open* with respect to the range of social agents and institutions that can be denoted by it. In other words, if the purpose of formulating a clear concept of this subject is to frame a research agenda in which we explore which of a range of candidate agents and institutions (states, IOs, NGOs, corporations, etc.) should be subject to the regulative demands of political legitimacy, then we need a concept of the subject that is sufficiently conceptually flexible to accommodate a range of plausible answers to the question at issue.

The second desideratum (D2) is also conceptual, and functions in a sense to counteract or place limits on D1. It is the requirement that our concept of the subject of principles of political legitimacy must be *sociologically non-inclusive* – that is, it must incorporate some kind of *conceptual criterion of differentiation* between the set of social agents and institutions that are to count as subjects of these principles, and the set of agents and institutions that are not. This desideratum is a function of the substantive view (outlined above) that principles of legitimacy are not intended to function as universal moral principles regulating the whole of social life, but rather have a more narrowly circumscribed regulative function connected to the specifically *political* values of achieving order, and regulating power within this order on terms that are politically acceptable to its participants.

The third desideratum (D3) refines, or places limits on, D1, in an even more specific sociological dimension: it requires that our concept of the subject, while remaining non-stipulative, must at least be *agent-centric*. By this, we mean that the subject must be some set of agents – or some set of social institutions through which groups of agents intentionally and systematically act – rather than some set of background social structures that generate social outcomes through *unintended* patterns of behaviour (or their effects). This desideratum reflects our general understanding, sketched briefly above, of the *purpose and function* of principles of political legitimacy – as one subset of a wider set of normative principles that may be invoked to regulate different aspects of social and political life. Whereas we would take principles of *distributive* justice to be exemplary of a scheme of normative principles concerned at least in part with the regulation of the patterned (though often unintended) social causes and effects constitutive of social structures, principles of political legitimacy (a sub-set of the broader set of principles of 'political justice') have a more narrowly *agent-centric* regulative purpose, namely: regulation of the *institutionalized social relationships between powerful agents and others within a political society*, in service of the political values of order and acceptability discussed above.

The fourth desideratum (D4) attaches a substantive empirical criterion to the demand for a conceptual criterion of differentiation (between the set of social agents and institutions that are to count as subjects of these principles, and the set of agents and institutions that are not) as specified at D2. This requires that any concrete social agent or institution that is to qualify as a viable subject for principles of political legitimacy must satisfy an empirical requirement of *causal efficacy in the protection of core political values* (associated with political order and acceptability, as specified in the discussion above). This desideratum reflects the fact that a principle of political legitimacy will be unable in practice to achieve its purpose of protecting these core political values if the social agents or institutions it 'goes to work on' with its regulative function themselves lack basic causal efficacy with respect to the protection of these values.

We can add to this a fifth desideratum (D5) which attaches an additional conceptual requirement to the empirical criterion of efficacy specified at D4: this is the requirement of *conceptual openness to both positive and negative readings of efficacy* in relation to the protection of key political values, where by 'positive' efficacy we mean an agent's or institution's *capacities to advance goods that are grounded in consensus and common interests*, and by 'negative' efficacy we mean an agent's or institution's *ongoing or likely detrimental impacts on some population's fundamental interests or autonomy*. In part this is a requirement that our conception of efficacy be reasonably non-stipulative, so that it is sufficiently conceptually open to permit consideration and investigation of a range of different agents and institutions (with widely variable social functions, capacities, and effects); this is important given the *pluralism* of the current global political order, which is one of our key empirical premises, as indicated above. In part, also, the requirement reflects a recognition of the importance of both positive and negative dimensions of the characteristically *political* values linked to normative principles of legitimacy, which are concerned *both* with the promotion and coordination of common interests within a social order *and* with the management of conflict, disagreement, and abuses of power.

Beyond concepts of 'states', 'basic structure', and 'governance'

With this understanding of political legitimacy and these desiderata for a concept of its regulative subject in hand, the next task is to evaluate and compare critically the prominent candidates for such a concept that we identified at the outset of this paper: states, global basic structure, and global governance.

The limitations of 'states' as subjects

Traditionally, the most prevalent concept of the subject of principles of political legitimacy – cutting across multiple normative and empirical disciplinary fields – has been that of the *state*. The idea that the state is the subject of political legitimacy, as the basic unit of political analysis generally, has been adopted by many in normative theoretical literatures; often this assumption is made explicit, such as in Robert Wolff's (1990, p. 20) claim that '[p]olitics is the exercise of the power of the state, or the attempt to influence that exercise', and consequently that political philosophy 'must begin with the concept of the state'. As noted earlier, it is common in philosophical analysis to incorporate constitutive features of states even into the very *concept* of political legitimacy, by *defining* it as the justification of state power, or of more specific feature of it, such as its coercive power or its 'moral power' to impose obligations on its subjects to comply with the law through the function of political 'authority'. The concept of the state (along with the related concepts of 'sovereignty', and 'government') has further served as a central subject of analysis for many *empirical* scholars concerned with questions of political legitimacy, in global as well as domestic domains. Questions asked here have been of the following kind: what range of activities is it legitimate for states and their diplomatic delegates to engage in within global politics – through direct foreign policy and through IOs – and what collective institutional constraints ought to be imposed upon states' conduct?

States of course remain centrally important actors on the global stage, and it seems that no plausible account of the subject of global political legitimacy could be formulated that did not incorporate some recognition of states and their IOs as prominent among the appropriate subjects of these political principles. However, there is a very straightforward problem with designating states as the sole subjects of global political legitimacy by invoking the idea of the state as the basic *concept* of subject: doing so precludes any conceptual framework for evaluating certain widespread, and potentially well-founded, intuitions that certain non-state actors and institutions may *also* be appropriate subjects for principles of political legitimacy – intuitions that are commonly held among real political actors in the context of our present pluralist global order.

The reality of political pluralism under conditions of globalization is such that states are no longer the sole bearers of the kind of decision-making power that have traditionally been subject to legitimating political control. Instead, non-state actors such as multinational corporations (MNCs), NGOs, and hybrid institutional actors constituted by both state and non-state actors, now wield many of these forms of decision-making power (in fields of law-making, economic development, public service-provision, and so on), alongside a plurality of states (Held 1995, Cutler, Haufler and Porter 1999, Strange 2003). In other words, there are now some firm grounds for judging that many non-state actors and institutions may now meet the crucial empirical criterion for qualification as subjects of principles of political legitimacy (D4): *causal efficacy in the protection of core political values* (associated with political order and acceptability, as specified in the discussion above). Correspondingly, this expanding and strengthening array of non-state actors is in practice now subject to many of the same political demands for greater legitimacy (through increased 'transparency', 'accountability', 'participation', and so on) as states.

Of course the fact that non-state actors are increasingly viewed by activists and stakeholders as appropriate subjects for principles of political legitimacy does not establish decisively that the state-centric view is misguided; it remains a theoretical possibility that it is the activists and stakeholders, rather than the state-centric theorists of legitimacy, who have got it wrong. These widespread political views do suggest, however, that the state-centric view of political legitimacy at the very least requires critical examination. And such critical examination clearly requires a broader analytic lens for evaluating the political status of these non-state actors than can be provided by the idea of 'states' itself; we need a concept of the subject of global political legitimacy formulated at a higher order of abstraction, through which we can evaluate arguments on both sides for viewing states as having a special status as such subjects.

In other words, the concept of state as subject fails to satisfy our first desideratum (D1), which requires that that our concept of the subject of principles of political legitimacy must be *sociologically non-stipulative* – that is, at least somewhat conceptually *open* with respect to the range of social agents and institutions that can be denoted by it. And underlying this objection is the widespread view (plausible enough to warrant at least a conceptual framework equipped to engage with and evaluate it) that it may not be only states but also many non-state actors which now meet D4: causal efficacy in the protection of core political values.

The limitations of the global 'basic structure' as subject

One such broader concept of the subject of principles of global political legitimacy, which has wide currency among normative political theorists influenced by the work of John Rawls (1999), is that of a global 'basic structure'. (In this literature the regulative principles in question are conceptualized as standards of 'justice', but these are often taken to incorporate some set of principles of political legitimacy as well as principles regulating the distribution of social goods.) Rawls (1999, pp. 6–7) defines the basic structure of a society as 'the way in which the major social institutions distribute fundamental rights and duties to determine the distribution of advantages from social cooperation', and claims that this is the primary subject of justice 'because its effects are so profound and present from the start'. Thomas Pogge (1989) has developed from this the broader concept of an 'institutional scheme', which he characterizes as any set of basic ground rules of a social system that constitute and constrain interactions in such a way as to produce morally significant 'effects'. Although Rawls himself resisted the proposition that there is an institutional structure of this kind at the global level, many others have maintained that there *is* such a 'global basic structure' already in existence, and accordingly designated this as the appropriate subject of global principles of justice (Pogge 1989,

Beitz 1999, Buchanan 2000). As Ronzoni (2009) has argued, we might also see the basic structure as subject of principles in a different sense: as something the principles obligate us to *create*, as a means of achieving the normative purposes embodied in the principles.

There are many ambiguities and difficulties surrounding interpretations of the sense in which a global basic structure can be regarded as a 'subject' of principles of justice, but here we focus on just one problem, which makes the idea of basic structure problematic specifically as a concept for the subject of principles of *political legitimacy*, given the desiderata set out above. The problem we wish to highlight here arises from the way in which the concept of 'basic structure' is linked to a strong form of theoretical 'holism'. By 'holism', we refer here to an approach to normative political theory – given this label by Samuel Scheffler (2003) which holds that all normative principles within a social order must be integrated within an overarching and cohesive framework of principles, systematically enacted through application to all social agents and institutions together, as a unified whole. Such 'holism' – which Scheffler argues Rawlsian theories of justice share in common with utilitarianism – can be justified on the grounds that, under circumstances of complex interdependence such as is experienced in domestic societies and arguably also global society, all social interactions have morally significant implications for other people, and thus cannot be morally assessed without consideration of the wider context.

A key problem with this kind of normative holism for thinking about the problem at hand is that it seems inhospitible to the general idea that there are distinct categories and sets of normative principles applicable to political life, each with its own purpose and function within some wider normative order, which may warrant different regulative subjects being attached to each.[3] On the brief account we offered above of the role of principles of political legitimacy within such a (functional) division of normative labour, these principles have the purpose of regulating institutionalized relationships between (more and less powerful) political actors, with the joint aims of political order and acceptability. This differs from the function of principles of *distributive* justice, which is to direct the production of whichever *distributions of goods* throughout society are deemed to be most morally justified.

Once we recognize this difference, we can see that the rationale for holism makes more sense with respect to the application of principles of *distributive justice* than with respect to those of *political legitimacy*. We can see, first, how a holist approach makes sense for thinking about distributive justice given the purpose of these particular principles: if our goal is to bring about some overall social distribution of goods, then a holistic approach to social regulation is best able to achieve this, since it can take account of distributions brought about through unintended structural effects as well as through intentional decisions of agents. Principles of political legitimacy, however, are not concerned with the production of some overarching social distribution, but rather with the regulation of political *relationships* among actors; an understanding of the purpose of these principles thus leads us away from a preoccupation with regulating unintended effects of actions embedded in social *structures*, and instead towards the direct regulation of powerful political *agents* in whatever form they are – as a matter of historical and sociological fact – actually constituted.

The purposes underlying principles of political legitimacy could in principle be achieved through the regulation of an agent or institution constituted at the most overarching global level (consistent with the holism of the basic structure idea) if one of two conditions obtained: either if some centralized or constitutionalized global agency or institution did already exist; or if it seemed a feasible prospect that some identifiable set of existing political agents could create one within some reasonable timeframe. As noted earlier, however, we take it as an empirical assumption that political pluralism is an important existing feature of the existing global order, and that this pluralism is likely to persist as a pervasive feature of world politics for some time. Given this assumption, we can conclude that – at least under present conditions of global pluralism – it is some fairly disaggregated set of actors and institutions that we need to target for regulation via principles of political legitimacy, rather the kind of unified structural entity associated with the basic structure idea.

To put this in the terms of the desiderata we set out earlier in the paper, we can say that the basic-structure-as-subject concept does not adequately satisfy our third desideratum for a concept of the subject of principles of political legitimacy (D3), which requires that such a concept must be *agent-centric*. This is so since it does not permit the targeting of principles of political legitimacy to particular agents, and within particular social relationships, within a pluralist political order of the kind we presently confront at a global level.

The limitations of global 'governance' as subject

While the concept of the global 'basic structure' is widely employed by normative theorists to characterize the subject of principles of global political legitimacy in non-state-centric terms, the concept most widely invoked by empirical analysts for this purpose is that of 'global governance'. At a very general level, the notion of global 'governance' denotes the various political institutions through which social coordination and control are maintained in global society, in the pursuit of some set of social goods. James Rosenau (2000, p. 171) defines governance as 'systems of rule, as the purposive activities of any collectivity that sustain mechanisms designed to insure its safety, prosperity, coherence, stability, and continuance'. Such governance occurs on a global scale, he argues, 'through both the co-ordination of states and the activities of a vast array of rule systems that exercise authority in the pursuit of goals and that function outside national jurisdictions' (Rosenau 2000, p. 172). These 'rule systems' can include informal and inchoate structures as well as established formal institutions, and can be generated and maintained by non-state actors as well as by state governments.

The concept of global 'governance' has been developed to frame empirical analysis of how these specified social *functions* (of coordination, promoting 'public goods', etc.) – which have conventionally been performed by states' governments – are being performed at the global level through institutions and processes very different from the hierarchical and centralized authority structures constitutive of states. Perhaps because the concept of 'governance' is employed in much empirical analysis as the functional equivalent of governments, many discussions of global political legitimacy are framed as discussions about the legitimacy ('accountability', 'transparency', 'democracy', etc.) of global 'governance' (Held and Koenig-Archibugi 2003, Buchanan and Keohane 2006).

Of the three concepts of subject we have examined here, the idea of 'governance' may in fact get the closest to satisfying the desiderata we set out above. To begin, the concept is non-state-centric and in general sociologically non-stipulative (satisfying D1). It is also sociologically non-inclusive (satisfying D2) in virtue of incorporating a functional criterion of differentiation between the set of social agents and institutions that are to count as subjects of these principles, and the set of agents and institutions that are not: agents and institutions count as elements of a framework of 'governance' if and only if they perform or contribute to the relevant functions (of coordination, promoting public goods, etc.). Finally, although there are some empirical analyses of governance processes that place more emphasis on structural than on agent-centric mechanisms for performance of governance functions, the concept of governance is at least able to accommodate agent-centric readings (through talk of particular 'governance agents' or 'governance institutions' for instance), and so has at least the potential to satisfy D3.

This concept does less well, however, in satisfying fully the requirements of D4 and D5. The functional character of the criterion of differentiation associated with the idea of governance does give it at least the potential to satisfy D4, which requires causal efficacy in the protection of core political values (associated with political order and acceptability); however, the substantive content of the functions most commonly linked to the idea of governance may not correspond fully with the substantive political values linked to the normative idea of legitimacy. Although a fuller normative theory of legitimacy than we have supplied here would be required to assess robustly the relationship between these respective functions and values, we can provisionally observe that the understandings of function entailed in the idea of governance place too much conceptual emphasis on the pursuit of goods that presuppose some harmony of interests and underlying consensus among members of the social order, and too little emphasis on the importance of the characteristically *political* values that are concerned instead with the management of conflict, disagreement and conflicting interests, and the curtailment of abuses of power.

We can perhaps capture this objection most succinctly by saying that the idea of governance does not adequately satisfy the requirements of D5, which demands *conceptual openness to both positive and negative readings of efficacy* in relation to the protection of key political values. This is so since there is too much emphasis on the positive dimensions of efficacy (concerned with an agent's or institution's capacities to advance goods that are grounded in consensus and common interests), and insufficient emphasis on the negative dimensions (concerned with an agent's or institution's ongoing or likely detrimental impacts on some population's fundamental interests or autonomy).

Towards a new conceptual framework: locating 'global public power'

In place of the ideas discussed so far, we propose the concept of *global public power* for capturing the subject of principles of global political legitimacy. The term 'public power' is one that is occasionally employed in both normative and empirical literatures on political legitimacy, but it has not been unpacked carefully or critically examined as a concept distinct from the alternatives we have discussed so far – and it has not (to our knowledge) been given any formal definition in these literatures. For our present purposes, we can define global public power both with respect to its *conceptual meaning*, and with respect to the *substantive normative and empirical criteria* that a concrete sociological entity must satisfy in order to qualify as an instance of global public power.

On the purely conceptual definition, we can say: global public power denotes *all forms of social power within the global domain that are proper subjects of principles of global political legitimacy.* On the substantive definition, we can say: global public power denotes all forms of social power within the global domain that: (a) are exercised through the institutionalized decisions and intentional actions of some *identifiable social agents* (as distinct from inhering in social structures); (b) possess significant *causal efficacy in the protection of core political values* (associated with political order and acceptability, as specified by some more fine-grained normative conceptions of these); and (c) satisfy some justified normative criteria specifying both the relevant thresholds of causal efficacy, and the appropriate conceptions of the core political values at issue – these are what we earlier called the *criteria of differentiation*, distinguishing *public* from *private* forms of social power.

Defined this way, we can see how the concept of global public power is able to satisfy all of the desiderata we identified earlier for a subject of principles of political legitimacy. It is not only that we have defined the concept here precisely *in order to* satisfy these desiderata (although it is true that we have done so – indeed this is just the point of the concept). It is also that this conceptualization points us towards richer traditions of thinking about both 'power' and the 'public'/'private' distinction in political life, which can further orient and expand our analysis of the subject of principles of political legitimacy. To see how this is so, it may help to hold the concept of public power directly against the five desiderata we elaborated earlier – as we did for the other concepts under consideration here – for purposes of critical comparison.

First, public power is a non-state-centric and (more broadly) sociologically non-stipulative concept, which can be employed to designate the subject of principles of political legitimacy, without pre-judging the question of whether, and under what conditions, non-state as well as state-based agents and institutions may qualify as subjects of principles of political legitimacy. As such, this concept straightforwardly satisfies the requirements of D1. Second, it is a sociologically non-inclusive concept, thus satisfying D2, in virtue of incorporating a conceptual criterion of differentiation whereby 'public' power denotes the political agents and institutions that qualify as subjects for principles of political legitimacy and 'private' power denotes those that do not. Third, it is a concept that is able to satisfy the requirements of D3 – that is, the requirement of agent-centrism – at least so long as the concept of power is given a relational (that is agent-relative) rather than a structural reading, which it commonly is and readily can be.

Finally, it is able to satisfy both D4 and D5 in virtue of the fact that the central concept of power is concerned very much with efficacy – in both the 'effective' and 'affective' readings of the concept of power (Morriss 2002). This last point can be strengthened by the recognition that it is not only different readings of the concept of power but also different traditions of political thinking about the character of 'publicness' which draw in both positive and negative readings of political efficacy. To simplify somewhat, we might say that positive readings of political efficacy are most strongly associated with certain aspects of 'republican' thinking about the 'public', concerned with joint action and the pursuit of common social goods (of which Buckinx's (2012) discussion in this collection provides a clear statement), whereas certain liberal traditions emphasize the importance of negative dimensions of efficacy – concerned with political conflict, coercion, and harm – in marking out the parameters of a 'public' or political sphere (such as in Macdonald 2008).

But of course the idea of public power gives us only an analytic concept of the subject of principles of political legitimacy, which in itself is devoid of much substantive normative or empirical content. Adopting the concept of global public power as subject is not sufficient to answer the substantive question of which agents or institutions within the global political domain ought to be subject to principles of political legitimacy, though it does succeed in equipping us with the analytic tools to frame the right kind of research agenda on this question, through which fuller answers can be sought via further normative and empirical research inquiry. An integrated (normative and empirical) research agenda on the scope of global public power would need to tackle the following questions in particular.

To begin with, there is a need to develop more fully the *normative theory of political legitimacy*, and the underlying values of political order and acceptability that we have identified as central to this. More would need to be said here both about how these characteristically political values should be interpreted and operationalized, as well as about the relationship between the 'political' forms of justification associated with political legitimacy and the 'moral' justificatory strategies and principles that are applied in non-political domains of practical decision-making.

Connected to this, there is a need to identify the substantive normative criteria for distinguishing 'public' from 'private' forms of power in global political life. First, this requires determining to what extent we should apply 'negative' criteria of publicness concerned with problematic impact of power (on autonomy, interests, and so on), and to what extent we should apply 'positive' criteria of publicness that demand an active role, by the power in question, in the promotion or protection of important collective interests. Second, it requires the specification of more fine-grained normative conceptions of publicness (such as the republican conception developed by Buckinx 2012) to guide the application of these criteria in more detail.

Once some suitable normative criteria have been established, there is then a need for further *empirical* analysis that investigates which concrete agents and institutions in fact satisfy these criteria – and thus qualify as the bearers of public power – in contemporary global politics. Traditionally, public power has been linked to institutional forms associated with statehood. In particular, it has been linked to the use of force (organized violence), centralized or hierarchical decision-making structures, and law-making. These institutional forms are commonly thought of as uniquely and definitively 'political' or 'public', while other institutional forms (markets, corporations, processes of economic 'production', institutionalized 'supply chains', 'civil associations', 'social movements', NGOs, etc.) are designated as private. But with an institutionally non-stipulative concept of public power and some associated normative criteria in hand, empirical analysts will be equipped to evaluate these common associations more critically.

Conclusions

Conceptualizing the subject of principles of global political legitimacy as global public power, rather than in terms of the conceptual alternatives we have considered here, comes with three key advantages for analysis of legitimacy in global politics. First, the idea of global public power supplies a concept of subject that can help to *unify* analysis of legitimacy across the multiple political sub-disciplines in which it is studied, thus facilitating the future development of a more methodologically diverse and integrated research agenda on the question of the scope of application of these principles than has been undertaken so far in the existing literature. Second, recasting our concept of the subject of principles of political legitimacy in the way we have proposed has important implications for how we conceptualize political legitimacy *itself*: insofar as the concept of legitimacy is commonly defined in part with reference to its subject (as the justification of certain specified forms of power), our proposed reconceptualization of this subject entails an argument for the reconceptualization of political legitimacy – as the (political) justification of public power. Third, this reconceptualization of political legitimacy and its subject provides analytic tools for grappling with the complex normative problems and dilemmas raised by the significant forms of power now exercised by non-state actors, as well as by states through the fragmented and disaggregated institutional architecture of the present global order. In sum, our arguments supply concepts better able to support robust political analysis of the problems raised by the *pluralism* of contemporary world politics than our existing theories of legitimacy have achieved.

Acknowledgements

Earlier versions of this paper were presented at the American Political Science Association Annual Meeting, Boston 2008, and at the Princeton/Oxford Workshop on Global Justice, University Center for Human Values, Princeton University, 2007. We thank the panellists and audiences at these events for helpful questions and feedback.

Notes

1. The question of which social practices in particular are salient here, and how the reasons articulated within them should be interpreted, is a much bigger question that we cannot settle here.
2. Whether this kind of justificatory practice can be regarded as properly 'moral' raises bigger questions than we can resolve here; but all that matters for our present argument is that political order and political acceptability are central

values in the justifications underpinning principles of political legitimacy, whatever we take the 'moral' status of such justifications to be.

3. We do not assume that these different sets of principles must be fully commensurable such that they together constitute a single unified and coherent normative order, but we cannot further elaborate and defend this view here.

Notes on contributors

Andrew Hurrell is Montague Burton Professor of International Relations at Oxford University, and a Fellow of Balliol College. He serves on the editorial boards of journals including *Political Studies* and *European Journal of International Relations*. He has authored and edited many books and articles on topics of global governance, law, and justice, including *On Global Order* (Oxford University Press, 2007).

Terry Macdonald is a Senior Lecturer in Politics and International Relations at the University of Melbourne, having previously held positions as Junior Research Fellow and Lecturer at Merton College, Oxford University, Research Fellow at the Centre for Applied Philosophy and Public Ethics at the ANU, and Lecturer in Politics at Monash University. Her previous publications include *Global Stakeholder Democracy* (Oxford University Press, 2008).

References

Beitz, C.R., 1999. *Political theory and international relations*. Princeton, NJ: Princeton University Press.

Buchanan, A., 2000. Rawls's law of peoples: rules for a vanished Westphalian world. *Ethics*, 110 (4), 697–721.

Buchanan, A., 2002. Political legitimacy and democracy. *Ethics*, 112 (4), 689–719.

Buchanan, A. and Keohane, R.O., 2006. The legitimacy of global governance institutions. *Ethics & international affairs*, 20 (4), 405–437.

Buckinx, B., 2012. Global actors and public power. *Critical review of international social and political philosophy*, 15 (5), 535–551.

Bull, H., 1977. *The anarchical society: a study of order in world politics*. London: MacMillan.

Cerny, P., 1999. Globalization and the erosion of democracy. *European journal of political research*, 35 (5), 1–26.

Cerny, P., 2006. Plurality, pluralism and power: elements of pluralist analysis in an age of globalization. *In*: R. Eisfeld, ed. *Pluralism: developments in the theory and practice of democracy*. Opladen; Farmington Hills, MI: Barbara Budrich Publishers, on behalf of the International Political Science Association, Research Committee No. 16 [Socio-Political Pluralism], 81–111.

Copp, D., 1999. The idea of a legitimate state. *Philosophy and public affairs*, 28 (1), 3–45.

Cutler, A.C., Haufler, V. and Porter, T., 1999. *Private authority and international affairs*. Albany, NY: State University of New York Press.

Held, D., 1995. *Democracy and the global order: from the modern state to cosmopolitan governance*. Cambridge: Polity Press.

Held, D. and Koenig-Archibugi, M., 2003. *Taming globalization: frontiers of governance*. Cambridge: Polity Press.

Hurrell, A., 2007. *On global order: power, values, and the constitution of international society*. Oxford: Oxford University Press.

Krisch, N., 2011. *Beyond constitutionalism: the pluralist structure of postnational law*. Oxford: Oxford University Press.

Macdonald, K. and Macdonald, T., 2010. Democracy in a pluralist global order: corporate power and stakeholder representation. *Ethics & international affairs*, 24 (1), 19–43.
Macdonald, T., 2008. *Global stakeholder democracy: power and representation beyond liberal states*. Oxford: Oxford University Press.
Morriss, P., 2002. *Power: a philosophical analysis*. 2nd ed. Manchester, NH: Manchester University Press.
Pogge, T., 1989. *Realizing Rawls*. Ithaca, NY: Cornell University Press, 1989.
Rawls, J., 1996. *Political liberalism*. New ed. New York: Columbia University Press.
Rawls, J., 1999. *A theory of justice*. Rev. ed. Oxford: Oxford University Press.
Ronzoni, M., 2009. The global order: a case of background injustice? A practice-dependent account. *Philosophy & public affairs*, 37 (3), 229–256.
Rosenau, J.N., 2000. Change, complexity and governance in a globalizing space. *In*: J. Pierre, ed. *Debating governance*. Oxford: Oxford University Press, 167–200.
Scheffler, S., 2003. Rawls and Utilitarianism. *In*: S. Freeman, ed. *Cambridge companion to Rawls*. Cambridge: Cambridge University Press, 420–459.
Simmons, A.J., 1999. Justification and legitimacy. *Ethics*, 109 (4), 739–771.
Strange, S., 2003. The declining authority of states. *In*: D. Held, ed. *The Global Transformations Reader: An Introduction to the Globalization Debate* 2nd Ed, Cambridge: Polity Press, 127–134.
Valentini, L., 2012. Assessing the global order: justice, legitimacy, or political justice? *Critical review of international social and political philosophy*, 15 (5), 593–612.
Wellman, C.H., 1996. Liberalism, Samaritanism, and political legitimacy. *Philosophy and public affairs*, 25 (3), 211–237.
Williams, B., 2005. Realism and moralism in political theory. *In*: G. Hawthorn, ed. *In the beginning was the deed: realism and moralism in political argument*. Princeton, NJ: Princeton University Press, 1–17.
Wolff, R., 1990. The conflict between authority and autonomy. *In*: J. Raz, ed. *Authority*. New York: New York University Press, 20–31.

Two conceptions of state sovereignty and their implications for global institutional design

Miriam Ronzoni

Centre for Advanced Studies 'Justitia Amplificata', University of Frankfurt, Germany

Social liberals and liberal nationalists often argue that cosmopolitans neglect the normative importance of state sovereignty and self-determination. This paper counter-argues that, under current global political and socio-economic circumstances, only the establishment of supranational institutions with some (limited, but significant) sovereign powers can allow states to exercise sovereignty, and peoples' self-determination, in a meaningful way. Social liberals have largely neglected this point because they have focused on an unduly narrow, mainly negative, conception of state sovereignty. I contend, instead, that we should more closely consider the positive aspects of sovereignty, understood as the capacity to maintain internal problem-solving capacities and make meaningful discretionary choices on a range of national issues.

1. Introduction: sovereignty, cosmopolitanism, or both?

The idea that the problem-solving capacity of the state is under strain is extremely widespread. What we need, many argue, are global solutions to global problems. Global institutional design – to address such issues as climate change, human rights, world poverty, and the regulation of migration, trade, labour, tax competition, and financial markets – strikes many as being the most pressing challenge of our time. Other participants in the debate, however, believe the point to be overstated, both from a diagnostic and from a normative perspective. Empirically, so the argument goes, the idea that the state in the era of globalization is powerless is a myth;[1] normatively, putting an end to the sovereign state would entail giving up the important value of self-determination (see, for instance, Miller 1995, Miller 2000, Macedo 2004).

As Katrin Flikschuh (2010, p. 469) has pointed out, this divide reveals a deeper consensus on the premise that one can either have state sovereignty or cosmopolitanism, but not both. Scholars disagree about whether the former or the latter ought to be sacrificed, but agree that a sacrifice is necessary. Flikschuh argues that this is not the case, in that Kant's cosmopolitan Right is only made possible by the morality of sovereign states. For Kant, however, cosmopolitanism is not the *institutional* project of establishing global institutions with independent powers of some sort, but rather the doctrine unpacking the obligations between states and individual citizens of other states – which can only, in his view, be honoured in a world of independent republics. Flikschuh's way of solving the dilemma, therefore, is by redefining the very concept of cosmopolitanism in a way that, by returning to Kant's original argument, moves away from contemporary institutional discourse.

My aim in this paper is to provide some preliminary work concerning how the dilemma addressed by Flikschuh could be solved in a converse way to her proposal; that is, by redefining sovereignty, rather than cosmopolitanism. The central claim of this paper is that, under a specific understanding of what sovereignty and self-determination are, and why they matter, only the establishment of supranational institutions with some sovereign powers can allow states to exercise sovereignty, and peoples' self-determination, in a meaningful way when certain empirical circumstances occur. This point, I shall argue, has so far been neglected because political theorists have tended to rely on an unduly narrow conception of sovereignty, understood in purely *negative* and formal terms – as the legal right to non-interference, which constitutes the crux of international law. My argument will rest on the premise that we should, instead, put more emphasis on the *positive* and substantive aspects of state sovereignty, which are central to the empirical study of statehood in such disciplines as history, international relations, and political science. The positive aspects of sovereignty point to the substantive problem-solving capacity of states and to their ability to make meaningful and genuinely discretionary choices on a range of issues.[2] The positive component of sovereignty, I suggest, not only enables a better fulfilment of the value of self-determination than negative sovereignty, but is also more compatible with a tighter institutional regulation of the global arena.

My fundamental concern, in making a case for global regulatory institutions, is one of *political*, rather than distributive, justice, and this is the case in two respects. Firstly, the fundamental *normative problem* addressed here concerns the problematic power relationships that global political and socio-economic dynamics might generate, rather than their distributive effects. Secondly, insofar as the paper advocates the establishment of supranational institutions with some independent powers, both the *rationale* for global institutional-building and the *kind* of institutions I shall advocate are political, rather than distributive, in nature. Rebalancing power, rather than redistributing resources, among global actors is of central concern here.

Needless to say, problematic power relationships are often due to socioeconomic inequality; lack of positive sovereignty can have poverty as one of its main causes; and global institutions aiming at giving a fair chance at developing positive statehood to all polities might have to engage in some redistribution. However, to the extent that distributive inequality is relevant to my argument, this is the case because it might generate political injustice, rather than because of its intrinsic distributive unfairness.

The paper unfolds as follows. In the next section, I discuss the analytical device of the domestic analogy, which consists of treating states as agents that are relevantly similar to individual actors in one or more respects, and using our convictions about individual interaction to construe normative arguments on international matters. I shall suggest that, although the domestic analogy should be used with caution, there is one aspect in which it has not been exploited *enough*, namely to highlight the analogies between individual freedom and positive sovereignty. In section 3, I expound the difference between negative and positive sovereignty in some detail, drawing on Robert Jackson's (1990) work on quasi-states. In section 4, I unpack the central normative argument of the paper, namely (1) that we should pay more attention to the threats to positive sovereignty that states face; and (2) that the establishment of supranational regulatory institutions might well turn out to be the best way to tackle some of the global systemic obstacles to positive sovereignty. Section 5 concludes by briefly discussing the danger that states might use their positive sovereignty for unjust purposes.

2. Taking the domestic analogy seriously

The so called 'domestic analogy'[3] is both an extremely controversial concept among scholars of international politics, and one that it is extremely difficult to relinquish. In its strongest form, it is 'the argument from the experience of individual men in domestic society to the experience of states, according to which states, like individuals, are capable of orderly social life only if, to use the Hobbesian expression, they stand in awe of a common power' (Bull 1977, p. 46). Bull, who first coined the term, argues that the 'domestic analogy' should be abandoned altogether, because international society is unique in character due to features that are specifically pertinent to the nature of sovereign states. Addressing this issue in a comprehensive manner is beyond the scope of this article; suffice it to say that I believe Bull to be right in several respects: the domestic analogy has been taken *too far* in many ways. This article, however, shall analyse one problem that arises from *not* taking the analogy *far enough* in one way: if sovereign states are to be understood as agents whose freedom ought to be respected, then *attention should be paid to the positive as well as to the negative aspects of their sovereignty.*

Statists typically have a more benign account of the state than advocates of the Hobbesian domestic analogy. They see it less as a self-interest maximizer and more as a moral agent in the global arena, whose agency should be respected. This is usually achieved by conferring upon them the status of *sovereignty*, which many statists take to be, at least in some respects, the functional equivalent of freedom for individuals. Self-governing polities should, just as free individuals, be respected qua (collective) moral agents. The conclusion follows that cosmopolitanism, understood as the establishment of robust global institutions with sovereign powers, unacceptably curtails state sovereignty.

In what sense does this argument not take the domestic analogy far enough? Quite straightforwardly, if it is appropriate to take state sovereignty as a proxy for some form of collective freedom, then it should be acknowledged that the debate on individual freedom is rich and multifaceted, and that more than one *conception* of freedom[4] inhabits it. My argument is that, under certain empirical circumstances, transnational and international dynamics can curtail the positive sovereignty of (some) states, whilst leaving their negative sovereignty untouched – and that, conversely, a carefully designed global institutional order could enhance, rather than endanger, the positive dimension of sovereignty. Once the task of global institutional-building is seen through these lenses, it is counterproductive for contemporary statists to oppose it. For some forms of global institutional-building – more ambitious than the existing global institutional order, yet still significantly limited in competence and scope – could promote, rather than threaten, the features of state sovereignty that statists themselves have reasons to value. Contemporary statists are not Hegelians; they do not believe that states are ultimate, organic units of moral concerns, whose *Geist* ought to be preserved for their own sake. They are, essentially, *liberals*:[5] they believe that states are good for individuals. States, therefore, ought to be considered as the primary units of moral concern in the global arena because we value what they mean *to* individuals – in particular, either because we believe that national identity is essential to promote individual autonomy, and nation-states are the best way to preserve nations (see again Miller 1995); or because individual autonomy can best be protected through forms of democracy and collective self-determination that, arguably, only states can realize. Moreover, statists argue, commonly binding political institutions generate, in turn, special obligations among the individuals subjected to them, and the preservation of states is the only way of making sure that fellow-citizens can honour such mutual obligations (see, for instance, Blake 2001, Nagel 2005, Risse 2006, Sangiovanni 2007). We need states to obtain certain important moral goods, and states themselves trigger special obligations. My argument shall be that only positively sovereign states can fulfil the two sets of functions that statists assign to them, and that under current global circumstances states need global institutional support to restore and/or maintain their positive sovereignty.[6]

This argument brings out one crucial reason why, for Bull and others, the domestic analogy is mistaken. States are not individuals because they are Janus-faced (Jackson 1990, p. 28): they interact both externally, with other states, and internally, with their own citizens or subjects. However, precisely because this is true – precisely because the domestic analogy is not perfect – a richer package of conceptions of individual freedom[7] should inform the debate on sovereignty. The domestic analogy should be taken further for the sake of highlighting the *very difference* between persons and states – and, in particular, the fact that states have individual citizens to respond to. If statists care about sovereignty because they care about internal self-determination, they should put more emphasis on the positive aspects of sovereignty, for these focus on the effective internal capacity of states to solve *internal* problems, and to do so with a sufficient degree of autonomy and discretion.[8] In so doing, positive sovereignty enables states to be more responsive to their citizens (and to their mutual special obligations) and less to external pressures. Negative sovereignty is focused on the freedom of sovereigns, whereas positive sovereignty is more responsive to those who are subject to sovereign power (Jackson 1990, pp. 26–28).

3. Negative and positive sovereignty

In this section, I unpack how the distinction between the negative and the positive aspects of freedom might contribute to our understanding of state sovereignty.[9] In so doing, I shall draw upon Robert Jackson's (1990) work on quasi-states.[10]

Jackson describes negative sovereignty as a 'formal-legal condition' (see Jackson 1990, p. 27 and Schwarzenberger 1967, pp. 54–55) indicating the immunity from external interference that a sovereign state enjoys. Negative sovereignty is arguably the central concept of contemporary international law; it is 'the legal foundation upon which a society of independent and formally equal states fundamentally rests' (Jackson 1990, p. 27). The rights/immunities that negative sovereignty confers over a state correspond to duties of non-intervention that other states bear. Like individual negative freedom, negative sovereignty can helpfully be described as a 'freedom from' and as an 'external' kind of freedom: a state is negatively sovereign when it enjoys immunity from external intervention, whether or not it is capable and has the necessary resources to use such an immunity to self-assigned ends. Positive sovereignty, instead, indicates a dimension of (institutional) self-mastery; it is, once again like its individual counterpart, a 'freedom to', and, crucially, an *internally* enabling condition; a state is positively sovereign when it possesses the internal resources to decide which *kind of polity* it wants to become and acts on it successfully. Unlike negative sovereignty, it is a *substantive* and *empirical* dimension, which negatively sovereign states may or may not enjoy. For this reason, it does not feature very prominently in international legal discourse but is, instead, central to those disciplines which study the empirical dimension of statehood and state-building, such as history and the social sciences. Positive sovereignty concentrates on statehood as a complex empirical phenomenon: it is something that a polity possesses in virtue of its empirical attributes, rather than a status which other states confer upon it as a matter of right. It indicates the capacity of states to be their own masters by making, and effectively implementing, meaningful discretionary choices on crucial institutional and policy matters. It is what 'enables states to *take advantage of* their own independence' (Jackson 1990, p. 29, emphasis added). Positively sovereign states are able to provide fundamental political goods (such as welfare, security, and the rule of law) to their own citizens, and to take advantage of their negative sovereignty in order to choose, pursue, and realize self-imposed goals by means of effective public policies. This should clarify why positive sovereignty is necessary to self-determination. It is positive sovereignty that enables the people to take advantage of the immunities conferred upon their state by means of negative sovereignty in order to achieve and nurture the political goods that statists, social liberals, and liberal nationalists value. Moreover, it is thanks to positive sovereignty that citizens can honour their mutual special obligations by establishing and upholding the appropriate institutional structures that allow them to do so.

In analysing the sovereignty discourse, Jackson (1990, pp. 13–49) argues that the interpretation of state sovereignty in mainly negative terms is fairly new. The positive understanding of sovereignty used to dominate the discourse of international society until the whole first half of the twentieth century. Of course, this does not mean that the *idea* of negative sovereignty did not exist – on the contrary, from the Peace of Westphalia onward, the international society of states has been grounded on the principles of territoriality and mutual non-interference. Indeed, this is what the Peace of Westphalia is famous for, and the concept of *Westphalian sovereignty* is, after all, another term for negative sovereignty. However, according to Jackson's reconstruction, negative sovereignty did not identify, back then, the very *core* of state sovereignty. Rather, the conferral of negative sovereignty was perceived as the acknowledgement, on the part of the international community, of a polity's success in achieving positive sovereignty; states which had *proven themselves* as securely in possession of empirical statehood were recognized as free as equals by the community of states, and therefore granted the immunity of non-intervention. Positive sovereignty was the core of statehood, and negative sovereignty its reward. Moreover, sovereignty was associated with a specific package of institutional qualities – effective control over territory, capacity to provide public goods and effectively implement the rule of law, etc. – that only one type of polity, the modern European state, was seen as possessing.[11] This is why the Westphalian system of non-intervention was not perceived as being in any tension whatsoever with processes of imperial expansion and colonialism. Alien control of extra-European territories was not seen as a violation of sovereignty: to the extent that certain communities were not seen as capable of ruling themselves through the complex institutional web of modern European statehood, they were simply not recognized as sovereign states, and no violation could therefore occur.

It is the process of decolonization itself, Jackson argues, that made the notion of negative sovereignty so central, thereby transforming sovereign statehood into a *normative*, rather than *empirical*, concept – that is, into an entitlement which every people has, rather than a status to be earned on the field by proving one's capacity to self-govern. Undoubtedly, those processes of decolonization that resulted from a successful revolt against the colonial West suggest a large level of positive sovereignty had already been achieved in some colonies (Jackson 1990, pp. 82–83). Many others, however, could not reasonably claim to possess the empirical features that characterise positive sovereignty; therefore, the case for the end of their colonial oppression could not rest on that. The status of sovereign state came therefore to be seen as a *right* to non-interference that every people has on the basis of an underlying right to self-determination, rather than as an *empirical quality* to be then rewarded through a legal status. Achieving positive sovereignty was now seen as a political goal of utmost importance for every sovereign state to pursue, rather than as a precondition for political independence. Understanding the reasons underlying this change in norms and beliefs is beyond the scope of this article;[12] what matters here is to point out that an exclusive focus on negative sovereignty is a relatively recent phenomenon originating from a very specific historical juncture.

The 'new sovereignty game', Jackson (1990, pp. 40–47) argues, has given rise to a very specific set of international political actors: *quasi-states*, which are characterized by the fact of possessing negative, but not positive, sovereignty – although, as recent history shows, states who lack positive sovereignty also face serious difficulties in enforcing their right to negative sovereignty when this is threatened.[13] Quasi-states are recognized as equals in the new sovereignty game, yet their lack of positive sovereignty prevents them from taking advantage of their juridical statehood to pursue self-determined ends.

4. Protecting positive sovereignty in a globalized world

It is now time to unpack how the concept of positive sovereignty can be helpful in understanding which problems of global political justice the current international setting raises. My argument shall proceed in three steps. (1) First, I shall argue that, on balance, the most promising view to hold with respect to the contrast between negative and positive freedom is a mixed one. (2) Secondly, I shall – as promised – take the domestic analogy further and argue that, just as in the individual case, positive sovereignty must contribute to informing our account of sovereignty. (3) Thirdly, I shall argue that a renewed, and revised, emphasis on positive sovereignty might highlight what is problematic about the current global order – namely the fact that it creates global systemic obstacles to the positive sovereignty of (some) states. If this is the case, *supranational regulatory institutions can be seen as a way of supplementing, rather than replacing, state sovereignty.*

4.1. Freedom: defending a mixed view

In 'Two Concepts of Liberty', Isaiah Berlin famously argued that the idea of positive freedom, understood as an internally enabling condition, might suggest that one's ostensive will and aims – influenced as they can be by social and environmental factors – are not necessarily one's 'true' will and aims. Thus, oppressive policies, aimed at 'forcing people to be free', can be justified in the name of positive freedom. Most scholars nowadays agree, however, that 'Two Concepts' must be read neither as a full-blown rejection of positive freedom altogether, nor as an unqualified defence of negative liberty. Berlin (1969) himself clarified that *monism* had been his intended target in 'Two Concepts'; his worry was directed at an account of positive liberty that did not leave space for any other political values. His historically contextualized concern was with how the rhetoric of positive liberty had been abused by totalitarian regimes during the first half of the twentieth century, and he later regretted not having discussed how negative liberty itself, if considered the only worthy political value, could be used to justify great evils, such as exploitation under laissez-faire capitalism (Berlin 2002).

Indeed, much of contemporary liberal theory accepts, either explicitly or implicitly, that some degree of both positive and negative freedom must be part of an appropriate account of freedom,[14] and that this is not necessarily as dangerous as some of Berlin's remarks seem to suggest.[15] If we shift the focus from liberal theory to the actual structure of liberal societies, the consensus becomes almost unanimous. Virtually all liberal societies are characterized by a package of institutions and policies aimed at promoting different variations on, and degrees of, a mixed model of freedom. Even in the most laissez-faire societies, institutions and policies acknowledge the need for individuals to be able to effectively take advantage of one's negative freedom – many welfare policies are justified on these grounds. Admittedly, most of these policies can be conceived as attempts to provide a richer interpretation of negative freedom itself, by relying on a more plausible and wider account of what count as 'constraints'. However, some are uncontroversially inspired by ideas of self-mastery and autonomy. For instance, the idea that each of us needs to 'become' the *kind of agent* who can make effective use of one's negative freedom to pursue self-assigned ends underlies many of the most widely shared policies among liberal-democracies and in contemporary liberal theories, such as the compulsory education of children up to a certain age and the rehabilitation of criminal convicts. There is nothing even remotely similar to a consensus regarding how exactly freedom should be defined, understood, and, promoted. But few would deny that negative freedom without *any* attention being paid to self-mastery, processes of preference formation, and the effective capacity to act on one's negative freedom is not only an empty concept, but one that can be used to justify unacceptable forms of exploitation and false consciousness.[16]

4.2. Taking the domestic analogy further: the benefits of positive sovereignty

In this section I am to suggest that, just as in the individual case, an account of sovereignty should be informed by its positive as well as by the negative dimension. An exclusive focus on negative sovereignty does not allow us to appreciate that an international society characterized by the co-existence of positively sovereign states and quasi-states is not a true society of equals.

Negative sovereignty by itself is just as purely formal, and more often than not as impossible to take advantage of, as negative individual freedom. Quasi-states have a formal equal status with other states, but are often forced to accept deals and agreements that they are not, objectively, in a position to refuse. They are often highly pressurized not only into accepting international agreements that favour stronger states, but also to run their *internal* affairs in a way that pleases them – by unilaterally opening their markets, reforming their own institutions according to specific and far from uncontroversial development agendas, and modifying their foreign policies in such a way as to please global and regional powers. In other words, their exercise of internal, empirical sovereignty is often guided by agendas that are not their own – the clearest sign of poor positive sovereignty. Finally, even when stronger states leave them in peace, quasi-states often cannot do much, if anything at all, with their negative sovereignty. Given their lack of empirical sovereignty, they cannot use their juridical statehood to pursue those goals for which sovereignty is deemed valuable to begin with. Therefore, positive sovereignty needs to supplement purely juridical statehood; a certain degree of positive sovereignty is a precondition to be able to enjoy the immunities granted by negative sovereignty.

Moreover, whereas a closer attention to positive sovereignty is a way of taking the domestic analogy further, it is also a way of doing justice to the very difference between individuals and states, and acknowledging that states have individual citizens to respond to. Positive sovereignty allows us to pay more attention to how being a sovereign state actually benefits the citizens of that very state, and allows them to honour their mutual special obligations of justice – in Robert Jackson's (1990, pp. 26–28) terms, negative sovereignty is biased in favour of sovereigns and against subjects, in a way that positive sovereignty is not. Positive sovereignty, unlike its negative counterpart, allows us to look *inside* states. Indeed, this is where the *analogy* between the individual and the state sheds light on a *substantive link* between them:[17] positive sovereignty is a necessary tool to enable states to secure both the negative and the positive freedom of their own citizens.

Many readers might worry, at this point, that just as positive freedom has been used to promote illiberal ideologies, positive sovereignty has its own dodgy pedigree and sinister sides. The idea that only one kind of polity – conveniently, the *European* modern state – could be seen as having positive sovereignty, and therefore as grounding an entitlement to juridical statehood, has traditionally been one of the most candid justifications for colonialism ('these people cannot rule themselves!') or West-biased development agendas. Positive sovereignty creates, perhaps, fewer biases in favour of sovereigns and against their subjects, but does potentially create biases in favour of some states. In other words, positive sovereignty can be used as a tool to "force some states to be free."

We should, indeed, use the notion of positive sovereignty with caution, yet not fully dismiss it – just as in the individual case. The justification of colonialism derives from a monistic interpretation of positive sovereignty as the *only* normatively relevant consideration – and indeed, most likely, on a narrow definition of positive sovereignty itself, excessively biased in favour of European-style institutions. This does not mean that the lack of positive sovereignty ceases to remain a problem; we should instead opt for a mixed model as our regulative ideal. Recognizing the crucial importance of positive sovereignty does not entail abandoning the normative language of the new sovereignty game, according to which sovereignty is a matter of *right* rather than of fact. A monistic approach towards positive sovereignty led to a paradigm where only empirically sovereign states were entitled to juridical statehood; a pluralistic model allows us to acknowledge that all polities are entitled to independence as a matter of right whilst defining independence in a richer sense. Moreover, it is worth noting that it is the 'new sovereignty games' itself, in current global circumstances, that generates biases in favour of stronger states, by obscuring not only real interstate inequalities behind equal juridical statehood, but also the variety of ways in which the sovereignty of quasi-states can be jeopardized other than through direct interference.

We must, therefore, acknowledge the lack of positive sovereignty as a very serious obstacle to the effective exercise of negative sovereignty – yet, learning from the domestic case, find ways to *support* and *promote* positive sovereignty, rather than consider it a *precondition* to juridical independence.

In the following sub-section, I shall argue that one way in which we could do so is by identifying specific global systemic obstacles to positive sovereignty and designing global regulatory institutions to tackle them.

4.3. Global background conditions and positive sovereignty: addressing global political injustice

In the previous two sub-sections, I have reached the intermediate conclusion that an account of state sovereignty cannot avoid taking its positive dimension into account. The argument I shall put forward in this subsection, which concludes my argument, is that *the global order might be politically unjust in that it creates unjustifiable systemic obstacles to positive sovereignty.*[18] As highlighted in my initial caveats, this is a form of political injustice: making a state's access to positive sovereignty unjustifiably difficult means making its people's access to self-determination – to the determination of its own *political fate* – equally hard.

In describing the status of quasi-states in international society, Jackson observes how state-building is a highly complex and primarily domestic process occurring over a prolonged period of time.[19] Negative sovereignty can simply be conferred upon a state by one legal or diplomatic act;[20] positive sovereignty, instead, cannot be bestowed by other actors. It is the outcome of a long and complex process, and achieving it is each state's own task – although several forms of international development aid can be interpreted as attempts to assist quasi-states in achieving positive sovereignty.[21] I do not wish to challenge this assumption. I agree that, if we want to take self-determination seriously, each country must be deemed responsible for achieving positive sovereignty and that this cannot but be a complex domestic institutional process. However, each country should enjoy reasonably favourable conditions for putting such a process into motion and following it through; in other words, *global background conditions* should not be such that they undermine the capacity of states to achieve or maintain positive sovereignty.[22] As I have argued elsewhere (Ronzoni 2009, Orrù and Ronzoni 2011), this might be precisely what is problematic about the current global order: its systemic role in imposing obstacles to an effective exercise of domestic sovereignty. This happens both (1) through the *imposition* of international rules and norms, and (2) through the *absence* of international rules and norms when these are needed.

(1) The former is embodied in the rules of *existing* global institutions. Some of these are biased in such a way that unduly limits the capacity of quasi-states to build their way out of poor positive sovereignty. Two examples could clarify this point. Firstly, forms of institutional aid and foreign assistance are very often conditional on borrowing countries opening their markets to lending ones (often to the detriment of a more balanced domestic economic development) or on implementing stringent and fit-for-all

'recipes for growth', usually characterized by a clear neoliberal agenda of controlled inflation, budget spending containment, and large-scale processes of privatization.[23] Scholars have questioned whether this is truly the best route for fragile countries to find their way out of poverty and poor institutional functioning (Stiglitz 2006); but what is equally if not even more important from the point of view of positive sovereignty is that these solutions prevent states from *experimenting* with institutions and policies (Rodrik 2006). Such a process of trial and error is both a *means* towards, and an *expression* of, positive sovereignty. On the one hand, the freedom to experiment with institutions and policies is considered by many as the only effective way to gain knowledge as to what works best in a specific national context, in order to achieve the effective control over a territory and the capacity to provide those public goods that are the hallmark of positive sovereignty (Rodrik 2006). On the other hand, positive sovereignty itself *consists in* the very capacity to tackle issues of domestic prosperity and justice with an acceptable degree of autonomy, discretion, and flexibility – to assign oneself ends and pursue them with freely chosen, and revisable, means.

A second example is the existence of a regime of global trade that allows escalating trade tariffs.[24] Escalating tariffs increase progressively as we move from unprocessed raw materials towards technology-intensive processed goods. Quasi-states are most likely to fall into the trap of escalating tariffs. A regime of escalating tariffs highly incentivizes resource-rich quasi-states to structure their economy around the production of one or several raw materials, in order to obtain immediate gains. When this happens, a country's economy becomes highly vulnerable to economic shocks, dependent on trade and export trends, and significantly impaired in its capacity to build a complex, stable, and internally diversified domestic economy. A complex and internally differentiated economy is a typical indicator, and milestone, of positive sovereignty, and it is precisely what quasi-states lack.

(2) The second way in which the current global order might create systemic obstacles to positive sovereignty is constituted by the *lack* of regulation of some of the most important political and socio-economic dynamics that characterize it. In other words: problematic forms of power are being exercised across borders, in the absence of any appropriate institutional way to bind and control them. This happens both in an international and in a transnational manner. Internationally, powerful states are often capable of influencing the domestic policies of weaker ones to their own interests, thus severely limiting their positive sovereignty. Transnationally, several kinds of powerful non-state actors are capable of acting in the global area in ways that favour their own interest and severely undermine the capacity of states to resist them.

According to some, the threats to positive sovereignty caused by the lack of accountability of powerful non-state actors are increasingly affecting not only quasi-states, but also – at least to some extent – affluent and established ones. Domestic welfare states, for instance, are suffering under the pressure of various forms of international tax competition (see, for instance, Avi-Yonah 2000, Genschel 2002, Rixen 2008, Dietsch 2011b, Dietsch and Rixen forthcoming). Established systems of labour rights protections, on the other hand, are increasingly undermined by the strategic decisions of transnational corporations, which can move their business elsewhere without much warning or many consequences. The extent to which this is happening is controversial, and European welfare states are far from being, and unlikely to become, quasi-states; but if positive sovereignty is a matter of degree, then their positive sovereignty has not remained immune from the increased public power, and still virtually absent accountability, of
non-state actors.

Both sets of obstacles to positive sovereignty point, broadly speaking, to the same direction: *global institutional regulation*. We need (1) *better* rules (different rules from the existing ones to regulate trade, international aid, and other areas such as, for instance, intellectual property law); and (2) *more* rules, to regulate global dynamics where lack of accountability dominates (e.g. limiting or prohibiting harmful tax and labour competition). Yet, this is not a full blown cosmopolitan argument. The domestic analogy is imperfect. The appropriate supranational regulatory institutions are those which, by putting constraints on all countries, give effective problem-solving capacities *back* to them.[25] If, for instance, binding global rules against harmful tax competition were to be implemented, then countries would lose the freedom to deviate from such rules (for instance, the freedom to be a tax haven), but would gain back the power to design and implement fiscal policies at more discretion within the constraints of those rules. States would lose part of their *negative* sovereignty in order to gain in terms of *positive* sovereignty. Moreover (and as already highlighted above), *if* it is true that the positive sovereignty of wealthy and established democracies can also be under strain under current global circumstances, an emphasis on positive sovereignty-promoting global institutional design has an additional strategic advantage. At least in some areas, both strong states and quasi-states might have, for instance, a joint interest in binding the power of transnational corporations and other non-state actors through global rules regulating tax breaks and labour conditions.[26]

Which systemic global obstacles to positive sovereignty are the most serious ones, and which specific institutional solutions could tackle them, is a task for another day – and, crucially, a complex interdisciplinary enterprise. The argument made in this paper, I hope, has nevertheless provided a sufficient initial grasp on what our agenda should be.

5. Conclusion

In this paper, I have argued that more attention ought to be paid to the positive aspects of sovereignty; that positive sovereignty can be hindered by globally systemic, as well as internal, factors; and that in order to tackle these, the establishment of more powerful and more independent global regulatory institutions might be needed.

By way of a conclusion, I shall point out one crucial way in which this argument should be qualified. Positive sovereignty can be exercised for evil ends. Although positive sovereignty allows us to look inside states and to pay attention to subjects as well as to sovereigns, states can be positively sovereign and yet oppressive, undemocratic, and deeply unjust (the Third Reich was by all means a positively sovereign state). Admittedly, a focus on positive sovereignty envisages the possibility for polities to genuinely make different choices, responding to context-sensitive needs, but also to different views about justice. Yet, the problem of establishing the *limits of state sovereignty* remains for advocates of positive sovereignty as well as for those who favour a purely negative account of statehood.[27] My point is not that, when states are capable of being positively sovereign, their positive sovereignty should not be bound and controlled in any way. Favouring positive sovereignty does not entail that sovereignty should not be limited through, for instance, international regimes of human rights and international criminal law. Indeed, I have argued that positive sovereignty is crucially important because it allows us to look within states, gives states the power to secure the negative and positive sovereignty of their citizens, and enables polities to be genuinely self-determining, thus realizing political justice. It follows, therefore, that positive sovereignty is valuable *if and only if* it is conducive to these goals, and that it must be regulated in such a way that will not allow its use for oppressive ends (both towards insiders as well as towards outsiders).

Yet, even within those limits, positively sovereign states can take different paths (that is the whole point!) and these paths might fare differently when assessed, for instance, through the lenses of specific conceptions of *distributive* justice. Granted, the protection of positive sovereignty will surely entail a good deal of redistribution of power and resources from wealthy to poor polities; in this respect, then, global political justice might go together with some of the demands of international distributive justice. However, positively sovereign states are entitled, within the limits imposed upon them by global standards of human rights and international criminal law, to a significant level of discretion over domestic socioeconomic choices; global political justice might, therefore, give polities the power to take some unjust decisions with respect to domestic social justice. This might well be where distributive and political justice come apart. If we believe in the good of political justice, and hold the view that accountable and not-too-distant institutions are necessary to achieve it, then we must bite an important bullet: there can be no political justice without positive sovereignty, even if this entails a less than perfect performance in terms of distributive justice according to one's favoured theory.

Acknowledgements

I am grateful to Peter Dietsch, Terry Macdonald, Peter Niesen, Ronen Shnayderman, Milla Vaha, Laura Valentini, Timothy Waligore, an anonymous reviewer, audiences at the Political Theory Research Seminar at the University of Pavia (particularly Ian Carter and Emanuela Ceva), at a workshop on 'Global Political Justice' at the Monash Campus in Prato, and at a panel on 'Global Justice beyond Redistribution' at the ECPR 2011 General Conference in Reykjavik for helpful feedback.

Notes

1. The argument was first made by Weiss (1998).
2. For an argument that focuses on the positive aspects of statehood in the specific case of *fiscal sovereignty* see Dietsch (2011a).
3. The term was first introduced by Hedley Bull as a criticism of 'Kantian' approaches to international relations, according to which the international arena must reach a 'civil condition' just as the domestic one (see for instance Bull 1968a and b). As Flikschuh (2010) has persuasively argued, however, this 'Kantian' argument is not Kant's own argument.
4. In this article, I shall always use the term 'freedom' rather than 'liberty'; this is a mere convention. More importantly, I shall speak throughout the paper about *conceptions*, rather than *concepts*, of freedom. I endorse MacCallum's argument that people who disagree about the right interpretation of freedom actually share the same concept of freedom, according to which 'a subject, or agent, is free from certain constraints, or preventing conditions, to do or become certain things' (Carter 2003). Different conceptions of freedom provide different accounts of what should count as important or relevant agents, constraints, and ends. See MacCallum (1967).
5. Hence the terms liberal nationalism (Miller 1995) and social liberalism (Beitz 1999).
6. In his insightful piece, Peter Dietsch argues that an additional fundamental way in which we should depart from the Westphalian model is by highlighting how state sovereignty entails obligations (to other sovereign states) as well as rights (to non-intervention). Although I do not focus *directly* on the obligations that follow from sovereignty here, the duty to establish global regulatory institutions could plausibly be construed as one such obligation (see Dietsch 2011a).
7. This paper deals with the extent to which positive sovereignty may help us understand what, if anything, is politically unjust about the international order. For congenial remarks regarding free statehood from a republican perspective, see Laborde 2010 and Skinner 2010.
8. I thus follow Dietsch in his account of sovereignty as fundamentally instrumental to individual well-being (and I take liberal statists to do so, as well); see Dietsch (2011a).
9. For the distinction between negative and positive freedom, see Berlin (1969).

10. For a partially different definition of the difference between positive and negative sovereignty, see also Schwarzenberger (1967, pp. 52, 564).
11. Jackson illustrates this point through a poignant imaginary story of time traveling. A British civil servant in 1936, he tells us, would be less surprised by our claim that we are time travellers from the late twentieth century (used as he is to eccentricity) than by the fact that all former colonies of the British Empire are now 'sovereign' states. It would take us a while to understand that he cannot get his head around what it even *means* for a colony with extremely poor institutional capacity to become a sovereign state, because he operates with an entirely positive account of sovereignty (Jackson 1990, pp. 13–15).
12. Jackson (1990, pp. 78–81) himself remains rather open on the matter, although he shows a certain predisposition towards the view that this was, at least to a certain degree, a genuine change in normative beliefs.
13. See, for instance, the interventionist politics of the United States in Latin America throughout the 1970s.
14. There are exceptions, and both purely negative and purely positive libertarian positions do survive in academic debates (see, respectively, Nozick 1974 and Taylor 1991, pp. 141–162).
15. Those who are familiar with the debate on freedom will probably find my remarks here naïve and superficial. It is not my aim here to make an informed argument within that rich and complex discussion, and I cannot possible make justice to it here. The debate has moved on immensely from the publication of Berlin's seminal essay. Indeed, several different interpretations of positive and negative freedom are currently put forward in the literature (see, for instance, Taylor 1991); several attempts to reconcile the two exist (see, for instance Christman 1991); and several schools of thought (most notably neo-republicanism) have tried to overcome the distinction altogether by proposing alternative conceptions of freedom (Pettit 1997, Skinner 2002). My aim here is, much more modestly, to see whether the broad distinction between negative and positive liberty can be of some use to highlight different conceptions of state sovereignty.
16. It has been pointed out to me that a revised account of negative freedom (and sovereignty) can account for even these problems, by having a richer and more pluralistic account of what count as constraints and acts of interference (for instance, by including internal –psychological and intellectual – constraints). This might constitute a strategic advantage (negative sovereignty is easier to swallow), but would lead, I think, to a neglect of the important phenomenological difference between the dimension of freedom that concentrates on not being constrained, and the one which focuses of *being a certain kind of agent*.
17. I am grateful to an anonymous reviewer for drawing my attention to this point.
18. For an insightful and broadly similar perspective, although within a slightly different conceptual framework, see also Valentini (2012).
19. See also Mathias Risse's (2005) 'institutional thesis', according to which the main cause of poverty are poor domestic institutions.
20. However, enforcing one's negative sovereignty when this is threatened by other actors might itself require a good deal of positive sovereignty.
21. And indeed, development sceptics may argue the fact that development aid often fails demonstrates that positive sovereignty can only be achieved internally by one's own means, over time.

22. This argument has a similar structure to Pogge's case about the causes of global poverty. Pogge does not deny the role of domestic factors, and in particular corruption and poor domestic politics, in perpetuating extreme poverty. His argument, however, is that we should acknowledge how much the global order *systemically incentivizes* such domestic politics (Pogge 2008, esp. chs. 4 and 5).
23. Ngaire Woods (2010) argues that this has remained relatively unchanged even after the financial and then economic crisis of the last few years.
24. I have discussed this case is some more detail in Ronzoni (2009).
25. Some of the most immediate implications of my approach are therefore close to those supported by Barbara Buckinx's 2011 incrementalist model.
26. The idea that the traditional winners and the perceived losers of globalization might have an overlapping long-term interest in global institutional design is also suggested by Dani Rodrik (2000).
27. Thus, we ought to distinguish between positive sovereignty understood as an *empirical* quality that we have normative reasons to value, and the *normative* constraints that empirically sovereign states must respect in order to be normatively entitled to negative sovereignty, i.e. to the juridical entitlement to non-interference (see Valentini 2011, ch. 8).

Note on contributor

Miriam Ronzoni is a Research Fellow at the Centre for Advanced Studies 'Justitia Amplificata', in Frankfurt. Her work mainly focus on issues of global justice and constructivism. Her publications include *Social Justice, Global Dynamics: Theoretical and Empirical Perspectives* (Routledge, 2011, co-edited with Ayelet Banai and Christian Schemmel) well as research articles appeared in journals such as *Philosophy and Public Affairs, Politics, Philosophy, and Economics*, and *Review of International Studies*.

References

Avi-Yonah, R.S., 2000. Globalization, tax competition, and the fiscal crisis of the welfare state. *Harvard law review*, 113 (7), 1573–1676.

Beitz, C.R., 1999. Social and cosmopolitan liberalism. *International affairs*, 75 (3), 515–529.

Berlin, I., 1969. Two concepts of liberty. *In*: I. Berlin, *Four essays on liberty*. Oxford: Oxford University Press, 118–172.

Berlin, I., 2002. *Freedom and its betrayal: six enemies of human liberty*, ed. H. Hardy. Princeton, NJ: Princeton University Press.

Blake, M., 2001. Distributive justice, state coercion, and autonomy. *Philosophy & public affairs*, 30 (3), 257–296.

Buckinx, B., 2011. Domination in global politics. reflections on freedom and an argument for incremental global change. *In*: L. Cabrera, ed. *Global governance / global government: institutional visions for an evolving world system*. Albany, NY: Suny Press, 253–282.

Bull, H., 1968a. Society and anarchy in international relations. *In*: H. Butterfield and M. Wright, eds. *Diplomatic investigations: essays in the theory of international politics*. Cambridge, MA: Harvard University Press, 35–50.

Bull, H., 1968b. The Grotian conception of international society. *In*: H. Butterfield and M. Wright, eds. *Diplomatic investigations: essays in the theory of international politics*. Cambridge, MA: Harvard University Press, 51–73.

Bull, H., 1977. *The anarchical society*. London: Macmillan.
Carter, I., 2003. Positive and negative liberty. *Stanford Encyclopedia of Philosophy* [online]. Available from: http://plato.stanford.edu/entries/liberty-positive-negative/. (accessed 4 October 2012).
Christman, J., 1991. Liberalism and individual positive freedom. *Ethics*, 101 (2), 343–359.
Dietsch, P., 2011a. Rethinking sovereignty in international fiscal policy. *Review of international studies*, 37 (5), 2107–2120.
Dietsch, P. 2011b. Tax competition and its effects on domestic and global justice. *In*: A. Banai, M. Ronzoni, and C. Schemmel, eds. *Social justice, global dynamics – theoretical and empirical perspectives*. London: Routledge, 95–113.
Dietsch, P., and Rixen, T. forthcoming, Tax competition and global background justice, Journal of Political Philosophy. Available on early view: http://onlinelibrary.wiley.com/doi/10.1111/j.1467-9760.2012.00419.x/full (accessed 4 October 2012).
Flikschuh, K., 2010. Kant's sovereignty dilemma: a contemporary analysis. *The journal of political philosophy*, 18 (4), 469–493.
Genschel, P., 2002. Globalization, tax competition, and the welfare state. *Politics & society*, 30 (2), 245–275.
Jackson, R.H., 1990. *Quasi-states: sovereignty, international relations and the third world*. Cambridge: Cambridge University Press.
Laborde, C., 2010. Republicanism and global justice. a sketch. *European Journal of Political Theory*, 9 (1), 48–69.
MacCallum, G.C., Jr., 1967. Negative and positive freedom. *Philosophical review*, 76 (3), 312–334.
Macedo, S., 2004. What self-governing peoples owe to one another: universalism, diversity, and the law of peoples. *Fordham law review*, 72 (5), 1721–1738.
Miller, D., 1995. *On nationality*. Oxford: Oxford University Press.
Miller, D., 2000. *Citizenship and national identity*. Cambridge: Polity Press.
Nagel, T., 2005. The problem of global justice. *Philosophy & public affairs*, 33 (2), 113–147.
Nozick, R., 1974. *Anarchy, state and utopia*. Oxford: Blackwell.
Orrù, E. and Ronzoni, M., 2011. Which supranational sovereignty? Socio-economic justice and international criminal law compared. *Review of international studies*, 37, 2089–2106.
Pettit, P., 1997. *Republicanism: a theory of freedom and government*. Oxford: Oxford University Press.
Pogge, T., 2008. *World poverty and human rights*. Cambridge: Polity.
Risse, M., 2005. How does the global order harm the poor? *Philosophy and public affairs*, 33 (4), 349–376.
Risse, M., 2006. What to say about the state. *Social theory and practice*, 32 (4), 671–698.
Rixen, T., 2008. *The political economy of international tax governance. transformation of the state*. Basingstoke; New York: Palgrave Macmillan.
Rodrik, D., 2000. How far will international economic integration go? *Journal of economic perspectives*, 14 (1), 177–186.
Rodrik, D., 2006. *What kind of global institutions will accelerate global economic catch-up?* [online]. Available from: http://www.docstoc.com/docs/273722/What-Kind-of-Global-Institutions-will-Accelerate-Global-Economic-Catch-Up—Conference-at-Harvard-University (accessed 4 October 2012).
Ronzoni, M., 2009. The global order: a case of background injustice? *Philosophy & public affairs*, 37 (3), 229–256.

Sangiovanni, A., 2007. Global justice, reciprocity, and the state. *Philosophy & public affairs*, 35 (1), 2–39.
Schwarzenberger, G., 1967. *A manual of international law*. London: Stevens.
Skinner, Q., 2002. A third concept of liberty. *Proceedings of the British Academy*, 117, 237–268.
Skinner, Q., 2010. On the slogans of republican political theory. *European Journal of Political Theory*, 9 (1), 95–102.
Stiglitz, J., 2006. *Making globalization work*. London: Penguin.
Taylor, C., 1991. What's wrong with negative liberty. *In*: D. Miller, *Liberty*. Oxford: Oxford University Press, 141–162.
Valentini, L., 2011. *Justice in a globalized world: a normative framework*. Oxford: Oxford University Press.
Weiss, L., 1998. *The myth of the powerless state*. Ithaca, NY: Cornell University Press.
Woods, N., 2010. Global governance after the financial crisis: a new multilateralism or the last gasp of the great powers? *Global policy*, 1 (1), 51–63.

Assessing the global order: justice, legitimacy, or political justice?

Laura Valentini

Department of Political Science, University College London, UK

Which standards should we employ to evaluate the global order? Should they be standards of justice or standards of legitimacy? In this article, I argue that liberal political theorists need not face this dilemma, because *liberal* justice and legitimacy are not distinct values. Rather, they indicate what the same value, i.e. equal respect for persons, demands of institutions under different sets of circumstances. I suggest that under real-world circumstances – characterized by conflicts and disagreements – equal respect demands basic-rights protection and democratic participation, which I here call 'political justice'. I conclude the article by considering three possible configurations of the global order – the 'democratic world-state', 'independent democratic states', and 'mixed' models – and argue that a commitment to political justice speaks in favour of the latter.

1. Introduction

The existing global institutional order is far from being morally faultless, but what standards ought to be employed to evaluate its moral failings and guide its reform? There are two main contenders for this role: standards of legitimacy, and standards of justice. Traditionally, *legitimacy concerns the right to govern, justice the moral quality of government.* A legitimate institution has the right to rule, a just institution exercises its rule consistently with its subjects' rights and entitlements (cf. Reidy 2007, p. 246).

Within the liberal tradition, discussions about justice and about legitimacy – whether in relation to the domestic or the global realm – have often proceeded separately.[1] In this paper, I argue that such a separation is regrettable, because the underlying concerns of a liberal account of legitimacy are the same as those of a liberal account of justice. From a liberal perspective, justice and legitimacy should not be treated as distinct values. Instead, they should be seen as expressing what the same value – equal respect for persons – demands of our institutions under different sets of circumstances.[2] When deciding how to evaluate domestic and global institutions, then, we need not choose between justice and legitimacy, but simply ask ourselves what equal respect demands under the circumstances at hand. Given existing circumstances, our answer to this question delivers what I call *principles of political justice*, namely principles of justice that are sensitive to the conflicts and power-dynamics characterizing real-world politics. I bring the paper to a close by examining the implications of this conceptual conclusion for our moral assessment of the global institutional order.

The paper is structured as follows. In section 1, I lay out the distinction between the *concepts* of justice and legitimacy. In section 2, I specifically focus on the *conceptions* of justice and legitimacy defended by *liberal* political theorists (in the domestic context): distributive egalitarianism and democracy.[3] In sections 3 and 4, I question the idea that there is a fundamental distinction between liberal justice and liberal legitimacy, and show that they are rooted in the same value, giving rise to different rules of conduct under different circumstances. I argue that, given the existing circumstances of reasonable disagreement about justice, a (politically) just state need not be distributively egalitarian, but must protect basic rights and democracy. This way of thinking about justice is eminently 'political' insofar as it takes seriously not only the distribution of material goods, but also that of political power. In section 5, I consider the implications of my argument for the debate on global justice. I suggest that the debate's focus on distributive equality is somewhat misguided, and that a politically just global institutional order is one that secures respect for basic rights and democratic participation for all its inhabitants. In section 6, I lay out three possible configurations of the global order which may all be thought to instantiate the outlook on justice I favour – the 'democratic world-state', 'independent democratic states', and 'mixed' models – and defend the latter in particular. I conclude by summarizing the paper's arguments.

2. The concepts of justice and legitimacy

What is *justice*? Even though philosophers disagree about the substantive answer to this question, they agree that principles of justice establish people's rights, they tell us who owes what to whom (Barry 1991). For example, to say that Bob owes Mary five pounds is to make a claim about justice. Similarly, to say that Christine owes Jacob compensation for damaging his car is to make a claim about justice, about what Jacob has a right to. This is a maximally general definition of justice, applying to all sorts of agents, be they individuals or collectives. But my focus in this paper is narrower than that: I am specifically interested in the justice of coercive political institutions. From this perspective, principles of justice determine what such institutions – rather than individuals or groups – owe to their subjects. When political institutions are just, they fully respect their subjects' rights.

Legitimacy indicates a different standard for institutional evaluation (cf. Rawls 1996, lecture IX). The function of legitimacy is not to tell us when a political institution gives its subjects what they are owed, but when it is entitled to exercise political power (Buchanan and Keohane 2006). A legitimate state may not be fully just, but it nevertheless has the right to rule (and to be obeyed).[4] For instance, from the perspective of an egalitarian political philosopher, the United Kingdom is not a perfectly just state: it is far from implementing distributive equality. Yet most egalitarian philosophers would probably argue that the British state has the right to rule (and be obeyed), namely that it is legitimate.

To sum up, we may distinguish between justice and legitimacy along the following lines:

- **Standards of justice**: indicate when institutions give their subjects exactly what they are entitled to (i.e. when they respect their rights).
- **Standards of legitimacy**: indicate when institutions have the right to rule (and be obeyed).

3. Liberal conceptions of justice and legitimacy

What do justice and legitimacy demand? In this paper, I focus on the answers given by the contemporary liberal-egalitarian tradition in particular, which is characterized by a commitment to the moral equality of persons *qua* rational and autonomous agents (Waldron 1987, Kymlicka 2001, p. 4). This commitment informs liberal accounts of both justice and legitimacy.

As far as *justice* is concerned, respect for persons' autonomy demands that institutions establish entitlements in such a way as to allow each to pursue her goals without preventing others from doing the same. In other words, a just society is one in which everyone enjoys the necessary social conditions to lead an autonomous life. Different theories of justice offer different articulations of this ideal. For instance, Rawls's justice as fairness (1999a), Dworkin's equality of resources (2000), and G.A. Cohen's equality of access to advantage (1989) can all be seen as attempts to operationalize what each person is owed by the state – or a functionally equivalent set of institutions – *given* the fundamental moral equality of all.

While justice demands the satisfaction of certain substantive requirements, *legitimacy* is associated with the satisfaction of procedural ones. Within the liberal tradition in particular, the right procedures are typically those that express equal respect for persons by attracting their *consent or acceptance*. Although this understanding of legitimacy is widespread among pre-twentieth-century liberals – specifically social-contract theorists – a contemporary and influential version of it is offered by Bernard Williams.

Williams (2005, ch. 1) argues that a state is legitimate when it 'makes sense' to its subjects as a political authority with the right to rule. That is, a state is legitimate when it is accepted as such. Crucially, only *genuine* acceptance – rather than acceptance resulting from subjugation – has legitimizing force.[5] A slave may regard his master as a 'legitimate authority', yet the slave's acceptance of the master's authority hardly counts as legitimizing. For similar reasons, any legitimate state must include guarantees against oppression.

Note though that even when such guarantees are in place, citizens rarely *all* consent to their government and regard it as authoritative. As anarchists have repeatedly pointed out, universal consent is chimerical.[6] This suggests that equal respect cannot feasibly require *de facto* unanimous consent/acceptance, but must demand something weaker, namely respect for the opinions and views of those who are governed (Waldron 1999, Christiano 2008).

These reflections have led many liberal philosophers to conclude that institutions can be legitimate only when they are *democratically* organized, thereby granting citizens equal participation in political decision-making.[7] As Buchanan (2002, p. 711) puts it: democratic theory does 'what consent theory claimed but failed to do but without the overdemanding requirement of consent: reconcile equality with the exercise of political power'. Of course, there are different forms of democracy, but certain minimal conditions such as freedom of speech, association, universal suffrage and majority rule have to be satisfied for a society to count as democratic. Unless these guarantees are robustly provided, a state cannot be legitimate from a liberal point of view.

From our short discussion it has emerged that, in contemporary liberal theory, justice by and large corresponds to substantive equality, while legitimacy to procedural equality. To be sure, legitimacy demands the satisfaction of certain 'substantive' rights making it possible for people to exercise their 'procedural' rights. When people are severely discriminated against, or denied access to basic goods, they are hardly able to participate as equals. What distinguishes legitimacy from justice – *to the extent that* they are treated as separate moral concerns – is that, from the perspective of legitimacy, substantive guarantees are seen as necessary for the satisfaction of procedural demands, rather than as independently valuable.

In sum, as Eamonn Callan (2001, p. 141) puts it, '[o]n the standard liberal construal of legitimacy, it requires the free consent of citizens in some sense. Justice [by contrast] depends on the extent to which democratic self-rule honors basic rights and realizes a fair distribution of benefits and burdens among citizens'.

4. Justice and legitimacy: two separate values?

Even though this picture of the distinction between justice and legitimacy is common in the contemporary liberal literature, I am going to challenge it. To give the challenge some initial plausibility, let me start by highlighting some puzzling features of this distinction as it is typically conceived of.

To begin with, liberal justice and legitimacy are depicted as competing values, but as the previous section has shown, they stem from the same fundamental commitment to equal respect. On the 'justice' reading, equal respect requires that all persons be given an equal sphere of agency (delimited by their rights to social goods) within which they can pursue their ends and goals. On the 'legitimacy' reading, equal respect demands that the institutional mechanisms which 'force' a certain distribution of rights on people be as consistent as possible with people's own views. The natural reaction to these different interpretations of the demands of equal respect is a suspicion that only one of them can be correct. Either a set of institutions instantiates equal respect because its rule meets independent distributive standards (justice); or it instantiates equal respect because its rule is democratically validated (legitimacy). If you believe in liberal justice, then it becomes unclear why you should also believe in liberal legitimacy and vice versa (cf. Davis n.d.).

The separation between justice and legitimacy is puzzling not only because they express the same underlying moral concern (i.e. equal respect), but also because they have the same function: that of justifying coercion. Legitimacy tells us when institutions have the right to rule, that is to coerce us into respecting particular laws. Justice tells us when institutions give their subjects what they are owed, and what they are owed as a matter of justice is *rightfully enforceable* (think of property rights, valid contracts etc.).[8] When coercion is used to protect people's justice-based entitlements, i.e. their spheres of agency, it is rightful precisely because its exercise is consistent with the autonomy of all (see Kant 1965, Blake 2001).

In sum, since liberal justice and legitimacy (i) stem from the same moral concern and (ii) have the same function, one may rightly wonder why they are treated as *entirely* separate values. Some liberal theorists – arguably Rawls (1996) and certainly Buchanan (2002, 2004, ch. 5) – have already offered a partial answer to this puzzle, by defending a justice-based account of legitimacy. On this account, institutions are legitimate when they sufficiently approximate the demands of justice (i.e. equal respect), without necessarily meeting them fully (Reidy 2007, p. 247). From this perspective, justice and legitimacy are not *entirely* separate, but legitimacy is a subset of justice. A state is legitimate if it protects certain fundamental rights, including the right to democratic political participation (assuming this is possible), but its protection of such rights need not be perfect, and the outputs of democratic decisions need not fully align with the demands of egalitarian justice (Buchanan 2002).

This account of the distinction between justice and legitimacy responds to our original puzzle, but it generates a different one, namely: how are we to distinguish those requirements of justice which are necessary and sufficient for legitimacy, from those which are not? Moreover, this account has the odd implication that the state may *rightfully* enforce some *unjust* laws, provided they are democratically chosen. But how can this be consistent with the claim that only demands of justice are rightfully enforceable? If I have an entitlement to X, how can the state rightfully enforce a law that denies my entitlement to X (Davis n.d.)?

In what follows, I suggest that these puzzles can be answered by no longer considering justice and legitimacy as (entirely or even partly) separate values. Justice and legitimacy are both expressions of what the same value (equal respect) demands of our coercive institutions *under different sets of circumstances*. In brief, what we typically call 'justice' articulates the demands of equal respect under the so-called circumstances of justice (moderate scarcity, limited altruism, and no reasonable disagreement about justice). What we typically call legitimacy articulates the demands of equal respect under the circumstances of 'political justice' (moderate scarcity, limited altruism, and reasonable disagreement about justice).[9] Which articulation of equal respect we should employ to evaluate our institutions thus depends on the circumstances at hand (cf. Valentini forthcoming).

5. Justice and political justice

My argument is based on the following assumptions.

(a) *A state is just (i.e. it complies with the duties of justice that apply to it) when it gives its citizens what they are owed qua moral equals.*

This premise has already been discussed and defended earlier in the paper, and simply restates the 'liberal' conception of justice.

(b) *Ought implies can: duties cannot exceed what is possible.*

This is a constraint on any genuine moral requirement. Plainly, individuals and institutions cannot have duties to do what they cannot do. The duties (of justice) that apply to them must align with the limits of human nature. Combining (a) and (b), we obtain:

(c) *A state is just when it gives its citizens what they are owed qua moral equals, to the extent that this is possible given the limits of human nature.*

But what are the limits in question? Traditionally, these correspond to the so-called Humean circumstances of justice: moderate scarcity and limited altruism (Rawls 1999a, pp. 109–112).[10] In a just society, resources must be so distributed as to express equal respect for persons, taking into account that resources are scarce and that humans are not fully altruistic creatures. The recommended distribution is typically egalitarian in form. Of course, what institutions have to do in order to realize the relevant conception of justice might vary depending on the social conditions at hand. For instance, in a society characterized by racial discrimination, justice might demand the introduction of affirmative action policies (see, e.g. Nagel 1977). But notice that variation here only concerns the *implementation* of the correct account of justice, not what the correct account of justice *is* in the first place. So far, we have reached the following conclusion.

(d) *Under conditions of moderate scarcity, and limited altruism (and no reasonable disagreement about justice), institutions are just – they give citizens what they are owed qua moral equals – when they realize distributive equality.*

Things look different, however, if instead of limiting the circumstances of human existence to moderate scarcity and limited altruism, we include another pervasive fact of social life: disagreement about what justice itself demands (Waldron 1999). This fact appears to be at least as pervasive as resource scarcity and human selfishness. Indeed, even among those committed to equal respect (the group I am focusing on for the purposes of this paper) there is serious disagreement concerning what social rules count as respectful of all. Disagreement between different *plausible* interpretations of equal respect, i.e. of what it is for people to have roughly equal spheres of agency, is what I here call 'reasonable' disagreement.[11]

Consider, for instance, variations on Rawls's difference principle. Even though Rawls (1999a) claims that this principle would be unanimously chosen in the original position, it is not clear that this is the only principle which could express equal respect for persons (but cf. Rawls 1999b). Indeed, Dworkin's equality of resources would seem to be another plausible candidate – or Sen's equality of capabilities, and so forth.

To be sure, we can readily exclude a number of possible social arrangements as inconsistent with persons' moral equality – i.e. those which would fail to respect certain fundamental rights, or those which would obviously unfairly discriminate against a particular social group. However, beyond certain limits, equal respect is open to different reasonable interpretations, and we do not seem to be in the epistemic position to single one out as being uncontroversially superior to the others. Under these circumstances, how should we organize our institutions for them to express equal respect to the extent that this is possible given the limits of human nature? The answer is: democratically.[12]

The line between the substantive and the procedural demands of equal respect is to be drawn in correspondence with those matters of justice over which there is reasonable disagreement. If we ask: what should institutions do to show equal respect towards their subjects, when their subjects reasonably disagree about justice? The answer is: they should enforce those demands of justice that are a *sine qua non* of equal respect (and I am assuming they are a non-empty set), and then let democratic procedures determine what else equal respect requires. Directly enforcing a partisan conception of justice on society would be inconsistent with equal respect, because it would treat holders of competing reasonable views as inferiors. When there are disagreements about justice, one of citizens' rights – which a just government ought to respect – is that to (approximately) equal political decision-making power, i.e. to democratic participation (Valentini forthcoming, cf. Gaus 1996, Waldron 1999, Christiano 2008).

Of course, democracy (on any specification of its requirements, a matter on which I remain silent in this paper) is less than perfect. Democratic outcomes inevitably favour the views of some (i.e. of the majority) over those of others. Since decisions cannot be postponed indefinitely or until consensus is reached, giving each person an equal say in political decision-making seems to be the best solution compatible with equal respect.[13] *If ought implies can, justice cannot require of institutions any more than what they can do to realize it.* Under circumstances of reasonable disagreement about justice, this corresponds to respect for basic rights plus democratic entitlements.[14] Strict distributive equality ceases to be the core of justice because its status as an enforceable moral demand is conditional upon its democratic approval. In sum:

(e) *Under conditions of moderate scarcity, limited altruism, and reasonable disagreement about justice, institutions are (politically) just, i.e. they give their citizens what they are owed qua moral equals, when they realize basic rights and democracy.*

This conclusion may seem to have a particularly unpalatable implication, namely that the different competing theories of distributive justice which constitute the bulk of the contemporary literature on the topic have no normative force, or no role to play in deciding how society should be organized. If my view really had this implication, it would be highly surprising and (possibly) problematic. But as I shall shortly explain, it does not. From the perspective I defend, Rawls's difference principle, or Dworkin's equality of resources are not 'thrown out of the window', so to speak, but are simply no longer allowed to take centre stage in thinking about justice. This seems fully appropriate, given their fragile normative status: they are all reasonable interpretations of equal respect, but there is no privileged perspective from which we can single one of them out as correct. On the view I have presented, the substantive egalitarian principles dominating the contemporary debate on justice do not primarily apply to institutional conduct, but to the political choices of individuals *within* just institutions (Waldron 1999, pp. 2–4). They represent competing accounts of what political programmes individuals should support (e.g. through democratic vote), not of how institutions ought to be structured at a fundamental level. Such institutional principles, sensitive to the existence of disagreement and conflict, and setting out enforceable entitlements, are what I call principles of *political justice*.

To sum up, if norms of justice indicate when an institution gives its citizens what they are owed *qua* moral equals, and justice is always constrained by the limits of human nature, under circumstances of reasonable disagreement about justice, *institutions* are politically just when they implement basic substantive guarantees and democratic rights. The values of justice and legitimacy are thereby brought together under the (more coherent) master-value of political justice. There are no longer two competing answers to the question 'What does equal respect demand of *our* institutions?', but one, integrated answer. In what follows, I explore the implications of this view for our assessment of the global order.

6. Reconsidering the debate on global justice

The debate on global justice has in large part focused on whether liberal-egalitarian distributive justice should apply globally. While cosmopolitans insist that this question should be answered in the affirmative, statists deny the global extensibility of egalitarian justice (for the former position, see, e.g. Pogge 1989, Beitz 1999, Moellendorf 2002, Tan 2004, Caney 2005; for the latter, see Rawls 1999b, Nagel 2005, Miller 2007). If my argument so far is correct, this focus on the global appropriateness of distributive equality is misconceived. On the assumption that there exists reasonable disagreement about the nature and content of justice, distributive equality cannot be the guiding value of an account of justice for institutions, whether local or global. From a liberal perspective, under circumstances of reasonable disagreement about justice, the world ought to be so organized as to respect each person's basic rights, and allow competing reasonable accounts of justice to confront each other fairly, through broadly democratic procedures (see Caney 2006, Buchanan 2002, 2004, ch. 7 sec. III).[15] When institutions satisfy these requirements, they are *as just as they can be*, and this is the case not only for domestic institutions, but also for global ones (given the undeniable existence of reasonable disagreement at the global level).

What is more, while democratic institutions already exist at the domestic level, they are lacking at the global one. When such institutions are present, a focus on 'what people should vote for' on the part of political philosophers is not practically idle. But such a focus becomes dubious in the global arena, where no democratic decision procedures exist. Absent such procedures, and the preconditions for their good functioning, egalitarian principles are normatively irrelevant. This is because, as we have seen, their status as enforceable demands of justice rests precisely on their being the output of such procedures.

In sum, my conceptual analysis of justice and legitimacy prompts us to *reorient the debate on global justice from a focus on distributive equality, to a focus on basic rights and democracy.* Theorists of global justice should ask how the global order can best guarantee both persons' basic rights, and their ability to participate in the institutional structures, and control the forms of power, that apply to them.

7. Towards a politically just global order

In this section, I consider three possible accounts of what a politically just global order – one that secures basic rights and democratic participation for all its inhabitants – might look like, and argue in favour of one of them in particular. The accounts describe, respectively: (i) a global democratic state, (ii) a system of independent and internally just states, and (iii) a system of states coexisting with a multiplicity of supranational institutions.

7.1. A democratic world state

The first account of a just global institutional order is modelled by analogy to domestic political-legal systems (see, e.g. Cabrera 2004, Tännsjö 2008).[16] It envisages a global state with a legislative assembly, an executive, a judiciary, global political parties, and global constituencies. To be sure, elaborating the details of this complex global political structure is a task largely bound to rest on speculative grounds. Still, the idea of a domestic state being somehow reproduced at the global level seems sufficiently clear to allow for critical discussion. As always when it comes to the evaluation of normative ideals, two perspectives have to be taken into account: that of desirability and that of feasibility.[17] Interestingly, most critics of the ideal of a democratic world state tend to focus on its infeasibility, while implying that, if a *just* global state were possible, it would be desirable. Contrary to this common stance, I will argue that fatal to the ideal of a democratic world state are not so much considerations of feasibility but of desirability. Let me start with feasibility.

Feasibility challenges to a global democratic state emphasize that the necessary background conditions for such a state to exist and function are lacking. A well-functioning democracy needs a demos, namely a set of people (constituting the electorate) capable of effectively participating in, and sustaining, democratic institutions (see List and Koenig-Archibugi 2011). This capacity presupposes a certain level of 'internal cohesion' and agreement on principle, mutual trust and fellow-feelings. Globally, such an internally cohesive demos does not exist, and is unlikely to exist for many years to come (see, e.g. Miller 2009, 2010). This being the case, global democracy is best seen as a chimera, akin to the ideal of a society of angels.

The feasibility sceptic seems right: there is no global demos, and there probably will not be one in the near future. But can we move from the actual non-existence of a global demos, to the conclusion that global democracy is altogether infeasible? It seems not (Valentini n.d.). Consider an analogous situation at the domestic level, such as the recent one in Iraq (List and Koenig-Archibugi 2010, p. 87). After the Second Gulf War and the trial of Saddam Hussein, Iraq entered a troubled political phase, leading to it being considered a case of a failed state (BBC News 2007). Attempts to establish a *well-functioning* democracy were not initially entirely successful, because the preconditions for a well-functioning democracy – peace, security and mutual trust – were not in place. In other words, there was no fully-fledged demos. Does this imply that we should reject the idea that just states must be democratic? It would seem not. What this fact implies is that it was hard to realize democracy in Iraq when conditions on the ground were not yet fertile. A move towards democracy should be a long-term goal, but the priority should be peace, security, and respect for basic rights. Only once these guarantees are in place can we genuinely institute a healthy democracy in the one-person-one-vote sense.

A similar reasoning applies at the global level. The fact that a global demos does not yet exist need not imply that it could never exist (List and Koenig-Archibugi 2010). Of course, there is an important difference in scale between domestic and global arenas. While we know that democracy is in principle possible at the state level (there are, after all, many democratic states) we cannot have the same confidence in the possibility of global democracy. Can the necessary fellow-feelings and shared norms develop across the world's population? These reflections invite caution, but once again they do not *demonstrate* that global democracy is altogether impossible (Koenig-Archibugi 2011). In fact, as Robert Goodin (2010) has argued, we might even interpret recent developments of the global order – especially in the form of an ever-more solid global rule of law – as first steps in the direction of global democracy. Feasibility considerations, then, cannot be invoked as *conclusive* arguments against a global democratic government.

What about desirability? The idea of a world state has often been objected to on the grounds that it would inevitably lead to global tyranny.[18]

For reasons already explored in the previous paragraphs, this argument also has little bite. Since we have no conclusive evidence to exclude the feasibility of global democracy, the worry about global despotism is at most an invitation to be cautious, rather than a knock-down argument against a democratic world state (Pogge 2009, Valentini 2011, sec. 2.4 and 2.5). Instead of focusing on the global despotism argument, I wish to focus on a less popular desirability-based objection to global democracy. This is that, for many, the withdrawal of state sovereignty and self-determination implied by the advent of global democracy would represent a loss of value. This is the value of determining our future jointly with our fellow-citizens, with whom we have a shared history (Miller 1995, cf. Stilz 2011, sec. V).

In light of this, if respect for basic rights and democracy could also be possible within a system allowing for national pluralism and self-determination, why move to one in which these values are not realized? This points in the direction of a second configuration of the global order.

7.2. A world of separate, independent and democratic states

This second ideal assumes that it is possible to build a just global order comprised of a multiplicity of independent and internally just states, without global institutions. Global political justice would then require states to refrain from undermining others' national self-determination, to respect international treaties, to help one another when in need, and largely to leave each other alone (cf. Rawls 1999b).

How does this picture of a just world order fare from the viewpoints of desirability and feasibility? From a desirability perspective, the pluralistic just world envisaged here seems very appealing, combining respect for communal ties and self-determination, with respect for basic rights and democracy. Of course, liberal-egalitarian cosmopolitans would object to this normative proposal because it allows for resource inequalities between societies (and individuals). But if my arguments about the status of distributive equality are correct, this does not pose a serious challenge to this more pluralistic normative proposal. Moreover, democratic decision-making is a morally required expression of equal respect only between those who exercise political power over one another, and in a world of independent states, citizens of different communities do not stand in such mutual power-relations. Under the circumstances envisaged here, democracy beyond borders is therefore not a requirement of equal respect.

What makes the proposed pluralistic picture of a just global order problematic, I argue, are instead considerations of feasibility. In our interdependent world, the ideal of a loose federation of self-sufficient political communities is a chimera. Globalization has undermined the state's capacity to perform the functions which justify its existence (Ronzoni 2009). States' domestic affairs are increasingly affected – whether deliberately or not – by decisions taken outside their borders. In an ever-more integrated world, political communities interfere with one another all the time, not so much through military means, but through economic and political ones (Dahbour 2005, p. 216).

Recurrent financial crises, and lower capital taxation aimed at attracting foreign investment, put significant pressure on the state's capacity to secure basic rights in both developed and (particularly) developing countries (Avi-Yonah 1999–2000, Dietsch 2011, Rixen 2011, Dietsch and Rixen n. d.). Similarly, states' ability to provide a safe environment for their citizens is increasingly threatened by international crime and terrorism, as well as by dangerous climate change.

To tackle these phenomena, states need coordination mechanisms in the form of supra-national agencies with the authority to generate binding regulations.[19] As recent history has shown, voluntary federations of states often lack the resources to respond to global challenges, and their decisions are highly susceptible to being skewed in favour of their most powerful members. Think of the United States' refusal to join the International Criminal Court (ICC), of World Trade Organization (WTO) subsidies for farmers in the United States and Europe, and of the disappointing outcomes of recent climate summits. International institutions must possess a certain level of independence and authoritativeness if they are to realize the ideal of a world in which each person enjoys basic-rights protection, and can participate in collective decision-making.

7.3. A world of democratic states and accountable supra-national institutions

It should not be surprising that the picture of the world order I advocate falls somewhere in between the previous two. I am thinking of a world in which multiple national communities retain some sovereign powers, while other sovereign powers are devolved upwards, to supra-national institutions with specific competences. This of course would involve somewhat compromising state sovereignty, but it would be done for the sake of those goods that state sovereignty is supposed to deliver in the first place (see Ronzoni 2009, Orrù and Ronzoni 2011, Valentini 2011, ch. 8). Let me explain.

Earlier I suggested that there is a value to national self-determination, and the ability of different peoples to affirm their communal ties and shape their future together. However, this value is premised upon their collective decisions being effective. There cannot be genuine self-determination without control (Ronzoni 2012). Under existing circumstances of global interdependence, control – the very control necessary for equal respect – is not possible without supra-national institutions. States' capacity to be self-determining is eroded, so that even though they *nominally* keep certain powers, *de facto* they cannot effectively exercise them. Ceding sovereignty upwards – for instance in matters of global financial regulation, or global climate and environmental risk-management, or global criminal law – would officially sanction something which is already the case in practice: namely that states are not in a position individually to cope with these world-scale problems (Orrù and Ronzoni 2011).

Crucially, I am not arguing for the establishment of a global government, but rather, for the creation of a multiplicity of supra-national institutions each in charge of authoritatively addressing particular types of coordination problems (economic, financial, criminal, environmental etc.) with global reach.

On the proposed model, states would still be able to operate freely *within* the constraints set by the relevant supra-national institutions on matters of global interest, in the same way in which citizens can act freely within the confines of domestic law regulating matters of national interest. Moreover, the type of organization I have in mind would be centred around the so-called 'subsidiarity principle', according to which there would be no need to transfer decision-making power to the supranational level, when decisions could be efficiently taken at the national or local one. Transfers of sovereignty 'upwards' would only be justified if necessary.

Interestingly, the intermediate model I am sketching is not so far from developments of the global arena we are already witnessing today. The idea of absolute state sovereignty is a myth not only at the level of empirical fact (due to the *de facto* influence of globalization processes on domestic affairs) but also at that of shared moral norms. As Goodin (2010) argues, international norms *above* the state are becoming more and more entrenched in the international community, for instance human-rights norms and principles of *jus cogens*. Moreover, international institutions are being created, and their membership increasingly expanded – think, for instance, of the European Union, the ICC, or the WTO (Goodin 2010). To be sure, such institutions are far from being fully just, and are often criticized because of their democratic deficit. These criticisms are good news though, for they express a healthy urge to move in the direction of democratization, and hence of political justice.

Of course, while we may have taken the first steps towards a more politically just global order, we are still far from having reached our target, and the question of how to get there most safely and efficiently is a hard one to address. I want to conclude by venturing a conjecture, and one that seems particularly fitting when we consider what democratic states ought to do in this respect. My sense is that there is little prospect for powerful democracies such as the United States, Canada, European countries and Australia to take the lead on global institution-building *unless* their citizens activate first (cf. Ypi 2011). Citizen-responsiveness is at the heart of democratic politics, and unless the majority of the electorate expresses global-justice-oriented preferences, democratic governments are unlikely to work towards global institution-building and fair decision-making. So although political justice is primarily a virtue of institutions, in well-functioning democratic states, responsibility for its global realization falls largely on citizens themselves. The hope is that, once a critical number of leading democratic states mobilizes in pursuit of global political justice, other powerful and less powerful states will follow. After all, addressing global problems is in everyone's interest, and once a dominant solution emerges, remaining outside the network of those who have adopted it comes at considerable costs (Goodin 2010, Grewal 2008). There is therefore reason to believe that the politically just global order here envisaged, though still far from the *status quo*, is not entirely utopian.

8. Conclusion

In this paper I have done three things. First, I have offered a conceptual analysis of the notions of justice and legitimacy, and concluded that, as part of a liberal account of morality, they are not genuinely distinct. In particular, I have suggested that principles of justice and principles of legitimacy indicate what equal respect for persons requires of institutional arrangements under two sets of circumstances: without and with reasonable disagreement about justice. I have then argued that since our world is characterized by many instances of such reasonable disagreement, the principles of justice that apply to it demand respect for basic rights and democratic participation. These I have called principles of 'political justice', to highlight their sensitivity to the conflictual and power-driven nature of politics.

Second, I have considered the implications of this conclusion for the debate on global justice, and argued that its focus on the question of whether economic equality should be seen as a global goal is somewhat misconceived. The ideal of a (politically) just world order that applies to us, given existing disagreement, is one on which both statists and cosmopolitans can converge, and includes respect for basic rights and democratic participation (cf. Caney 2006).

Third, I have turned to the question of what type of institutional configuration the global order ought to exhibit in order to best realize the normative goal of global political justice. I have contrasted three different possible configurations, and opted for the ideal of a world in which separate states with limited sovereignty coexist with issue-specific and democratically organized supra-national institutions in charge of making binding decisions on coordination problems with global reach. Even though we are far from realizing the ideal proposed, with the commitment of democratic citizens, we might be able to get there sooner than we think.

Acknowledgements

My interest in this topic was partly sparked by Terry Macdonald's (2011) work on international/global legitimacy. I am grateful to the audiences at the SPT Seminar (ANU, April 2011), the Visiting Speakers' Seminar (Monash University, April 2011), and the ECPR General Conference (Reykjavik, August 2011) for questions and comments. I also thank Luis Cabrera, Emanuela Ceva (who revealed her identity as a reviewer), Terry Macdonald, and Miriam Ronzoni for their extremely helpful written comments on an earlier version of the paper, and Christian List for discussion.

Notes

1. On this see Ceva (2012). Ceva rightly argues that accounts of justice should include procedural considerations which are typically confined to the realm of legitimacy. Note that, unlike other theorists, Buchanan (2004) discusses justice and legitimacy together.
2. Rawls (1996) acknowledges that liberal justice and legitimacy originate from the same normative concerns, however he still insists in keeping them separate, by suggesting that the former is more demanding than the latter. See Peter (2010) for discussion. For a similar view, see also Buchanan (2002, 2004).
3. For the distinction between concepts and conceptions see Rawls (1999a, p. 5).
4. The notion of legitimacy can be given more or less demanding readings. On one reading, an institution is legitimate if it has the (liberty) right to rule. On another, more demanding reading, a legitimate institution has the (claim or power) right to rule *and* its subjects have a duty to obey it. My argument is neutral between these two accounts. On this see the contributions in Meyer (2009), and Durning (2003).
5. This is due to what Williams calls the 'critical theory principle'.
6. This point applies to both express and tacit consent alike. For defences of anarchism see, e.g. Simmons (1976) and Wolff (1970), the former in particular for a critique of consent theory.
7. Williams would disagree. I agree with Matt Sleat (2010, p. 496), however, that Williams's attempt at distancing himself from liberalism is unsuccessful. For a defence of liberal democratic legitimacy see Buchanan (2002), and the review by Peter (2010), which confirms that the dominant liberal view on political legitimacy is broadly 'democratic'.
8. On the enforceability of justice see, e.g. Buchanan (2002, p. 704), Nardin (2005) and O'Neill (1996). This distinguishes justice, for instance, from other moral demands such as charity.
9. Cf. what Jeremy Waldron (1999) calls the 'circumstances of politics'. For further discussion see note 11.
10. Exactly identifying such limits is a complex matter, and different proposals are bound to be somewhat controversial.
11. Rawls (1996) introduces the notion of reasonable disagreement between conceptions of the good. The Rawlsian framework has been famously extended to disagreements about justice by Waldron (1999, ch. 7). Note, however, that for Waldron reasonable disagreements about justice need not be characterized by a commitment to equal respect. Rather, they need to be 'good faith' disagreements between rational/conscientious people. While my notion of reasonable disagreement is partly normativized (arguably in line with Rawls's own under-

standing of it), Waldron's appears to be more directly epistemic. See also Gaus (1996).

12. I have offered a more sustained defence of this claim in Valentini (forthcoming), on which the following paragraphs partly draw. There I emphasize that democracy can be defended as a demand of justice only if reasonable disagreements about justice extend to the truth conditions of claims about justice. This proviso (implicitly) applies to the present discussion too.
13. Some think that random procedures (e.g. lotteries) also express equal respect. I briefly explain why I am generally sceptical about this view in Valentini (forthcoming).
14. Emanuela Ceva has suggested to me that reasonable disagreement might also extend to constitutional rights and democratic institutions (see Waldron 1999, Reidy 2007, esp. pp. 259ff.). This is an important worry, yet one I believe is less pressing in my case than, say, in Waldron's, because my notion of 'reasonable disagreement' is more strongly normativized than his (see also note 11). By reasonable disagreement about justice I mean disagreement between views that are compatible with equal respect. While there may be disagreement, at the margin, about the best shape of basic rights and democratic decision-making, a certain set of guarantees (i.e. basic rights and democracy *broadly* construed) will have to be in place for a society to be a plausible instantiation of equal respect. If, by contrast, one's understanding of reasonable disagreement does not refer to an independent normative criterion such as equal respect, then the scope of reasonable disagreement will be broader than what I suggest, possibly also encompassing non-liberal views.
15. Caney's and Buchanan's arguments though seem to presuppose the distinction between justice and legitimacy which I challenge. For discussion of Caney's position in particular see Valentini (2013).
16. For the discussion of the so-called domestic analogy, and a tri-partite distinction between different configurations of the global order along the lines drawn here, see Suganami (1989).
17. On desirability and feasibility in relation to the global arena see Gilabert (2012).
18. This worry is shared, for example, by Immanuel Kant (1970), Rawls (1999b), and Nagel (2005).
19. For a proposal concerning the relevant agencies in the fields of criminal and socio-economic justice see Orrù and Ronzoni (2011), and in that of tax competition see Dietsch and Rixen (n.d.). This type of proposal has also been advocated by theorists of global democracy, such as Held (1995), and of cosmopolitan justice, such as Pogge (1992).

Note on contributor

Laura Valentini is Lecturer in Political Philosophy at University College London. Her research focuses on international political theory, democratic theory, and methodologies in normative theorizing. Her book *Justice in a Globalized World: A Normative Framework* has recently appeared with Oxford University Press, and her work has appeared in journals including *Political Theory, Economics & Philosophy, American Political Science Review, Journal of Political Philosophy,* and *Politics, Philosophy & Economics.*

References

Avi-Yonah, R.S., 1999–2000. Globalization, tax competition, and the fiscal crisis of the welfare state. *Harvard law review*, 113 (7), 1573–1676.

Barry, B., 1991. Humanity and justice in global perspective. In: B. Barry, *Liberty and justice*. Oxford: Clarendon, 182–210.

BBC News, 2007. Iraqi rises up failed states index [online], 19 June. Available from: http://news.bbc.co.uk/2/hi/6766877.stm [Accessed 21 December 2011].

Beitz, C., 1999 [1979]. *Political theory and international relations*. Princeton, NJ: Princeton University Press.

Blake, M., 2001. Distributive justice, state coercion, and autonomy. *Philosophy and public affairs*, 30 (3), 257–296.

Buchanan, A., 2002. Political legitimacy and democracy. *Ethics*, 112 (4), 689–719.

Buchanan, A., 2004. *Justice, legitimacy and self-determination*. Oxford: Oxford University Press.

Buchanan, A. and Keohane, R.O., 2006. The legitimacy of global governance institutions. *Ethics and international affairs*, 20 (4), 405–437.

Cabrera, L., 2004. *Political theory of global justice: a cosmopolitan case for the world state*. London: Routledge.

Callan, E., 2001. Liberal legitimacy, justice, and civic education. *Ethics*, 111 (2), 141–155.

Caney, S., 2005. *Justice beyond borders*. Oxford: Oxford University Press.

Caney, S., 2006. Cosmopolitan justice and institutional design: an egalitarian liberal conception of global governance. *Social theory and practice*, 32 (4), 725–756.

Ceva, E., 2012. Beyond legitimacy: can proceduralism say anything relevant about justice? *Critical review of international social and political philosophy*, 15 (2), 183–200.

Christiano, T., 2008. *The constitution of equality*. Oxford: Oxford University Press.

Cohen, G.A., 1989. On the currency of egalitarian justice. *Ethics*, 99 (4), 906–944.

Dahbour, O., 2005. Three models of global community. *The journal of ethics*, 9 (1/2), 201–224.

Davis, R., n.d. Justice. Do it. Manuscript.

Dietsch, P., 2011. Tax competition and its effects on domestic and global justice. *In*: A. Banai, M. Ronzoni, and C. Schemmel, eds. *Social justice, global dynamics: theoretical and empirical perspectives*. London: Routledge, 95–114.

Dietsch, P. and Rixen, T., n.d. Justice and international tax competition. Manuscript.

Durning, P., 2003. Political legitimacy and the duty to obey the law. *Canadian journal of philosophy*, 33 (3), 373–389.

Dworkin, R., 2000. *Sovereign virtue*. Cambridge, MA: Harvard University Press.

Gaus, G., 1996. *Justificatory liberalism*. Oxford: Oxford University Press.

Gilabert, P., 2012. *From global poverty to global equality*. Oxford: Oxford University Press.

Goodin, R., 2010. Global democracy: in the beginning. *International theory*, 2 (2), 175–209.

Grewal, D., 2008. *Network power: the social dynamics of globalization*. New Haven, CT: Yale University Press.

Held, D., 1995. *Democracy and the global order*. Cambridge: Polity.

Kant, I., 1965 [1797]. *Metaphysical elements of justice. Part I of the metaphysics of morals*. Indianapolis, IN: Bobbs-Merrill.

Kant, I., 1970 [1795]. *Perpetual peace: a philosophical sketch*. *In*: H. Reiss, ed. *Kant's political writings*. Cambridge: Cambridge University Press, 93–130.

Koenig-Archibugi, M., 2011. Is global democracy possible? *European journal of international relations*, 17 (3), 519–542.
Kymlicka, W., 2001. *Contemporary political philosophy: an introduction*. Oxford: Oxford University Press.
List, C. and Koenig-Archibugi, M., 2010. Can there be a global demos? An agency-based approach. *Philosophy & public affairs*, 38 (1), 76–110.
Macdonald, T., 2011. Citizens or stakeholders? Exclusion, equality and legitimacy in global stakeholder democracy. *In*: D. Archibugi, M. Koenig-Archibugi, and R. Marchetti, eds. *Global democracy: normative and empirical perspectives*. Cambridge: Cambridge University Press, 47–68.
Meyer, L.H., ed., 2009. *Legitimacy, justice and public international law*. Cambridge: Cambridge University Press.
Miller, D., 1995. *On nationality*. Oxford: Clarendon.
Miller, D., 2009. Democracy's domain. *Philosophy & public affairs*, 37 (3), 201–228.
Miller, D., 2010. Against global democracy. *In*: K. Breen and S. O'Neill, eds. *After the nation: critical reflections on post-nationalism*. Basingstoke: Palgrave Macmillan, 141–160.
Moellendorf, D., 2002. *Cosmopolitan justice*. Boulder, CO: Westview Press.
Nagel, T., 1977. Equal treatment and compensatory discrimination. *In*: T. Nagel, M. Cohen, and T. Scanlon, eds. *Equality and preferential treatment*. Princeton, NJ: Princeton University Press, 3–18.
Nagel, T., 2005. The problem of global justice. *Philosophy & public affairs*, 33 (2), 113–147.
Nardin, T., 2005. Justice and coercion. *In*: A.J. Bellamy, ed. *International society and its critics*. Oxford: Oxford University Press, 247–364.
O'Neill, O., 1996. *Towards justice and virtue*. Cambridge: Cambridge University Press.
Orrù, E. and Ronzoni, M., 2011. Which supranational sovereignty? Criminal and socio-economic justice compared. *Review of international studies*, 37 (5), 2089–2106.
Peter, F., 2010. Political legitimacy. *In:* E.N. Zalta, ed. *The Stanford encyclopedia of philosophy* [online]. Available from: http://plato.stanford.edu/archives/sum 2010/entries/legitimacy [Accessed December 2011].
Pogge, T., 1989. *Realizing Rawls*. Ithaca, NY: Cornell University Press.
Pogge, T., 1992. Cosmopolitanism and sovereignty. *Ethics*, 103 (1), 48–75.
Pogge, T., 2009. Kant's vision of a just world order. *In*: T. Hill, ed. *The Blackwell guide to Kant's ethics*. Oxford: Blackwell, 196–208.
Rawls, J., 1996. *Political liberalism*. New York: Columbia University Press.
Rawls, J., 1999a [1971]. *A theory of justice*. Oxford: Oxford University Press.
Rawls, J., 1999b. *The law of peoples*. Cambridge, MA: Harvard University Press.
Reidy, D., 2007. Reciprocity and reasonable disagreement: from liberal to democratic legitimacy. *Philosophical studies*, 132 (2), 243–291.
Rixen, T., 2011. Tax competition and inequality – the case for global tax governance. *Global governance*, 17 (4), 447–467.
Ronzoni, M., 2009. The global order: a case of background injustice? A practice-dependent account. *Philosophy and public affairs*, 37 (3), 229–256.
Ronzoni, M., 2012. Two conceptions of state sovereignty, and their implications for global institutional design. *Critical review of international social and political philosophy*, 15 (5), 573–591.
Simmons, A.J., 1976. Tacit consent and political obligation. *Philosophy & public affairs*, 5 (3), 274–291.

Sleat, M., 2010. Bernard Williams and the possibility of a realist political theory. *European journal of political theory*, 9 (4), 485–503.
Stilz, A., 2011. Nations, states, and territory. *Ethics*, 121 (3), 572–601.
Suganami, H., 1989. *The domestic analogy and world order proposals*. Cambridge: Cambridge University Press.
Tan, K.-C., 2004. *Justice without borders*. Cambridge: Cambridge University Press.
Tännsjö, T., 2008. *Global democracy: the case for a world government*. Edinburgh: Edinburgh University Press.
Valentini, L., 2011. *Justice in a globalized world*. Oxford: Oxford University Press.
Valentini, L., 2013. Cosmopolitan justice and rightful enforceability. *In*: G. Brock, ed. *Cosmopolitanism vs non cosmopolitanism*. Oxford: Oxford University Press.
Valentini, L., forthcoming, Justice, disagreement and democracy. *British journal of political science*.
Valentini, L., n.d. No global demos, no global democracy? Manuscript.
Waldron, J., 1987. Theoretical foundations of liberalism. *Philosophical quarterly*, 37 (147), 127–150.
Waldron, J., 1999. *Law and disagreement*. Oxford: Oxford University Press.
Williams, B., 2005. *In the beginning was the deed*, ed. J. Hawthorne. Princeton, NJ: Princeton University Press.
Wolff, R.P., 1970. *In defense of anarchism*. New York: Harper & Row.
Ypi, L., 2011. *Global justice and avant-garde political agency*. Oxford: Oxford University Press.

Creating cosmopolitans

Patti Tamara Lenard

Graduate School of Public and International Affairs, University of Ottawa, Canada

Cosmopolitan principles of justice tell us that it is the responsibility of the wealthy to ensure the immediate transfer of resources to the poor. Yet, it cannot be denied that most countries, and most individual citizens, seem unwilling to act as these principles demand. At issue is motivation: although many people would agree that cosmopolitan principles of justice are right, at least to some extent, few seem motivationally inspired to act upon them. This paper evaluates one set of proposals for securing the transfer of resources from the wealthy to the poor, namely, those that suggest that the right way to achieve cosmopolitan objectives is to generate institutions that will, over time, produce cosmopolitans. I argue that we should focus, doubly, on the generation of supra-national institutions as a way to create a 'global demos' and on harnessing the motivational resources available at the nation-state level.

Few would disagree that the disparities in wealth that separate the wealthiest countries from the poorest countries, and the insufferable poverty faced by those living in the poorest countries, are morally objectionable. Cosmopolitan principles of justice tell us that it is the responsibility of the wealthy to ensure the immediate transfer of resources to the poor; this responsibility derives from a commitment to the equal moral worth of all individuals, who are arbitrarily divided by national borders into wealthy and poor communities. Yet, even though these principles seem compelling, it cannot be denied that most countries, and most individual citizens, seem unwilling to act as these principles demand. At issue is *motivation*: although many people would agree that cosmopolitan principles of justice are *right*, at least to some extent, few seem motivationally inspired to act upon them.[1]

There is one caveat to note before I begin. Whereas we may have agreement that some form of cosmopolitan principles are right, whatever agreement we have nevertheless masks considerable controversy about the specific content of these principles. Some argue merely for a duty of mutual assistance, which is consistent with permitting inequalities between nations to persist; others insist on a non-exploitation principle according to which the goal is to enable the self-determination of independent nations; and others argue for equality of opportunity at the global level. What these debates reveal – and this is all I need to rely on here – is that whatever principles are agreed, they all demand more redistribution across borders than we presently witness.[2] I leave it to others to determine the content of these duties and assume only that, whatever the depth and scope of the duties, we can all agree that one important problem we face is an unwillingness to carry them out. In what follows, the terms 'a just society' or 'duties of justice' are used broadly, and do not signal commitment to any particular principles of cosmopolitan redistribution.

In light of this unwillingness to carry out duties of justice across borders, many have sought ways to overcome these motivational challenges, in particular with a view to remedying them, and therefore to securing a commitment to the transfer of resources from the wealthy to the poor. This paper evaluates one set of proposals for securing these transfers, namely, those that suggest that the right way to create cosmopolitans, and therefore to achieve cosmopolitan objectives, is to generate institutions that will, over time, produce cosmopolitans. The editors of this volume observe that insufficient attention has been paid to the constitution of the global political order, along two dimensions: first, the management of power and conflict; and second, the structure and function of 'cooperative arrangements for collective decision-making' (Macdonald and Ronzoni 2012). This essay aims to provide a contribution to the second of these dimensions, by considering the attitudes that must underpin, and can be produced by, the institutions that facilitate cooperative relations at the global level.

In particular, I express scepticism with respect to approaches that emphasize, only, the building of global institutions as a way to create cosmopolitans; in particular, I suggest that although we should not abandon attempts to develop global institutions that will, over time, create global citizens, we have good reason to believe that this process will be slow to provide the motivational resources on which the success of the cosmopolitan project depends; I will suggest that we can look to the progress of the European Union (EU) to confirm this observation. I thus argue that we have good reason to focus, doubly, on the generation of supra-national institutions as a way to create a 'global demos' – a term I will define in more detail later, but which for now can be understood as a mutually-recognized community of individuals who share interests, values and norms – and to harness the motivational resources available at the nation-state level.[3] It is this latter proposal that worries cosmopolitans, who believe that nationalism is too frequently a source of injustice; although the injustice that has been perpetrated at the hands of so-called nationalists cannot be denied, I argue that it is a mistake to reject all nationalism as a result. I conclude with a cautious optimism; while I agree that institution-building of the right kind can aid the cosmopolitan political project, I shall argue that institutions which produce cosmopolitan consequences, without altering the motivations of individuals, will inevitably be unstable.[4] Thus, for the foreseeable future, we cannot ignore the motivational resources that are available to be harnessed, towards cosmopolitan ends, at the nation-state level.

The paper begins with a brief account of a debate among political philosophers concerning the right relation between just institutions and the attitudes of the citizens whose behaviour is shaped and constrained by them. I then consider proposals according to which a global demos can be created and sustained over time by the self-interest of the relevant parties; I suggest that solutions that rely exclusively on self-interest may be motivationally *efficacious*, and therefore that we can and ought to rely on them to motivate initial cooperation at the global level, but that they are not motivationally stable over time. In their haste to dismiss the insights we can derive from the nationalist argument (roughly put, the argument that nations are the proper site of distributive justice), these thinkers fail to heed the strength of the relations among co-nationals, relations that motivate the willingness to participate in cooperative ventures, including redistributive policies, over time. I conclude that attempts to build a motivationally stable global demos should focus on the ways in which relationships serve to motivate our willingness to carry out duties of justice. Institutions can therefore serve the cosmopolitan project to the extent that they highlight existing relations and forge new ones, all of which can ground our willingness to carry out (increasingly extensive) obligations of justice.

The stability of global institutions

There is a range of global institutions – including the United Nations (UN), the International Monetary Fund (IMF), and the World Bank – that serves to coordinate state activities. Moreover, as Thomas Nagel (2005, p. 136) observes, there is considerable pressure to develop or strengthen international institutions, in three domains in particular: 'the protection of human rights; the provision of humanitarian aid; and the provision of global public goods that benefit everyone, such as free trade, collective security, and environmental protection'. I shall say more about this below, but these institutions are generally motivated by state self-interest; it is in the interest of individual states to coordinate their activities, and to create a context in which each state can be compelled to perform a particular task or set of tasks. Global justice theorists are engaged in an ongoing debate with respect to whether these complex interactions, mediated by institutions, in fact serve to *create* duties of justice among the participating states. Thomas Nagel for one, is doubtful, and suggests that these institutions, alongside the increasingly complex rules and regulations of international trade, fail to 'trigger demands for justice, even in diluted form. The relation remains essentially one of bargaining, until a leap has been made to the creation of collectively authorized sovereign authority', of the kind that exists in domestic society (Nagel 2005, p. 141). Others suggest instead that as interdependence among nations increases, and as the capacity to meet duties of justice becomes easier across borders, the duties of justice we have therefore expand and grow deeper.[5] I highlight this broader discussion simply to point out that my concerns are connected to, but are somewhat tangential to, this debate. I am not concerned with whether the institutions themselves, if expanded, would *create* duties of global justice where they do not yet exist. I am concerned instead with whether and by what mechanism institutions, if organized in the right way, can serve to motivate individuals, via states, to carry out these duties of justice.

Of course, there are reasons to explain the failure of individuals to carry out duties of justice that do not attempt to explain the motivational gap between attitude and behaviour. For example, the failure of individuals to act as they ought to do, given their stated principles, may be traced to inadequate information about the effects that their choices – say with respect to the options they have presented to them by political actors seeking re-election – will have on the pursuit of justice. At the very least, we may like to refrain from blaming individuals for this inadequate information, and to say that they cannot be held entirely responsible for their failure to realize that their votes will serve to perpetuate injustices that they would, with full information, choose against. Alternatively, individuals may not be able to act in the service of justice as a result of deficient political systems that deprive them of justice-compatible options that they would seize, if they were made available. Again, here, we might like to avoid blaming individuals who face restricted political alternatives as a result of a deficient electoral system (for example, first-past-the-post systems typically produce an unrepresentative distribution of seats, and it could be that those who are under-represented are those who support just political agendas).[6] Thus, while inadequate motivation may be insufficient to account for the failure of citizens to carry out their duties of justice, any attempt to account for this failure must confront it.

Institutions in the ideally just society will be such that actions that conform to their rules will necessarily produce just results. Insofar as an ideally just society is populated by people who are, to some extent (or even to a considerable degree), motivated by self-interest in their private lives, just institutions will function by 'correcting the outcomes of market transactions among people' in such a way that justice is preserved over time (Murphy 1998, p. 257).[7] As a result, individuals are by and large absolved of having to be concerned with the justice of their individual actions; if a citizen is concerned that her actions conform to the principles of justice, all she needs to do is ask whether the institutions to which she is subject permit the action. If so, she can be reasonably confident that the action is consistent with justice. Yet, the danger with an exclusive (or near exclusive) institutional focus is that it ignores the complex ways in which attitudes interact with institutional support over time. Says Thomas Nagel (1991, p. 26), for example, 'political theory must take into account the individual conduct it demands of people in the creation and operation of political institutions, and the character of the motivation required for that conduct'. Attention to our motivational structure will not only dictate what kind of institutions we ought to construct, it will equally remind us that these institutions can sustain support over time only if those who are subject to them are willing to comply with their demands. In order to sustain justice, we need not only for our institutions to be just, we also need for individuals themselves to be willing to comply with these institutions.

The lesson to draw from efforts to account for the relationship between attitudes and institutions is that it is a mistake to ignore the attitudinal components of institutional support over time. At least on its face, this lesson – that (just) institutions demand attitudinal support from those subject to them – warns us against implementing institutions that demand more from citizens, justice-wise, than they are prepared to accept except under coercive conditions. It may simply be that, for now, a 'strongly egalitarian [or cosmopolitan] society populated by reasonably normal people is difficult to imagine and in any case psychologically and politically out of reach' (Nagel 2005, p. 128). Instead, a commitment to working towards a cosmopolitan order of some kind implies a kind of justice-gradualism: the focus should be on implementing institutions that slowly press citizens towards accepting duties towards the distant poor, rather than on institutions that demand too much from citizens – given their present motivational structure – and therefore are likely to fail as a result of a failure to gain widespread support.

Motivation, self-interest and the (global) demos

Above, I suggested that there is a strong connection between the attitudes of citizens and the institutions with which they comply; citizens are willing to comply with institutions that coordinate their behaviours in ways that they recognize and accept as just, even when their self-interest, understood strictly in terms of material wellbeing, may not perfectly be served by this coordination. At issue, however, is how citizens come to be motivated to comply with institutions that facilitate the carrying out of these duties over time. As I shall argue, this motivation does not stem simply from the belief that the principles supported by these institutions are right; in this sense, my view is not the conception-dependent view that many others have endorsed, i.e. the view that compliance depends only on the perception that a set of principles are just and therefore worthy of our adherence. Instead, the *motivation* to abide by these principles stems from a shared commitment among members of a *demos* to each other and to the interests and values that define it.

Conventionally, democracies are defined by a *demos*, that is a 'territorially delimited people' where there is 'symmetry between governmental institutions and the governed territorially defined people' (Moore 2006, p. 25).[8] Members of a demos, typically, are thought to 'feel bound together', by shared interests, values and norms, or by a commitment to a shared purpose of some kind (Bellamy and Castiglione 1997, p. 160). These shared interests, values and norms give rise to trust relations among members, and these trust relations facilitate cooperation among them; in particular, these shared norms and values motivate them to make sacrifices on each other's behalves. It is difficult to specify the content of the interests, norms and values that will give rise to trust; they are idiosyncratic to specific nations and are what distinguishes one nation from another. We might say, for example, that one of the shared values that defines the Canadian nation is a commitment to universal health care and that one of the shared values that defines the American nation is a commitment to a rugged individualism.[9] When scholars wonder whether it is possible to create a global demos – a community in which shared interests, norms and values, which give rise to the trust relations that facilitate large-scale cooperative ventures – they are demonstrating a concern to find the resources on which we can build this motivational commitment at the global level.

At the nation-state level, there is a well-rehearsed story for the emergence of the demos (for example, see Yack 2001). Nations are historical communities, defined by a shared history, a shared language, and oftentimes shared religions and cultures as well, and over time institutional structures develop around them to enable them to be politically self-determining. Nations too are the kinds of communities that produce meaningful and valuable relationships, which give rise to obligations that co-nationals recognize and carry out.[10] When nationalists confront our failure to carry out what are taken to be cosmopolitan duties of justice, they respond by observing that the relevant community – the human community – fails to give rise to strong obligations to all members, and thereby fails to generate the concomitant motivation to carry them out. For nationalists, humans are thought to be naturally partial – they believe they have strong obligations towards those with whom they have intimate relations, and they are willing to act on these obligations (Miller 1995, chapter 3). In responding to the motivational challenge in this way, nationalists are not committed to denying the possibility (only the likelihood) that an obligation-generating community could emerge at the global level. They thus leave open the possibility that a global community might, in time, emerge. Their scepticism about the emergence of a sufficiently robust global community, however, is such that they advocate instead the protection of national bonds (within all nations), to what is perceived by their critics to be the detriment of egalitarian justice at the global level.[11]

Cosmopolitans express discomfort with the nationalist commitment to a 'natural' or 'prepolitical' nation, and therefore with the view that national partiality (or possibly any form of partiality beyond family and friends) is an inevitable feature of humanity. The history of nationalism reveals, instead, that nations are largely the product of artifice: 'most successful states have had to undergo a phase of nation *building* in order to create identities capable of sustaining institutions of solidarity without recourse to illiberal and undemocratic means' (Weinstock 2009, p. 95).[12] That nation-building was an essential element of the history of nations is presented as evidence that there are no natural or prepolitical bases to nations as they presently exist.[13] Moreover, when nation-builders tackled their project, they were not motivated to create 'sites of justice' in which citizens carried out duties towards each other; instead they were motivated by 'geostrategic considerations … nations were then largely constructed through a range of deliberate state policies in order to satisfy the political and economic needs of newly created states' (Weinstock 2009, p. 95). Thus, one of the frequent charges made against nationalists by cosmopolitans, or advocates of global democracy, is that they make an unreasonable assumption about human nature. According to their critics, nationalists assume that human nature is 'static [and] unvarying', as a consequence of which they are unable to entertain the possibility that citizens' sphere of concern could expand over time (Caney 2005, p. 175). In making this assumption, nationalists fail to acknowledge the extent to which 'people's inclinations are influenced by the prevailing norms and political and social institutions. They are, that is, not fixed in stone and inflexible but are, at least in part, endogenous' (Caney 2005, p. 175). It is a mistake to think of the duties we have towards others as given, since 'how much of a duty people are psychologically able to bear is not fixed but malleable' (Goodin 1986, p. 167).

The complaint made against nationalists as reported above thus has two dimensions which are frequently run together and which are worth distinguishing. First, nationalists assume that partiality is limited in scope; we are motivated to carry out duties only towards those within some set of boundaries, which delineate a subset of people with whom we share meaningful relations. Second, for those nationalists who concede the possibility that we have some duties that extend beyond these boundaries, the thinness of the relations that bind them to these 'others' are such that they are perceived to be less demanding. We are, according to nationalists, 'naturally' disposed to ('naturally disposed to share with', that is) a bounded set of people, and these ties serve to motivate our willingness to carry out duties towards them. To the extent that we are not bounded to others by meaningful relationships, therefore, we are unable to locate the motivation to carry out more than the thinnest of duties towards them.

In illustrating the non-naturalness of nations, Daniel Weinstock asks us to consider what might transpire if we removed the institutions that structure the decisions we make, in particular those that require us to participate in demanding redistributive programmes. In his estimation, we can conclude only that we participate in redistributive programmes because coercive institutions govern our behaviour: we know very little about 'how disposed people are to redistributing resources towards their less well-off co-nationals' (Weinstock 2009, p. 94). We simply cannot know how citizens will behave if these institutions are lifted: our compliance with redistributive institutions in the present cannot be taken as evidence that we are 'naturally disposed to share with one another in ways that people from different countries are not' (Weinstock 2009, p. 94). There is an element of truth here – the fact of coercive institutions that bind individuals into reciprocal relationships does not tell us whether, absent these institutions, individuals would remain committed to reciprocal *behaviour*. But, we know enough about human moral psychology to know that the willingness to engage in such behaviour is typically constrained by a desire to avoid being a 'sucker' – i.e. the only person who chooses to contribute to some cooperative scheme when others do not. The coercive institutions are providing just that incentive among co-nationals; how people would behave absent these institutions tells us little about the role that shared relationships among co-nationals is playing.

The accusation at the heart of this critique is misdirected, therefore: nationalists do not claim that human nature is static in the way that cosmopolitans claim, nor that it will prompt altruistic behaviour towards all co-nationals in all instances. Nationalists instead emphasize a series of observations Benedict Anderson recorded over 20 years ago: nations are imagined communities and the development of nations over time is and was in large part about expanding our national imagination to include larger and larger numbers of people. The lesson we can draw from this history is that our goal should be to work towards additional expansion of our imagination, in ways that extend our 'partiality' to include greater and greater numbers of people. Our disposition towards partiality – towards caring about those with whom we share meaningful relations – is natural, but the scope of this partiality is not fixed. To the extent that we can forge meaningful relations beyond borders, and even globally, we can alter the perception that carrying out duties beyond borders is too challenging or someone else's responsibility. Cosmopolitans tend to emphasize the dark side of nationalism, according to which robust nations gain their strength from denigrating and excluding others; on this view, the prospects for global justice are, presumably, dim. Yet, in general, nationalists, like cosmopolitans, recognize that the duties we have towards others can and do change over time, and that the emergence of nation-states is one prominent example of expanding our sphere of concern, as well as the reach of our duties towards others.[14] As John Rawls (1999, p. 113) observes, 'the relatively narrow circle of mutually caring peoples in the world may expand over time and must never be viewed as fixed'.

I thus believe that the lesson we are to draw from Weinstock's initial observation – that nations are the product of construction – is that the proper institutions may well over time build citizens who are motivated in the right way. In other words, Weinstock's scepticism with respect to (what he takes to be) the nationalist claim – that we cannot be sure whether people's redistributive tendencies are connected to feelings of partiality towards co-nationals rather than simply a response to coercive institutions – tells against his ultimate conclusion, namely, that if nationalist institutions built a national demos and then nationalists, then cosmopolitan institutions (whatever these might be) may well build a global demos and, thereby, cosmopolitans. If the point is that we can claim the existence of nationalists in virtue of effective institutions, we (obviously) must believe that institutions are capable of altering our motivations over time, and not simply that they change the pattern of our behaviours.[15] And, if our motivations are capable of changing in response to the right institutions, we have reason to believe that, somehow, cosmopolitan institutions will be able to generate citizens who are stably motivated to carry out duties of justice towards the global poor, rather than simply subjecting them to institutions that cater to their self-interest first, and only secondarily, and as a happy coincidence, to the needs of the global poor.

If we examine some of the most pressing issues in developed countries, there is some reason to be optimistic in this regard. There is increasing agreement that tackling global poverty may well serve, indirectly, to resolve many of the problems we face as a global community, including the spread of infectious disease, environmental degradation, and even the spread of terrorism. We may be encouraged by the deployment of 'prudence-based arguments … for a global egalitarian agenda' – that is, that we may be led towards ameliorating global poverty by a serious focus on ameliorating infectious disease, and so on. These 'prudence-based arguments' can as a result serve as 'motivational hooks to which the cause of global demos building might be hitched' (Weinstock 2009, pp. 99–100). Thus, states' pursuit of their self-interest will unintentionally generate positive consequences at the global level. Since we can reliably predict that states will be inclined to act in their own self-interest, we can rely on the production of whatever global goods can emerge if institutions properly direct this self-interest towards them, even if these global goods are produced as an afterthought (they are not produced, however, unintentionally – these goods are aimed at intentionally, but not because they are good in and of themselves).

Prudence is of course a tremendously powerful motivator, and I agree that we ought to rely on it as an intermediary that facilitates the move from reluctance to distribute resources beyond borders towards an acceptance that this is an obligation that must be fulfilled. But, the trouble with the story reported above, according to which states have prudential reasons to cooperate in a way that focuses their attention on remedying global poverty, is that there are tremendous contextual considerations in play as states determine what in fact is in their best interest. If our central concern is ameliorating global poverty – and if we genuinely believe that doing so is a moral obligation, rather than a matter of charity – we risk relying on a merely contingent commitment to remedying global poverty. While self-interest is unambiguously motivationally efficacious, in other words, it is unstable for our purposes in an important sense: although states can be relied upon to seek their self-interest, they will do so even when doing so conflicts with (or is neutral with respect to) remedying global poverty. It will simply be a happy coincidence, if the pursuit of state interests demands attention to global poverty.

In order for these cosmopolitan benefits to be provided consistently, we require a motivational transformation of some kind. Yet, evidence of cooperation at the global level, in the form of economic exchange, suggests that 'however dense and intense economic exchange may be, it does not translate easily or automatically into a shared awareness of a common identity, a shared community, or a common ethos' (Hurrell 2001, p. 34). Similarly, Richard Bellamy and Dario Castiglione (1997, p. 162) observe sceptically:

> it is reasonable to suppose that globalization will produce forms of interstate cooperation in those areas such as defence, the environment and the economy where the capacity of states to act in autonomous ways has been seriously impaired. However, in most cases these cooperative schemes will be regarded as mechanisms for preserving rather than undermining national interests and self-determination, with transfers of decision-making power being largely conditional on the extent to which involvement in the relevant international body makes that possible.

Simple self-interested cooperation may not, in other words, be sufficient to generate a shift towards a sense of community – towards the emergence of an 'objective community interest or of the common interest of global society' (Hurrell 2001, p. 39), i.e. towards a global demos – that will in turn serve to transform our sense of to whom we have obligations.

Thus, on the one hand, the lesson we are meant to draw from the history of nation-building properly understood is that, just as prudential reasons underpinned the development of nation-states, prudential reasons may be the foundation upon which we can build cosmopolitans. Moreover, if nations are constructed rather than natural, we have no reason to believe that the project of cosmopolitanism cannot, also, avail itself of institutions to build cosmopolitans, just as nationalists (if they are honest about the history of nationalism) have relied on institutions to create nationalists.[16] Nation-building provides us a model which, if followed, may permit cosmopolitan building – it might, in other words, create and then 'motivate a global demos'. On the other hand, we are advised to avoid relying entirely on global institutions to transform self-interested motives into justice-based motives, since at least historically we have little evidence that, at the global level, such a transformation is possible. The danger, say the sceptics, is that institutions that encourage merely self-interested cooperation among states will work to preserve national boundaries and the importance of national self-determination, as a result of which they are not self-evidently good candidates for the kinds of motive transforming institutions that we are after.

Institutions and motivation-building

At issue then is whether institutions are able to play a *transformative* role – that is, whether, if properly designed, they can serve to transform the motivations of those whose behaviour is constrained by them in the first place, and if they are able to do so, how they do so. It will be essential to understand the mechanics, and conditions, of this transformation in order to apply the lessons we have learned at the national level to the global level. We are seeking, in Andrew Hurrell's (2001, p. 37) terms, a 'dynamic view of the link between institutions and morally relevant communities'.

An optimistic account of how this transformation takes place is as follows: once cooperative institutions are in place, they may generate positive consequences from a cosmopolitan perspective. These positive consequences may be intended, but they are pursued for instrumental reasons alone, i.e. because they contribute to the self-interest of the cooperating parties. Above, I worried that this was an unstable solution to the problems of global poverty: even if this cooperation produces goods from the perspective of ameliorating global poverty, it is not clear that this cooperation can serve to shift attitudes in such a way that, when self-interest no longer dictates cooperation in a particular case, the cooperation continues. In order for the institutions to persist over time, I am suggesting, it is insufficient that they produce positive outcomes as a byproduct of self-interested cooperation; they must work to expand the sphere of concern to an ever-greater circle of needy global citizens, with whom we believe we share a community, and therefore to whom we feel motivated to carry out extensive duties of justice. In the ideal, participation in cooperative institutions will generate a sense of 'formal obligations that arise from being members of an institutionalized scheme of political cooperation' (Bellamy and Castiglione 1997,

p. 162) – the sense of obligations arises, in other words, in response to participation in the institutionalized scheme, but it does not motivate initial participation in this scheme.[17] Participation generates this sense of formal obligation by creating a 'sense of identification among a given group of people between whom it comes to be felt both legitimate and plausible that collectively binding decisions ... should take place' (Bellamy and Castiglione 1997, p. 163). At the global level, then, we will have to begin with rather 'thin' relationships – merely cooperative (but fair) relationships – that do not appear to give rise to thick obligations; and over time, we may witness a 'thickening [of the relevant sentiments, and therefore of obligations] in various ways depending on the nature and degree of their interaction and involvement ... and even international allegiances possibly developing in some instances' (Bellamy and Castiglione 1997, p. 165).

On the one hand, it seems evident that existing institutions with global reach – the UN, the World Trade Organization (WTO), the IMF – are riddled with unfairness and inequity, even if they produce benefits for many of those who participate in them. These institutions are frequently derided by poorer countries for being deeply unjust, and their acceptance of the rulings as compelled by the unjust distribution of power and wealth in the world. Thus, as constructed now, there is no reason to believe these institutions will underpin a demos that will prove stable over time.

On the other hand, as evidence that this transformation is possible, scholars point to the European Union. The EU is a regional institution, originally intended to enable European states to coordinate monetary and trade policy, which has expanded to encompass more policy domains over time. The purpose of the institutions is expressly to enable cooperation among European states and to allow for coordinated decisions that are in the best interest of all member states. The hypothesis therefore was that, as a result of this structured cooperation, initially intended to secure compliance by relying on the self-interest of European nations, a sense of community among Europeans would eventually emerge – a community in which members would find themselves motivated to carry out obligations across state borders on the grounds of participation in, and commitment to, a shared sense of community. On the one hand, some limited evidence does suggest that there is a growing sense of European identity among European citizens, and that this sense of identity is accompanied by the feelings of trust that are at the foundation of a democratic political community. The evidence is, however, limited: it ebbs and flows over time (reports of possessing a European identity have declined in recent years among British people, for example, and reports of trust in the British by continental Europeans have similarly declined) and reports of European identity among citizens are nationally dependent. The six original member states display the largest proportion of citizens who conceive themselves as partly European, while enthusiasm for Europe varies considerably among newer members. Authors

Angelika Scheuer and Hermann Schmitt (2009, p. 563) conclude an analysis of identities and feelings of belonging in the European Union by asking 'have the people of Europe grown together into a political community; is there a "sense of community" among EU citizens?', and respond to their own question as follows: '[t]he general answer is yes. Over half a century after World War II, a majority of EU citizens identifies with the new political community in the European Union'. An optimistic reading of the data presented by the European Union therefore suggests that, in a relatively short period of time, properly structured institutions can serve to expand the community of individuals who recognize each other as members of a shared demos as I defined it earlier, and therefore can create appropriately motivated individuals.

Yet, there are at least two pessimistic readings as well: one suggests that the European Union has failed to produce a demos in the first place and another suggests that it is unique and therefore unavailable as a model for building global institutional structures more generally. For those who subscribe to the first pessimistic reading, the EU has ultimately failed in producing a European community. Emphasis is placed instead on the Dutch and French rejections of the Constitutional Treaty and the difficulties the EU is facing in remedying its financial crisis, where the remedies include redistribution of resources from the wealthiest to the poorest of members.[18]

The second pessimistic reading emphasizes that, although not bound by a shared language, European states are bound by an extensive shared history and shared cultural referents (Přibáň 2009). As much as some liberal political theorists are uncomfortable acknowledging the way in which shared history and culture serve to underpin and support the solidarity that defines political communities, and which support democratic practice therein, it is a mistake to ignore the possibility that the (thus far limited) successes we see in the European project will prove difficult to recreate in environments where this cultural and historical basis does not exist. The observation that a European identity, and a European community, may be emerging after 50 years of institutionally structured cooperation, may not be a good indication of the likely path of global institutions more generally.

As a result, the project of creating cosmopolitans – i.e. people who are adequately committed to redistributing resources to poor nations – must be understood to be a long-term project, and it is a mistake to focus our energies solely on the construction of global institutions. Global institutions, which build on the self-interest of individual participating states, may well serve to build a global demos over time; this is the lesson we learn from a review of the nation-building literature, where national institutions served over time to create nationalists. Over time, it may well be that the establishment of the right kinds of institutions at the global level can, under the right conditions, generate members of a global community, who are motivated to pursue global justice through these institutions.

Instead, however, we need to think more seriously about how, and whether, domestic institutions can be modified in ways that generate the motivation to pursue a fairer redistribution of wealth, and so reduce the economic gap between rich and poor countries.[19] At issue here is whether domestic institutions can create the motivation among its citizens to pursue global justice, and this is where we must focus. The strategy for doing so in general, which unfortunately space prevents elaborating here, is to highlight the ways in which the values that underpin democracies at the national level do not stop in any obvious way at national boundaries.[20] Democratic citizens may eventually be persuaded that the equality and freedom to which they are committed internally are values that must, also, be pursued beyond boundaries; doing so, however, does not require that the significance of boundaries as defining valuable communities be entirely eroded. Indeed, historically, something like this has transpired across Western democratic nation-states, where we have witnessed a steady inclusion in the set of people who are included in the demos, as members entitled to the full range of rights and privileges associated with membership status. Expanding the set of people who compose the demos expanded, as well, the set of people to whom obligations of justice (rather than, simply, obligations of charity or protection – as was the case for example with respect to women) were owed. By analogy, then, we have reason to be optimistic that the thickening of sentiments that develop as a result of initially self-interested (but fair) cooperative ventures at the global level may, equally, serve to expand the set of people to whom we believe we owe obligations. There is an additional consideration here, and this is that there is a genuine reluctance to *deny* the goods to members, once these goods have been provided in the first place. In other words, even if the benefits to the global poor are provided simply because they are essential to secure a self-interested good (say, limiting the spread of infectious disease) pursued by the states in question, we have reason to be hopeful that there will be a reluctance to reduce provisions of these goods once the objective is achieved. It is much more difficult to deny benefits once they have been provided, than it is to deny their provision in the first place.

Thus, the lessons we can learn from the success of institutional mechanisms in building national loyalties, which have in turn underpinned a commitment to domestic justice are two-fold: (1) it may be possible to rely on properly designed transnational institutions, in the long term, to produce the motivational resources we need to pursue global justice; and (2) we should rely on properly designed domestic institutions, in the short term, to produce the motivational resources we need to pursue justice beyond borders. In the first case, we aim to develop a new community, from which the motivation will emerge; in the second case, we aim to build on an already existing sense of community to expand our justice commitments beyond domestic borders.

Conclusion

Institutions are stable when the citizens whose behaviour they coordinate support the outcomes they intentionally produce. Moreover, institutions frequently reflect the attitudes of the citizens whose behaviour they coordinate. Yet, as many observe, institutions also serve to shape the attitudes of those whose behaviour they coordinate. This paper has considered, namely, whether global institutions might be able, over time, to create a global demos that motivates its members to carry out thick duties of justice in relation to each other. I have suggested, first, that it is misleading to condemn the nationalist view of human nature as static and unvarying; although nationalists do (in my view rightly) believe that humans are by nature partial to those with whom they have relations, there is nothing inherent in a commitment to nationalism that denies the possibility of an emergent global demos. I suggested, second, that institutions are stable in virtue of coordinating individuals who are committed to the values that underpin and regulate these institutions, in virtue in particular of creating an adequately motivating demos. When individuals are not so bound, the stability of these institutions is at risk.

When we translate these observations to the global sphere, I suggested that whereas we can initially rely on self-interest to motivate participation in global institutions of various kinds, we cannot rely on self-interest to sustain commitment to these institutions. Doing so, in my view, is inherently unstable. Yet, there is some hope that these institutions will, over time, shift our attitudes – this is, after all, what happened at the national level. In particular, institutions properly constructed may serve to build a sense of community, even if limited, which can underpin the motivation that is essential to securing a commitment to carrying out thick(er) duties of global justice. In the meantime, and indefinitely, we are wrong to ignore the motivational power provided by the deep commitments that obtain among co-nationals. The strength of these commitments, which history suggests expand to include more and more people over time, and which motivates a commitment to providing justice to those outside of national membership, should be celebrated, rather than mourned, by cosmopolitans.

Acknowledgements

I would like to thank Terry Macdonald and Miriam Ronzoni for the invitation to participate in the workshop for which I prepared this paper and for their very helpful written comments on the paper itself, as well as Zofia Stemplowska for very helpful comments delivered at this workshop. I would also like thank Rogers Smith and Alistair Macleod both of whom commented on an earlier version of this paper at APSA 2009 and ECPR 2009 respectively. Stefan Bird-Pollan, Nahshon Perez and Scott Staring provided helpful written comments on an earlier draft. Finally, I'd like to thank an anonymous reviewer to this journal for helpful comments.

Notes

1. The term 'cosmopolitan' has many meanings. Here I am using the term to refer to those who believe that the wealth inequalities that divide nations are unjust and therefore that it is incumbent on wealthy nations to redistribute resources to those nations that are less well-off.
2. David Miller is typically cast as the anti-cosmopolitan. Regardless of whether this characterization is just, even Miller agrees that duties of justice across borders are presently unfulfilled.
3. This way of characterizing the problem is taken from Weinstock (2009).
4. This paper will steer away from discussing specific institutional structures that might be implemented at the global scale. It is rather concerned with the theoretical and normative implications of relying on institutions to build cosmopolitans.
5. See for example several of the contributions to the October 2011 issue of the *Monist*, edited by Gillian Brock, titled 'Cosmopolitanism: For and Against'.
6. I thank Alistair McLeod for the observations I make in this paragraph.
7. This is Murphy's characterization of John Rawls.
8. For a critique of the conventional view, see List and Koenig-Archibugi (2010).
9. I examine the claim that nations are defined by idiosyncratic interests, values and norms in *Trust, Democracy and Multicultural Challenges* (2012), chapter 4. The claim is not that the existence of shared interests, norms and values is sufficient to give rise to trust; they are necessary only.
10. More generally, the term 'associativist' defines those who believe that relations in associations more generally can be valuable and give rise to duties. Nationalists are therefore one type of associativist.
11. For a sceptical view with respect to the value and possibility of egalitarianism at the global level, see Miller (2005).
12. Arash Abizadeh makes this claim, as well in Abizadeh (2002).
13. I have some trouble with the imprecision of this argument – it is often not clear which features of the people who, over time, become co-nationals are relevantly 'natural' or 'prepolitical'. It is too fast to conclude from the fact most states undergo nation-building projects that nations are the product of artifice alone (or that the 'artifice' of these projects is what carries all the relevant moral weight).
14. I thank Rogers Smith for pointing out this distinction between the two ways of framing questions about 'partiality'.
15. Thus, there is an inconsistency here – it would make more sense if Weinstock expressed confidence rather than scepticism with respect to our willingness to participate in redistributive programmes that target co-nationals, even in the absence of coercive institutions.
16. I believe that many, including Weinstock, exaggerate the extent to which nationalists argue that *national* feelings in particular are natural. Rather, most nationalists argue that partiality of some kind is natural, and that in contemporary times, this natural propensity to partiality is best expressed at the nation-state level.

17. Though, some – e.g. Thomas Nagel – are sceptical that cooperation of this kind can do this kind of work. He writes, 'something more [than the pursuit of common interests] is needed to move us up toward the higher standard of equal consideration. It will not emerge merely from cooperation and the conventions that make cooperation possible' (Nagel 2005, p. 143). Compare Nagel's observations with Rawls' (1999, p. 112), however: 'relations of affinity are not a fixed thing, but may continually grow stronger over time as peoples come to work together in cooperative institutions they have developed'.
18. For two among many critiques of the EU as a demos-building project, see Bohman (2004) and Moravcsik (2006).
19. Space considerations prevent consideration of what these institutions look like, here, but see Ypi (2008)
20. Careful readers here will have noticed a transition from 'domestic' communities to 'democratic' communities. This is because, for now, the burden of wealth redistribution falls largely on the shoulder of democratic communities, and the relevant motivational question therefore applies most urgently within them. Non-democratic states may also be motivated to discharge cosmopolitan duties, but the mechanisms by which this motivation is built outwards will be distinct in ways that space prevents me from discussing here.

Note on contributor

Patti Tamara Lenard is Assistant Professor of Ethics in the Graduate School of Public and International Affairs, at the University of Ottawa. She is the author of *Trust, Democracy and Multicultural Challenges* (Penn State, 2012), and her work has been published in journals such as *Political Studies, Journal of Moral Philosophy*, and *Review of Politics*. Her current research focuses on migration across borders, multiculturalism, trust and social cohesion, and democratic theory more generally.

References

Abizadeh, A., 2002. Does liberal democracy presuppose a cultural nation? Four arguments. *American political science review*, 96 (3), 495–509.

Bellamy, R. and Castiglione, D., 1997. Between cosmopolis and community. *In*: D. Archibugi, ed. *Re-imagining political community*. Cambridge: Polity Press, 152–178.

Bohman, J., 2004. Constitution making and democratic innovation. *European Journal of Political Theory*, 3 (3), 315–337.

Brock, G., ed., 2011. Cosmopolitanism: for and against. *The monist*, 94 (4).

Caney, S., 2005. *Justice beyond borders: a global political theory*. Oxford: Oxford University Press.

Goodin, R., 1986. *Protecting the vulnerable*. Chicago, IL: University of Chicago Press.

Hurrell, A., 2001. Global inequality and international institutions. *In*: T. Pogge, ed. *Global Justice*. Oxford: Blackwell Publishing, 32–54.

Lenard, P.T., 2012. *Trust, democracy and multicultural challenges*. University Park, PA: Penn State University Press.

List, C. and Koenig-Archibugi, M., 2010. Can there be a global demos? An agency-based approach. *Philosophy and public affairs*, 38 (1), 76–110.

Macdonald, T. and Ronzoni, M., 2012. Introduction: the idea of global political justice. *Critical review of international social and political philosophy*, 15 (5), 521–533.

Miller, D., 1995. *On nationality*. Oxford: Oxford University Press.
Miller, D., 2005. Against global egalitarianism. *Journal of ethics*, 9 (1–2), 55–79.
Moore, M., 2006. Globalization and democratization: institutional design for global institutions. *Journal of social philosophy*, 37 (1), 21–43.
Moravcsik, A., 2006. What can we learn from the collapse of the European constitutional project? *Politische Vierteljahresschrift*, 47 (2), 219–241.
Murphy, L., 1998. Institutions and the demands of justice. *Philosophy and public affairs*, 27 (4), 251–291.
Nagel, T., 1991. *Equality and Partiality*. Oxford: Oxford University Press.
Nagel, T., 2005. The problem of global justice. *Philosophy and public affairs*, 33 (2), 113–147.
Přibáň, J., 2009. The juridification of European identity, its limitations and the search of EU democratic politics. *Constellations*, 16 (1), 44–58.
Rawls, J., 1999. *The law of peoples*. Cambridge, MA: Harvard University Press.
Scheuer, A. and Schmitt, H., 2009. Dynamics in European political identity. *European integration*, 31 (5), 551–568.
Weinstock, D., 2009. Motivating the global demos. *Metaphilosophy*, 40 (1), 92–108.
Yack, B., 2001. Popular sovereignty and nationalism. *Political theory*, 29 (4), 517–536.
Ypi, L., 2008. Statist cosmopolitanism. *Journal of political philosophy*, 16 (1), 48–71.

The injustice of territoriality

Paul Muldoon

School of Political and Social Inquiry, Monash University, Melbourne, Australia

In recent works Nancy Fraser has developed a model of 'metademocracy' that promises to reconcile the competing claims of universal justice (grounded in human rights) and localized democracy (grounded in popular sovereignty). By instituting a global democratic procedure in which all enjoy participatory parity, Fraser hopes to ensure that some people are not denied standing as 'subjects of justice' simply because of their territorial location while keeping faith with the democratic commitment to autonomy and self-legislation. Despite the compelling nature of this model, I argue that Fraser fails to bridge the gulf between justice and democracy because her model of metademocracy is built on the 'meta-norm' of 'participatory parity'. Drawing on the work of Hannah Arendt, I claim that this foundationalist move re-asserts the priority of justice over democracy because it takes equality as a moral given rather than the ever-precarious achievement of human organization.

Claims that globalization has exacerbated a long-standing tension between justice and democracy are now commonplace.[1] While political philosophy has, from the very beginning, been subject to a schism that positions truth, reason, universal norms, and humanity on one side of a fissure and opinion, will, customs and manners, and the demos on the other, the globalization of social relations appears to have invested it with a new salience.[2] In an increasingly interdependent world shaped by transnational flows of all kinds – goods, capital, information, technology, people, hazards, emotions – the need to adjudicate between the moral claims of universal justice (commonly understood in terms of the concept of human rights) and the sovereign claims of territorial communities (commonly understood in terms of the concept self-determination) has become increasingly urgent. Sharpened, in particular, by the gulf between the rich and poor and the precarious position of displaced people, the tension between justice and democracy resists satisfactory resolution because every move in one direction or the other seems to entail the sacrifice of something important. To do as justice dictates is effectively to foreclose the space of democratic contestation and deny the members of historically constituted political communities the experience of self-determination. Yet to allow political communities to continue (as best they can) to control their own affairs is to license exclusion and restrict rights on the grounds of territorial divisions that are entirely arbitrary from a moral point of view.

One of the most imaginative and engaging responses to this problem to emerge in recent times has come from the pen of Nancy Fraser. In a series of works, culminating in the publication of *Scales of Justice* (and overflowing from it), Fraser *2008b) has developed and refined a model of 'metademocracy' whose great virtue lies in the fact that it does not simply address the new realities of the globalizing world, but capitalizes upon their immanent potential to reconcile the competing claims of justice and democracy. Inadvertently, according to Fraser, globalization has brought critical attention to the question: who counts as a subject of justice? As more and more of the social processes that determine 'life chances' have started to flow across territorial borders, the presumption that it is only members of territorially bounded political communities who can make claims upon one another (whether this be for economic redistribution or cultural recognition), is beginning to be called into question. In this context, old arguments about the rights of persons *qua* citizens are being revisited. Rather than simply cast her lot for one of these options, however, Fraser has sought to synthesize the moral demands of justice and the political demands of self-determination by allowing questions about the scale of justice (the level at which it should operate) to be opened up to contestation. In her metademocracy, precisely 'who' is entitled to claim standing as a subject of justice is not determined a priori, but through a process of democratic deliberation procedurally regulated by the principle of participatory parity.

Despite the compelling nature of this model, I argue that Fraser does not succeed in her attempt to seize the new opportunities provided by globalization to reconcile the competing claims of justice and democracy. Fraser pins her hopes for this reconciliation upon a rejection of the 'monological approach' according to which philosophers seek to ascertain the requirements of justice theoretically, denying any role to those who would be subject to them.[3] By allowing critical components of justice (what it entails and whom it concerns) to be contested within the terms of a fair and open procedure governed by the norm of participatory parity, Fraser hopes to keep faith with the democratic idea that the addressees of the law should also be its authors, while at the same time ensuring that the conditions of justice are met. However, in the following sympathetic critique, as much inspired by Fraser as it is critical of her, I suggest that Fraser's 'dialogic turn' fails to overcome the rift between justice and democracy. By anchoring her model to the 'overarching normative principle' of participatory parity, Fraser effectively turns the object of political struggle – equality – into the basis of political struggle. Drawing on the work of Hannah Arendt, I argue that this foundationalist move prevents her from coming to a proper appreciation of 'the political' as the space in which struggles over equality are waged. Paradoxically, I suggest that this attempt to secure equality by naturalizing it threatens to sap the very democratic energies that Fraser extols for exposing the exclusionary effects of territoriality.

A theory of justice for abnormal times

Nancy Fraser's recent work is at base an attempt to come to terms with the impact of globalization on the way we think about justice. Until very recently, according to her, political theorists (including, it would seem, Fraser herself)[4] had tended to assume that it was only relations among citizens that could be configured according to principles of justice. Under the sway of the Westphalian 'political imaginary', they took it for granted that the primary purpose of normative theory was not to decide who was entitled to justice, but to work out what justice entailed by way of economic redistribution and, in a subsequent development, cultural recognition for the members of bounded political communities.[5] However, thanks to a heightened awareness of globalization, this territorial presumption is 'losing its aura of self-evidence' (Fraser 2005, p. 71). As Fraser characterizes it, the contemporary moment is 'abnormal' in the sense that the existing 'grammar of justice', composed of those hidden assumptions that in any given epoch give intelligibility to justice claims (e.g. assumptions about who constitutes an appropriate subject of justice), has been brought to the surface and exposed to politicization. In the transnational public sphere, deep disagreements now exist as to who is entitled to make justice claims upon whom (Fraser 2008a, pp. 393–397). Under these circumstances, according to Fraser, it is incumbent upon normative theorists to look beyond 'first order' questions of substance, those relating to *what* justice demands by way of redistribution and recognition, to 'second order' questions of framing – those relating to *who* is entitled to make claims for justice in any given situation.

Fraser's starting point for thinking through this problem of 'the who' is the concept of 'participatory parity' which she defines as a 'radical democratic interpretation of the principle of equal moral worth' (Fraser 2005, p. 73).[6] Stated as a general principle, participatory parity asserts that only those social arrangements that permit all people to participate as peers in social life can be counted as just (Fraser 2005, p. 73). In its original iteration, participatory parity was designed to furnish normative theorists with a single evaluative standard against which to test what Fraser considers the two major families of justice claims: those for redistribution arising out of economic inequalities and those for recognition arising out of status hierarchies. The effect of applying the norm of participatory parity in either case was to make an entitlement to remedy dependent upon claimants being able to 'show that current arrangements prevent them from participating on a par with others in social life' (Fraser 2003, p. 38). As Fraser has subsequently made clear, however, participatory parity is not simply an 'outcome notion' (that *towards which* decisions regarding social arrangements must be aimed), but also a 'process notion' (that *according to which* deliberations about social arrangements must be guided). If follows that decisions made in relation to claims for redistribution or recognition can only carry legitimacy as the product of a fair process of democratic deliberation in which all the 'implicated parties' are able to participate as peers (Fraser 2005, pp. 87–88).[7]

Fraser is the first to acknowledge that this conception of justice has an inbuilt circularity: claims for redistribution and recognition must be justified with reference to the norm of participatory parity through a democratic procedure in which the legitimacy of the decision requires all deliberators to enjoy participatory parity. Rather than consider this circularity reflective of a certain defect of conceptualization, however, she takes it to be expressive of 'the reflexive character of justice as understood from the democratic perspective' (Fraser 2003, p. 44). One of the recurrent problems with normative theory for Fraser is that it has endeavoured to ascertain the requirements of justice theoretically on the basis of some abstract conception of human flourishing (Fraser characterizes this as a 'monological approach'). To be consistent with democratic principles, however, justice cannot be 'an externally imposed requirement' – it binds 'only insofar as its addressees can also rightly regard themselves as its authors' (Fraser 2003, p. 44). Within this 'dialogical approach' the norm of participatory parity plays a double role as both a substantive and a procedural norm. On the one hand it serves as the substantive standard from which arguments over 'first order' claims for redistribution or recognition must take their bearings: do current social arrangements prevent certain individuals or groups from participating on a par with others in social life? On the other hand it acts as the procedural standard for the deliberative forums in which such first order claims are adjudicated and resolved: do such forums provide for the full and free participation of all implicated parties? Indeed participatory parity recommends itself as a 'meta-norm', according to Fraser, precisely because it is capable of identifying injustices at both the substantive and procedural levels.

For the time being I will bracket questions about this conception of 'democratic justice' to explore the way Fraser makes use of the norm of participatory parity to contest the current division of political space based upon the territorial principle. By arguing that the norm of participatory parity should be applied to the processes by which decisions about social arrangements are made, Fraser has been able to do two important things. In the first place she has been able to isolate misrepresentation as an analytically distinct species of injustice (separate from both maldistribution and misrecognition) that requires its own specific form of remedy: changes to the structures of representation. In her recent work, Fraser has deployed the concept of misrepresentation to capture to those 'distinctively political obstacles to parity' whose source lies neither in the distributive inequalities of the economic system nor in the status hierarchies of the cultural realm, but in the constitutional structure of the political order. In her account, the injustice that goes by the name of 'misrepresentation' can result from one of two sources: either the procedures by which decisions are made are biased in a way that denies parity to all participants (Fraser refers to this as the 'decision-rule' aspect of representation) or the criteria used to determine who is included in the decision-making process are distorted in a way that wrongly excludes some people from participating altogether (Fraser refers to this as the 'boundary-setting' aspect of representation). For Fraser (2005, pp. 75–76), in other words, a specifically *political* kind of injustice arises where people are denied full representation in decision-making processes where substantive questions of justice (e.g. how should wealth be distributed) are under discussion.

Secondly, Fraser has been able to turn a critical spotlight on the assumption that such claims of 'wrongful exclusion' can only be launched by citizens and only in relation to the constitutional order of the state in which they claim membership. For Fraser one of the clearest indices of the power of the Westphalian political imaginary is the scant attention hitherto paid to the boundary-setting aspect of representation in discussions of justice. In effect, according to her, the question of who might claim representation in deliberations about justice was determined *a priori* by the territorial principle. To the extent that normative theorists concerned themselves with the problem of misrepresentation at all, therefore, it was primarily in relation to situations where the decision rules *internal* to a polity wrongly denied some of its members the chance to participate fully as peers (Fraser calls this 'ordinary political representation'). However, the more that processes of globalization have placed people at the mercy of transnational forces, the more questionable it has become to allow the boundary-setting aspect of representation to be resolved, by default as it were, on the basis of territoriality. Fraser herself is firmly of the view that the globalization of social relations has exposed a 'deeper level' of misrepresentation which, for the sake of conceptual differentiation, she coins 'misframing'. Misframing, on this account, occurs whenever political boundaries are set 'in such a way as to wrongly exclude some people from the chance to participate *at all* in its authorized contests over justice' (Fraser 2005, p. 76, Fraser 2010, p. 367). Fraser does not suggest that the injustice of misframing arises in every instance where citizens and only citizens are afforded standing as subjects of justice, but she does leave open the possibility that there are situations in which it will.

Far from being a marginal issue, according to Fraser (2005, p. 88), misframing is fast emerging as 'the central question of justice in a globalising world'. As people have become ever more exposed to the consequences of decisions taken outside their domestic political spaces, their ability to make effective claims for redistribution and recognition has declined dramatically. More and more, individuals are finding that some relevant aspects of justice have been placed beyond their reach by their exclusion from the political spaces where decisions with wide-ranging implications for social relations are made (Fraser 2005, p. 77). Of special interest to Fraser in this regard is the situation of the 'global poor'. Measured against the norm of participatory parity, the global poor can legitimately claim to be the victims of a global economic system that distributes resources inequitably and a global status order that denies recognition to all but a select few. These economic and cultural injustices are, however, compounded by the fact that the global poor are denied the opportunity to challenge the social arrangements that prevent them from participating as peers in social life. Subject to injustices in all three of its dimensions – the economic, the cultural *and* the political – they have little chance of ever altering their position as the wretched of the earth (Fraser 2010, p. 366). More than anything else, according to Fraser (2005, p. 78), the situation of the poor and despised makes it clear that 'struggles against maldistribution and misrecognition cannot proceed, let alone succeed, unless they are joined with struggles against misframing'.

Fraser's response to the problem of misframing – the problem of *who* is entitled to claim standing as a subject of justice – is to advocate a 'metademocracy' in which an already transnationalized civil society movement is supplemented by 'new global democratic institutions where disputes about framing can be aired and resolved' (Fraser 2008a, p. 416). Fraser is the first to acknowledge the transnational public sphere as the site of a vibrant 'politics of framing', where political actors are already engaged in 'efforts to establish and consolidate, to contest and revise, the authoritative division of political space' (Fraser 2005, p. 80). Her own work is in fact clearly indebted to social movements which have used the transnational public sphere to contest the territorial principle on the grounds that it 'insulates extra- and non-territorial powers from the reach of justice' (Fraser 2005, p. 81). Her worry, however, is that such contestation will be equated with emancipation, ignoring the way in which contests over the territorial principle continue to be resolved in the interests of the powerful rather than in the interests of justice. In order to avoid such an outcome, according to Fraser, it is necessary to establish new democratic institutions at the global level where the arguments and counter-arguments over territoriality that are constitutive of global civil society can be formally adjudicated according to clear normative guidelines. She thus follows Habermas in advocating a 'two-track solution', according to which justice claims arising from the informal networks of civil society are subjected to a formal, institutional procedure that is capable of resolving them in an authoritative way (Fraser 2008a, p. 415).

It is at this formal institutional level that we reach the fulcrum of Fraser's theory of democratic justice for abnormal times. At this level the primary issue is not so much *what* justice entails, nor *who* is entitled to claim standing as a subject of justice, but *how* are disputes about 'the who' to be resolved? Here Fraser takes the radical step of suggesting that this question of 'the who' cannot be answered by philosophical fiat. It must instead be resolved through a process of democratic contestation. In practical terms, this entails the creation of a metademocratic procedure, situated above the level of the state, where everybody can exercise their moral right to participatory parity in order to argue their case to be treated as a subject of justice in relation to a specific institution or governance structure (e.g. the World Trade Organization). The only restriction that Fraser seeks to place upon these contests over 'the who' is that they be resolved with reference to the 'all *subjected* principle'. Her preference for this determinative norm over the better-known 'all *affected* principle' is based on the belief that the former does not make a group of people fellow subjects of justice merely on the basis of their 'objective coimbrication in a web of causal relationships'. As Fraser would have it, the all affected principle is susceptible to the *reductio ad absurdum* of the butterfly effect, according to which everyone is affected by everything. Accordingly, it is not a particularly useful tool for 'identifying *morally relevant* social relations'. The all subjected principle ostensibly overcomes this problem by granting moral standing only to those who are 'jointly subjected to a governance structure that sets the ground rules governing their interaction' (Fraser 2008a, p. 411, 2009, pp. 287–294).[8]

The evident merit of this way of approaching things for Fraser lies in its openness and flexibility. In contrast to the stand taken by liberal cosmopolitans and civic republicans, both of whom insist upon a specific subject of justice in every instance (humans and citizens respectively), the model of metademocracy opens up the possibility of different decisions being reached in different contexts with regard to who can claim standing as a subject of justice. In this de-territorialized deliberative procedure, each potential subject of justice (sub-national groups, citizens of states, members of regional associations, humanity as a whole) has an opportunity to prove through public argument that they are entitled to be included in more localized deliberative forums where substantive claims for redistribution and recognition are aired and adjudicated. The obvious advantage of going about things in this way for Fraser is that it removes the presumption in favour of the territorial state as the appropriate 'frame' within which to consider questions of justice, while at the same time leaving open the possibility that the exclusion of non-members as subjects of justice will continue to be justifiable in some instances. Rather than simply abolish or protect the territorial state as a frame of justice, in other words, this model of metademocracy works 'to democratize the process by which the frameworks of justice are drawn and revised' (Fraser 2005, p. 84, 2008a, p. 414).

The right to have rights

At first blush this model of metademocracy appears to be a productive way of resolving the tension between justice and democracy that continually resurfaces in relation to problems of poverty and displacement.[9] By adopting participatory parity as a universal norm, grounded in the equal moral worth of human beings, Fraser ensures that nobody will be denied the opportunity to make claims for redistribution and recognition simply on the basis of their territorial location. The substantive rights (to a fair distribution of resources and an appropriate recognition of status) that have hitherto been placed beyond the grasp of the 'poor and despised' will now fall within their reach on account of their right to representation in a metademocratic procedure. At no point, however, does Fraser impose a specific normative account of exactly who is entitled to be treated as a subject of justice in relation to any particular structure of governance or of what they are thereby entitled to claim. In her model of metademocracy, the norm of participatory parity merely secures people a general *procedural right* to argue their case for inclusion in specific decision-making forums where *substantive rights* to redistribution and recognition are at stake. It does not assume that they enjoy such substantive rights on the basis of some abstract account of what is required for human flourishing. In this way, Fraser is able to simultaneously answer criticisms coming from the democratic perspective that normative accounts of global justice leave no room for contestation or disagreement and criticisms coming from the justice perspective that current practices of democratic contestation violate the principle of equal moral worth by arbitrarily privileging members above non-members.

However there are grounds for doubting whether this reconciliation between justice and democracy is as successful as it first appears. The warrant of this paper is that cracks in Fraser's theory of democratic justice begin to appear when we return to Arendt's original problematization of 'the right to have rights' in *The Origins of Totalitarianism* (Arendt 1976). At various points, Fraser acknowledges her debt to Arendt's seminal study of statelessness, characterizing the loss of the right to have rights as the most striking manifestation of misframing. Her model of metademocracy could in fact be legitimately characterized as an attempt to preclude the kind of 'political death' suffered by those who lost the right to membership in *any* political community and thereby became 'non-persons with respect to justice' (Fraser 2005, p. 77). As I seek to show, however, her attempt to institutionalize the right to have rights by reference to the procedural norm of participatory parity dissolves the paradoxical framework in which the concept was originally formulated, thereby robbing it, not simply of its pathos, but of the insight it provides into the nature of 'the political'. Arendt, as we shall see, saw equality as the artificial product of human organization, a specifically political relation between people constituted through collective action and restricted to members of a community. By basing her procedural right to engage in contests over justice in the norm of participatory parity, therefore, Fraser turns the product of politics into the ground of politics. In her model, equality is treated as a moral given rather than the object of political struggle and the achievement of political action. The tension between justice and democracy that she claims to have escaped through her dialogic turn thus re-emerges in the form of a tension between foundationalism and anti-foundationalism in relation to the norm of equality.

In *The Origins of Totalitarianism* Arendt treats the plight of the stateless during the inter-war years as revelatory of the nature of 'the political'. For her no paradox of contemporary politics was filled with more poignant irony than the discrepancy between the efforts of 'well-meaning idealists' who insisted upon the inalienability of human rights and the actual situation of the stateless themselves (Arendt 1976, p. 279). As the victims of totalitarian strategies of de-nationalization soon discovered to their horror, expulsion from their national communities did not bring them under the protection of a different, more universal law. It plunged them into a political abyss in which they were robbed of *all* legality (i.e. all rights). Deprived even of the ancient 'right of asylum', which collapsed under the weight of the sheer number of displaced persons, their de-nationalization became equivalent to a 'total loss' of political status (Arendt 1976, p. 295). For Arendt, the true mark of the perversity of this situation could be found in the fact that the best (indeed the only) way for the stateless to improve their legal position was to break the law. As innocent victims they found themselves outside the scope of 'all tangible law' and subject to an entirely arbitrary police rule. As guilty criminals they found their legal status renewed in the form of the very same procedural rights (e.g. to a fair trial) available to citizens of the national community in which they were exiled (Arendt 1976, p. 286).[10]

Far from pointing to the value of human rights, according to Arendt, the plight of the stateless simply underscored the importance of membership in an organized political community to the enjoyment of equality. Paradoxically, the rights which all human beings enjoyed in the abstract, and which served as the *de jure* foundation of all civil rights, became *de facto* the rights to which one appeals in hopeless and desperate circumstances and generally to no avail. As the victims came to understand better than anyone, their inalienable rights, supposedly independent of any government, effectively disappeared at the same moment as their national rights for the very simple reason that they were unenforceable (Arendt 1976, p. 293).[11] While natural rights to freedom of movement and freedom of speech could not, technically speaking, be taken away, they proved utterly meaningless to the stateless once they were deprived of a political community in which their actions were effective and their opinions significant (Arendt 1976, p. 296). From that point onwards they ceased to be political beings because their treatment at the hands of others no longer bore any relation to what they did or said. Contrary to what might be expected, therefore, the situation of the stateless actually turned out to be worse than that of slaves who, as Arendt (1976, p. 297) points out, were protected from 'the abstract nakedness of being human and nothing but human' by virtue of the demand for their labour. While slaves maintained a certain, diminished standing as members of a community interested in exploiting them, the stateless were rendered completely superfluous. 'Their plight', wrote Arendt (1976, p. 296), 'is not that they are not equal before the law, but that no law exists for them; not that they are oppressed but that nobody wants even to oppress them'.

In her concluding remarks, Arendt took the calamity of the stateless in support of Edmund Burke's claim, proffered in his *Reflections on the Revolution in France*, that there was no such thing as the abstract rights of man, only the rights of Englishmen. Inadvertently the tragedy of totalitarian denationalization had driven home the fact that the critical determinant of human dignity was not the rights individuals possessed in the abstract, but the existence of a community willing and able to guarantee at least some of those rights.[12] For Arendt it was only when millions of people emerged who had lost their human rights and could not regain them that 'we became aware of the existence of a right to have rights' – of a right, that is, to belong to some organized political community where people assume the status of equals and are judged by their actions and opinions (Arendt 1976, p. 296). Nothing illustrated this more clearly for Arendt than the concentration of the stateless in internment camps where they assumed the appearance of so much unwanted human matter. Declared 'the only practical substitute for a non-existent homeland', the internment camps proved, ironically enough, to be the only 'country' the world had to offer those who had been expelled from their own (Arendt 1976, p. 284). For Arendt, the sheer arbitrariness of the treatment meted out to the stateless in the camps only went to prove that the equality given in the natural order was little more than the equality of naked bodies exposed to the elements. 'Equality', she was led to conclude,

> in contrast to all that is involved in mere existence, is not given us, but is the result of human organisation insofar as it is guided by principles of

> justice. We are not born equal; we become equal as members of a group on the strength of our decision to guarantee ourselves mutually equal rights. (Arendt 1976, p. 301)

The conclusion to which Arendt's analysis leads is that equality, insofar as it is understood as a status conferred by rights, is wholly artificial. The upshot of her analysis of statelessness is that the right to participate on a par with others is a contingent political achievement founded upon nothing more solid than a collective decision to guarantee each other 'mutually equal rights'. For Arendt, the public realm – the only space in which people recognize one another as equals – only exists because a conscious choice is made to override the manifold differences that mark each person as a unique beginning in the world. This is what makes it such an extraordinary (and extraordinarily precarious) achievement. As a product of human artifice, the public realm is forever exposed, not only to the vast reaches of the merely given which press in upon it, but to the possibility that individuals will decide to order their relations otherwise (i.e. not in accordance with principles of justice). For Arendt, in other words, equality (or participatory parity) was not the basis upon which one becomes included in decision-making processes where substantive matters of justice are debated and adjudicated. It was rather the product of one, wholly exceptional decision-making process: the one that founds the political community as such. In her persuasive account, built on the all-too-real history of the stateless, the specificity of 'the political' is not to be found in the unique character of the obstacles it poses to the realization of participatory parity. It is rather to be found in the very achievement of participatory parity.

It is the sense of vertigo created by this anti-foundationalist view of equality that drives philosophers to find a more secure footing for social relations. Fraser, her democratic sympathies notwithstanding, seems to be no exception.[13] In the 'theory of democratic justice', the concept of participatory parity plays the vital role of a philosophical backstop. Grounded in the principle of 'equal moral worth', it assumes the status of a *grund-norm* – a norm, in other words, which is capable of legitimating other norms, but which is not itself in need of legitimation (Fraser 2005, p. 73). It is by no means clear, however, that the principle of equal moral worth has any meaning (or enforceability) outside of those communities where a conscious decision has been made to respect it. Viewed from an Arendtian perspective, Fraser's error in treating participatory parity as an 'overarching normative principle' is more or less the same as the idealists who sought to respond to the problem of statelessness by promulgating a new charter of human rights. The mistake in both cases is to assume that the wellbeing of the 'poor and despised' rests upon the abstract rights they possess as human beings rather than the existence of a community willing and able to guarantee them. Tragically, as the stateless discovered, the 'human community' does not (and arguably cannot) perform this function because it is not the artificial product of any collective decision. The obligations we owe to other humans *simply by virtue of their humanity* are not compelling because we never chose to take them on.

Constituent power and the injustice of territoriality

Nothing I have argued in the preceding section is intended to cast doubt on the suggestion that structures of representation require urgent re-examination in a globalizing world where forms of oppression emanate from a variety of sources in and beyond the state. In a field where the issue of global justice has tended to be characterized in purely distributive terms, Fraser brings welcome attention to the distinctively political questions of membership (the boundary-setting aspect of representation) and procedure (the decision-rule aspect of representation). Both her critique of the default status of the nation-state as the frame of justice and her argument that decisions about framing (that is, about who is entitled to claim standing as a subject of justice) must be opened up to democratic contestation are well taken. The argument being advanced here is not that the issue of representation is insignificant, but that Fraser's attempt to ground a right to representation on a moral norm prevents her from appreciating 'the political' as the space in which struggles over equality are waged. By treating participatory parity as a moral right, she creates the impression that the only remaining problem is to give it an appropriate institutional expression. Arguably, however, the most pressing issue is not the institutional shape that deliberations about justice should take among people already recognized as peers, but the struggle groups are waging to achieve this kind of recognition.

One of the more banal, but nonetheless telling, manifestations of Fraser's misconception of the political can be found in her metaphors of political space. To suggest, as she does on many occasions, that the Westphalian system 'gerrymanders political space' or 'partitions political space along territorial lines' is to presume that the whole world is already a political space with moveable internal boundaries. Within this framework of continuous public space, territorial divisions can hardly but assume the appearance of morally arbitrary barriers to the extension of economic and cultural entitlements. The risk with this view of things is that the struggle entailed in constituting political relations, in carving political space out of vast reaches of human possession, disappears from view. To accept the terms of Fraser's metaphors is to assume the task ahead is not to constitute new political spaces, spaces where relations of equality are established through organization, but to re-partition the political space that is already there in ways that render it more just. If nothing else, however, the calamity of statelessness that Arendt illuminated so powerfully in *The Origins of*

Totalitarianism belied the presumption of continuous political space. The political paradox revealed in their condition of superfluousness is that territorial divisions are simultaneously constitutive of political relations *and* barriers to the universal enjoyment of rights. As Arendt herself notes in relation to the Ancient Greeks, the walls of the polis do not just function to deprive the barbarians of voice. They also define the artificial space of the public realm within which individuals recognize one another as equals (*isoi*) (Arendt 1958, p. 198).

What difference would it make to our thinking about the problems of representation exposed by Fraser if we abandoned participatory parity as a meta-norm and began instead from the Arendtian premise – for her the assumption upon which our whole political life rests, that equality is produced through organization? Exactly how Arendt's anti-foundational conception of equality might be articulated with her inspiring, yet still enigmatic, formula of the right to have rights is now a deeply contested topic that I cannot explore in any detail here (see, for instance, Ingram 2008). At a very general level, however, it is possible to identify two different lines along which Arendt's thought can be developed. The first begins from the premise that it is necessary to accept exclusion as constitutive of political relations of equality and seek to ameliorate the effects of such exclusion by ensuring that all human beings are members of an organized political community *somewhere*.[14] It was on this basis that Arendt herself argued that citizenship was the one, truly universal, right, the one that 'does not spring from "within the nation" and which needs more than national guarantees' (Arendt 1949, p. 34, see also Cohen 1999, p. 254, Menke 2007). By declaring citizenship a human right, Arendt appeared to have exposed herself to the criticism that she was taking precisely the backward step into nature that her conception of equality as the artificial product of human organization had foreclosed. As she endeavoured to make clear, however, this right to citizenship could, like all other rights, only exist through mutual agreement and guarantee. If it held the status of a universal right, therefore, it was only because the entire 'comity of nations' had agreed, through mutual promises, to underwrite it (Arendt 1949, p. 37). Regardless of how well this solution to the aporia of human rights works conceptually, however, it remains contingent upon the historical emergence of this comity of nations (itself an uncertain event) and does little to address the problem of misframing that Fraser has illuminated.

A second and, in the current juncture, arguably more productive development of Arendt's anti-foundationalist conception of equality focuses upon the role of political action. More than simply expose the unreality of natural rights, the premise that equality is artificial, the product of human organization insofar as it is committed to principles of justice, brings into sharp relief the productive potential of political agency. To acknowledge equality as the product of a decision 'to grant one another mutually equal rights', is to become aware of a human capacity to constitute political spaces through the practice of promising. As Arendt highlighted in her study *On Revolution*, individuals do not simply inherit political arrangements from the past. They also begin them anew through the power that comes from 'acting in concert'. For her, the promise of politics, ever open to redemption as a consequence of human natality, consists in the possibility, not simply to engage in contests over rights, but to constitute a public space of appearances in which citizens disclose who they are. It belongs to the power of political action, according to Arendt (1963), to bring something new into being that did not exist before, with the most radical manifestation of this constituent power being the constitution of political community itself. Crucially, for Arendt, this power of initiatory action is always in excess of the institutional arrangements that, at any given moment, codify it in legal form. In an important sense, it remains unbound by whatever institutional shape it currently takes and whatever territorial location it currently inhabits (see Ingram 2008, p. 411).[15]

Perhaps the most critical expression of this kind of initiatory action in the current period is the stand political actors are taking against the default status of the territorial principle. As William Connolly (1993, p. 250) noted some time ago, the 'democratic ethos', the essence of which lies in the spirit of egalitarianism, is being extended 'beyond the territorial state even while institutions of electoral accountability remain confined within it'. For Connolly, following in the spirit, if not the letter of Arendt, the very possibility of democratic agents engaging across territorial borders rests on the fact that democracy is not simply a structure of governance bound to a certain territory, but 'an egalitarian constitution of cultural life'. Ultimately it is this egalitarian constitution of social life:

> that encourages people to participate in defining their own troubles and possibilities, regardless of where these troubles originate and how narrow or broad they are in scope; it is moreover, an ethos through which newly emerging constellations might reconstitute identities previously impressed upon them, thereby disturbing the established priorities of identity/difference through which social relations are organized. (Connolly 1993, p. 265)

For Connolly, in other words, democratic states are underpinned by an ethos that allows them to break free, not only from traditional patterns of authority, but from their own entrenched assumptions. The same 'politics of democratic disturbance' that allowed the people to revolt against the authoritarian systems of the past are now being turned back, reflexively, upon democratic states themselves to draw into question the relations of identity/difference coordinated through the territorial principle (Connolly 1993, p. 265).[16]

There is little doubt that the pressure applied by this politics of democratic disturbance, at once realist and idealist, is beginning to impact on what Arendt (1976, p. 282) called the 'old trinity of state–people–territory'. As Connolly (1993, p. 250) notes, a 'creative disaggregation of elements' is taking place in the 'contemporary democratic imagination' that is helping to break this nexus between state–people–territory and, in the process, to revivify democracy itself. 'To disaggregate elements in the democratic imaginary', he writes, 'is to identify features that can exceed its state territorialisation' (Connolly 1993, p. 266). Among the more important of these for Connolly (1993, p. 267) are social movements that are 'not impelled to halt at the boundaries of a particular state' and non-state political organizations that 'crack through the walls of the state'. Of course, Connolly (1993, p. 263) is not so naïve as to think that the 'mystique of territorial democracy' will be broken anytime soon. If social movements and non-state political organizations are encouraging signs of a revivification of democracy through territorial transgression, there is also a great deal of democratic thought and practice that points to 'the tenacity of state territorialisation in contemporary politics' (Connolly 1993, p. 261). At the very least, however, one can point to 'democratic energies' that are exceeding the boundaries of the state and holding out the promise of new relations of equality created solely on the basis of contingent political decisions.

On the strength of these developments Fraser (2005, 85) is surely right to assert the existence of 'deep internal connections between democracy and justice'. Paradoxically, however, her attempt to overcome the problem of misframing by building upon the universal norm of participatory parity may actually work to sap rather than embolden these democratic energies. By institutionalizing a right to representation in a metademocratic procedure, Fraser undercuts the need for political action at exactly the moment when it is most urgently required. Since, in her model, representation at the meta-political level is guaranteed on the basis of the principle of equal moral worth, the struggle currently being waged to constitute the transnational sphere as a political space becomes entirely redundant. Representation ceases to be something to be fought for as a condition of autonomy and becomes instead an entirely instrumental good whose only function is to give the global poor an opportunity to press their claims for distribution and recognition in relation to structures of governance from which they are now excluded. Clearly we should not follow Arendt in treating all this as a disdainful exemplification of the denaturing of politics that occurs when the 'rise of the social' makes the satisfaction of needs more important than the experience of freedom.[17] By the same token we should not lose sight of her understanding of constituent power as the 'action in concert' that opens up a political spaces where people recognize one another as equals.

Notes

1. The tension between justice and democracy underpins a number of recent critical engagements with the normative status of national or territorially-based forms of citizenship in an age of globalisation (see, for instance, Bader 1995, Cohen 1999, Benhabib 2005).
2. This characterization of the schism is indebted primarily to Walzer (1981) but it owes something also to Arendt's (1990, p. 73) well-known claim that '[t]he gulf between philosophy and politics opened historically with the trial and condemnation of Socrates'.
3. This distinction between a monological and dialogical approach is generally attributed to Habermas and emerges out of his critical engagement with John Rawls in the essay 'Reconciliation through the Public use of Reason' (see Habermas 1998).
4. See Fraser (2005, p. 74).
5. As is well known, Fraser's earlier work is largely focused on the rise of recognition as a discrete dimension of justice and the way it stands in relation with more conventional understandings of justice as redistribution. In her later work she continues to refer to redistribution and recognition as the 'two major families of justice claims' (see Fraser 2005, p. 69)
6. Fraser (2003, p. 36) describes participatory parity as the 'normative core' of her theory of justice.
7. I return to the question of who can be considered an 'implicated party' later in the paper.
8. Although I do not have space to explore this problem here, the distinction between being affected and being subjected frequently looks in danger of collapsing. Fraser acknowledges that it is possible to be subjected to a structure of governance, like a state, even though one does not fall within its jurisdiction. To be subjected to a governance structure would thus appear to entail being affected by it (see Fraser 2009, p. 293).
9. Fraser makes reference to Arendt's concept of 'the right to have rights' in several places (see Fraser 2005, p. 77, Fraser 2008b, p. 132).
10. 'As a criminal even a stateless person will not be treated worse than another criminal, that is, he will be treated like everybody else. Only as an offender against the law can he gain protection from it. As long as his trial and his sentence last, he will be safe from that arbitrary police rule against which there are no lawyers and no appeals. The same man who was in jail yesterday because of his mere presence in this world, who had no rights whatever and lived under threat of deportation, or who was dispatched without sentence and without trial to some kind of internment because he had tried to work and make a living, may become almost a fully-fledged citizen because of a little theft. Even if he is penniless he can now get a lawyer, complain about his jailers, and he will be listened to respectfully. He is no longer the scum of the earth but important enough to be informed of all the details of the law under which he will be tried. He has become a respectable person' (Arendt 1976, pp. 286–287).
11. As Arendt points out, this was true even of those countries whose constitutions were built on them.
12. 'Man', wrote Arendt (1976, p. 297), 'can lose all so called Rights of Man without losing his essential quality as a man, his human dignity. Only the loss of polity itself expels him from humanity'.

13. Thus one of the concerns Fraser has about the collapse of Westphalian–Keynesian grammar of justice is that leaves 'no firm ground upon which to stand' (Fraser 2008a, p. 402).
14. As Ingram (2008, p. 410) notes, Arendt doubted that the sphere of politics could be universalized 'for that would entail extending this specifically political form of recognition and interaction to literally everyone'.
15. As Arendt points out in *The Human Condition*, 'The *polis*, properly speaking, is not the city-state in its physical location; it is the organization of the people as it arises out of acting and speaking together for this purpose, no matter where they happen to be' (Arendt 1958, p. 198).
16. 'A democratic ethos', writes Connolly (1993, p. 265), 'balances the desirability of governance through democratic means with a corollary politics of democratic disturbance through which any particular pattern of previous settlements might be tossed up for grabs again'.
17. Arendt's well-know critique of 'the rise of the social', which see perceives as a form of submission to the forces of necessity (i.e. 'mere' biological needs), is most clearly laid out in the second chapter of *On Revolution*. There she compares the American Revolution favourably against the French on the basis that the latter, in seeking to respond to the 'ocean of misery', managed only to 'drown the foundations of freedom' (Arendt 1976, p. 90).

Note on contributor

Paul Muldoon is a lecturer in Politics in the School of Political and Social Inquiry, Monash University. His current research concerns the attempts political communities make to deal with the past and the light those attempts shed on the nature of the political.

References

Arendt, H., 1949. 'The rights of man': what are they? *Modern review*, 3 (1), 24–37.

Arendt, H., 1958. *The Human Condition*. Chicago: University of Chicago Press.

Arendt, H., 1963. *On revolution*. London: Faber and Faber.

Arendt, H., 1976. *The origins of totalitarianism*. Orlando, FL: Harcourt Brace.

Arendt, H., 1990. Philosophy and politics. *Social research*, 57 (1), 73–103.

Bader, V., 1995. Citizenship and exclusion: radical democracy, community, and justice. or, what is wrong with communitarianism?' *Political theory*, 23 (2), 211–246.

Benhabib, S., 2005. Border, boundaries, and citizenship. *PS: political science and, politics*, 38 (4), 673–677.

Cohen, J.L., 1999. Changing paradigms of citizenship and the exclusiveness of the demos. *International sociology*, 14 (3), 245–268.

Connolly, W., 1993. Democracy and territoriality. *In*: Fredrick M. Dolan and Thomas L. Dumm, eds. *Rhetorical republic: governing representations in American politics*. Amherst, MA: University of Massachusetts Press, 249–275.

Fraser, N., 2003. Social injustice in the age of identity politics. In: N. Fraser and A. Honneth, eds. *Redistribution or recognition? A political–philosophical exchange*, trans. Joel Golb, James Ingram, and Christine Wilke. London: Verso, 7–109.

Fraser, N., 2005. Reframing justice in a globalising world. *New left review*, 36, 69–88.

Fraser, N., 2008a. Abnormal justice. *Critical inquiry*, 34 (3), 393–422.
Fraser, N., 2008b. *Scales of justice. reimagining political space in a globalising world*. New York: Columbia University Press and Polity Press.
Fraser, N., 2009. Who counts? Dilemmas of justice in a postWestphalian world. *Antipode*, 41 (1), 281–297.
Fraser, N., 2010. Injustice at intersecting scales: on 'social exclusion' and the 'global poor'. *European journal of social theory*, 13 (3), 363–371.
Habermas, J., 1998. *The Inclusion of the Other: Studies in Political Theory*. Cambridge MA: MIT Press.
Ingram, J.D., 2008. What is a 'right to have rights'? Three images of the politics of human rights. *American political science review*, 102 (4), 401–416.
Menke, C., 2007. The 'aporias of human rights' and the 'one human right': regarding the coherence of Hannah Arendt's argument. *Social research*, 74 (3), 739–762.
Walzer, M., 1981. Philosophy and democracy. *Political theory*, 9 (3), 379–399.

Cosmopolitan justice and the league of democracies

Avia Pasternak

Government Department, University of Essex, UK

Cosmopolitan justice calls for extensive institutional transformations at the international level. But in the absence of a global enforcing authority, such transformations are bound to be hampered by a range of obstacles, including non-compliance and coordination problems. What solutions can a cosmopolitan thinker offer to address these challenges? In answering this question, the paper focuses on the role that international cooperation between the world's democracies can play in promoting cosmopolitan aspirations. It argues that such cooperation has a crucial role to play in executing global justice reforms; and furthermore, that the world's democracies have a moral duty to lead the way in implementing cosmopolitan justice. The paper then suggests that a 'League of Democracies' – an intergovernmental organization which is open exclusively to the world's democracies – could potentially facilitate the type of democratic cooperation that is necessary for cosmopolitan justice.

Around the 2008 US presidential campaign, American international relations theorists hotly debated the direction which US foreign policy should take. According to one set of policy proposals, the United States should have promoted the creation of a 'League of Democracies': an intergovernmental organization (IGO) that would bring together the liberal democracies of the world, and allow them to make joint policy decisions on issues such as security, democracy promotion and human rights. This idea gained some support from both sides of the political campaign (e.g. Daalder and Lindsay 2006, Slaughter and Ikenberry 2007, Kagan 2007). At the same time, it was heavily criticized as politically dangerous and as rooted, at best, in a naïve or simplistic worldview (e.g. Carothers 2008, Kupchan 2008).

In this paper I seek to reassess the idea of a democratic cooperation generally, and of the 'League of Democracies' specifically, from a cosmopolitan perspective. Cosmopolitans call for the redesign of national and international institutions, so that they treat all persons across the globe on a fair and equal basis. As Macdonald and Ronzoni (2012) highlight in their introduction to this issue, the political realization of any vision of global justice, including a cosmopolitan one, is bound to be hampered by a series of political obstacles, including deep disagreements between relevant actors on the desired ends, unwillingness of real-world actors (individuals, business corporations, states) to act upon moral requirements that do not serve their immediate interests, and the absence of a central authoritative system at the global level. In the face of such formidable challenges, the question I ask in this paper is what role cooperation between the world's democracies – of the type envisioned by the supporters of a 'league of democracies' – could play in promoting the realization specifically of cosmopolitan aspirations. My core suggestions are: first, that cosmopolitans should (and to some extent do) consider cooperation between democratic states as a key vehicle for executing cosmopolitan policy proposals; and second, that such cooperation could be enhanced and facilitated by an IGO such as the League of Democracies. If these arguments are correct, it follows that cosmopolitans should pay more attention to the way in which international democratic cooperation can and should be organized and institutionalized.

The paper develops as follows: section 1 considers the role that international democratic cooperation plays in current cosmopolitan thinking. It shows that, while cosmopolitans do not pay much attention to this issue, they do at times imply that international cooperation between democracies is a step in the implementation of cosmopolitan policy proposals. Section 2 expands on this idea, suggesting that it is plausible to argue that democracies have a strong duty to lead the way in implementing global justice, in light of democracies' unique capacities, as well as their own democratic values. Section 3 turns to the idea of the League of Democracies, arguing that an IGO for the democracies of the world could help to promote successful cooperation between democracies, by facilitating joint agreements and by increasing their commitments. Section 4 addresses critiques to this line of thought. Section 5 concludes.

1. International democratic cooperation in cosmopolitan literature

Like many sophisticated moral views, cosmopolitanism is not easy to define.[1] For the purposes of this paper, I focus on what Thomas Pogge (2002, pp. 169–171) calls 'institutional cosmopolitanism', namely a political outlook that is comprised of two parts: first, a cosmopolitan moral principle, according to which every human being is the subject of ultimate moral concern for everyone; and second, an institutional agenda, which argues for the redesign of national and international practices and institutions in light of the moral premise about the equal moral worth of persons across the globe (Pogge 2002, p. 170).

Institutional cosmopolitans offer different visions of the type of transnational institutions that follow from the cosmopolitan moral premise. For example, some believe that cosmopolitanism entails, at the institutional level, a full global democratic government (e.g. Cabrera 2004, pp. 94–96), or at least the creation of various strong supra-national democratic institutions, from international law to a global parliament (e.g. Held 1995, Archibugi 2004); others focus their attention on redistributive schemes from rich to poorer nations (e.g. Pogge 2002). The role that democratic states should play in bringing about such visions is not discussed at length in this abundant literature. However, a close reading reveals that cosmopolitans do sometimes mention that the implementation of cosmopolitan policy proposals would involve intergovernmental democratic cooperation.[2] Consider, for example, proponents of cosmopolitan democracy, who offer a range of democratic institutional reforms at the global level. Here we find that practical discussions of the implementation of such reforms often suggest that the first step entails cooperation between democratic states. For example, David Held (1995, p. 232) suggests that 'in the first instance, cosmopolitan democratic law could be promulgated and defended by those democratic states and civil societies that are able to muster the necessary political judgement ... Such an association of states and societies would be an association of democratic nations which might draw in others over time...'. Similar statements appear in discussions of a 'world parliament': here too the idea is that a global parliament is to be created in the first instance by a coalition of willing democracies and civil society agents from across the world (Held 1995, pp. 273–274, Falk and Strauss 2001, p. 219, Strauss 2005, p. 9).

References to international democratic cooperation appear also in the rich literature on global distributive justice. When they discuss the reforms entailed by egalitarian notions of global justice, institutional cosmopolitans tend to focus their attention on the democratic states of the world. For example, Leif Wenar (2008), who proposes to reform international trade law so that it disallows trading in natural resources with states that fail to respect their citizens' basic human rights, hints that a successful revision of the law should start with the cooperation between democratic governments – specifically, he mentions the United States, the United Kingdom, France, and 'all other major Western governments' (Wenar 2008, p. 27). Once these democracies collectively endorse the proposed legal change, as well as penalties for non-compliance, a full global revision may be achieved.[3] Similarly, Pogge (2002, pp. 211–213) points out that a 'global resource dividend' – a scheme for the transfer of resources from developed to developing countries – depends on the coordinated action of leading developed democracies.

We can conclude, then, that cosmopolitan authors sometimes mention intergovernmental cooperation between democracies as a component of the realization of their policy proposals. However, it is hard to deny that their reflections upon this idea are minimal and unspecified. In the next section I turn to expand on the notion of international democratic cooperation, making the stronger claim that, from a cosmopolitan point of view, it is plausible to argue that the democracies of the world have the duty to lead the way in implementing institutional cosmopolitanism.

2. Democracies to the lead

The 'duty to lead the way' implies that democracies ought to start looking for ways to implement cosmopolitan reforms, and to act upon them, without waiting for the acceptance or the cooperation of all states or other agents around the world, and with the hope that, as David Held put it, in time those others will join their efforts. In other words, the idea here is that democracies have a *special* responsibility to begin implementing cosmopolitan reforms, and that (to the extent that they are motivated by normative considerations) this responsibility gives them a strong reason to act. In my view, cosmopolitans have two reasons to require democracies to lead the way in promoting global reforms. The first reason concerns democracies' record of relative success in building relationships of trust and cooperation at the international level. The *capacity* to cooperate generates the *positive duty* to lead the way in promoting global justice and democracy (at least under certain conditions). The second reason concerns democracies' shared values and norms, which should generate a special commitment to the cosmopolitan agenda.

The claim that democracies' capacities generate a duty to lead the way in promoting cosmopolitan projects is comprised of three premises. The first premise is that, at least as far as cosmopolitans are concerned, global institutional reforms are morally required, *inter alia*, because they would contribute to the protection of rights and the alleviation of human suffering across the world. The second premise is that such reforms, whether in the area of global democracy, international law or distributive justice, require the collective collaboration of a sufficient mass of states. We already saw an expression of this premise in the aforementioned proposals of Pogge and Wenar, the success of which requires, according to these authors, the collaboration of the world's leading democratic nations. Similar conclusions apply to other leading cosmopolitan accounts. Consider, for example, David Held's (1996, p. 354) proposal for a cosmopolitan democracy, which entails, *inter alia*, 'the creation of new political institutions … which would override states in clearly defined spheres of activity where those activities have demonstrable transnational and international consequences'. Or consider the tasks which Simon Caney (2005, pp. 162–163) lists as necessary in order to move towards a more just international system: the 'creation of a new economic institutions with an overview for all economic matters that can coordinate the IMF, WTO and the World Bank in the pursuit of global norms of distributive justice'; the creation of a 'permanent UN volunteer force' for dealing with human rights abuses across the globe; the strengthening of the International Court of Justice so that it includes mandatory membership for states; and the creation of a 'cosmopolitan court for transnational corporate wrongdoing' to 'arbitrate on issues concerning corporate wrongdoing'. Clearly, such tasks cannot be fulfilled by independent, uncoordinated actions of individual states. Rather, their realization necessitates intense levels of international cooperation and coordination by a sufficient number of the states of the world. Moreover, many of these tasks are likely to entail sacrifices from the participating parties without the guarantee of immediate benefits. The nature of the tasks at hand requires, then, relatively high levels of trust between the participating parties and willingness to cooperate in the face of uncertainty.

Finally, the third premise which grounds the capacity argument is that, at the international level, the highest levels of trust and ability to cooperate exist between democratic states (as opposed to non-democratic states).[4] It is beyond the scope of this paper to investigate the reasons why democracies fare better at international cooperation. What matters for the purposes of the discussion here is the fact that, among themselves, democracies are in the best position to engage in the type of collective action necessary in order to realize the cosmopolitan projects. In the world as it is today, democracies, and democracies alone, can engage in the cooperation necessary to execute tasks that are urgently required, according to cosmopolitans. This capacity encumbers them with the duty to act. This latter claim rests on the simple observation that if doing X can prevent great suffering, and if D is in the best position to do X, then assuming that doing X does not entail unreasonable costs for D, D ought to do X.[5] Of course, one could argue that, in principle, non-democratic states too have the *capacity* to cooperate at the international level. All they need to do is give democracies sufficient grounds to trust them, or (even better) become democratic themselves. But the question we are concerned with here is that of the duties that democracies have in the present world, a world in which non-democratic states are not inclined, or perhaps unable, to turn democratic or build a relationship of trust with democracies. In *this* world, while non-democracies surely have the duty to change their ways, the fact that democracies *already* have the capacity to act together, arguably without incurring unreasonable costs, implies that they do not have a normative justification to prolong the execution of their duties until such time as non-democracies would execute their own.

The second reason why democracies ought to promote cosmopolitan principles is that, arguably, these principles are generated by core democratic values. The idea here is that core democratic values dictate not only how societies should treat their own citizens, but also how they should treat members of other societies.[6] We find this idea articulated in many cosmopolitan demands for global justice and global democracy. For example, David Held (1995) grounds his call for a global democracy in the principle of democratic autonomy; Simon Caney (2005) bases his account of global justice on the idea of the equality of persons; Robert Goodin (2007) bases his call for global democratic procedures on the claim that political institutions' key function is to protect the interests of those who are subject to them. These are all foundational democratic normative principles. By basing their global duties accounts on them, cosmopolitan thinkers imply that the citizens and governments of the world's democracies ought to accept the requirements of cosmopolitan justice and global democracy precisely because these requirements are entailed by their own principles and values. Of course, democracies all too often fail to comply with the most elementary requirements of international law and decency (Archibugi 2004). But, from the cosmopolitan perspective, by acting so democracies not only cause undue harm and suffering, they also behave *inconsistently* and *hypocritically* – endorsing one set of values at home and at the same time undermining this very same set of values in their foreign policy (Bonanate 1995). At a normative level, then, one could argue that – because they profess allegiance to the core democratic norms – democracies have a special responsibility to promote them both at the national and international levels (Pasternak 2009).

3. Organizing democratic cooperation

In the previous section I suggested that there are good reasons for cosmopolitans to focus attention on the special responsibilities of democratic states in bringing about various cosmopolitan proposals. As we saw, such proposals necessitate intense cooperation between a sufficient mass of states, and there are good reasons to think it is democracies' responsibility, at least in the first instance, to engage in such cooperation. If this argument is correct, then an important follow-up question is: what can be done in order to facilitate such successful cooperation? At this point we can return to the idea of a 'league of democracies'. As mentioned in the introduction, supporters of the League envisioned an exclusive IGO for the democracies of the world, whose goal would be to further cooperation between democracies in light of their shared values and interests. The proposals developed along these lines in the context of the US presidential debate were by no means unitary, either in terms of agenda or institutional design. My point here is not to comment on them in detail. Rather, inspired by the driving idea behind these proposals, I would like to suggest that an international league of democracies, whose principal agenda would be to identify and to execute democracies' international responsibilities as they are generated from their shared values, could be beneficial in promoting cosmopolitan policy proposals. Such an organization could assist in meeting some of the global political challenges mentioned earlier that cosmopolitanism must face – for example, disagreement about the desired end-state of affairs, or the lack of compliance in the absence of central global enforcement mechanisms.

Generally speaking, it is a very familiar claim that IGOs facilitate interstate cooperation. Simply put, 'compared with a decentralized approach based on ad hoc contracting, a formal organization provides efficiency gains that outweigh the accompanying costs in terms of money, human resources, and constraints on unilateral action' (Abbott and Snidal 1998, p. 12). There are of course multiple ways in which IGOs promote cooperation,[7] but going back to the specific challenges that cooperation for the promotion of global justice raises, I would like to highlight two benefits that a League of Democracies could generate.

First, a League of Democracies could be beneficial for the promotion of institutional cosmopolitanism by helping to resolve inevitable disagreements about the direction that democracies' efforts should take. I mentioned before the difficulties in resolving global disagreements on how national and global institutions should be designed, which Macdonald and Ronzoni (2012) also highlighted. From a cosmopolitan point of view, we can distinguish between two levels of such disagreement. The first is disagreement between those who accept the democratic moral premises upon which cosmopolitanism rests, and those who reject these very premises. For simplicity's sake, I will characterize this as a disagreement between democratic and non-democratic states. The argument advanced here side-steps that disagreement, since its starting point is the claim that we may begin to implement cosmopolitan moral requirements by focusing on the collective international duties of those states that *already* share agreement on fundamental democratic premises.

But even if we concentrate on those states alone, they are still likely to encounter disagreement at a second level, namely disagreement on the specific cosmopolitan interpretation that democratic values have at the international level. Indeed, the ongoing debates between cosmopolitan thinkers indicate that there is no single straightforward answer to this question – neither in terms of the desired end-state, nor in terms of the political changes that are necessary to bring it about. Needless to say, such confusion is detrimental to the realization of any of the cosmopolitan projects I mentioned in the previous section, since they require the cooperation of a sufficient mass of democratic states. An IGO for the democracies of the world can help to resolve this confusion, by serving as a forum in which democracies deliberate, amongst themselves, on their conflicting visions of global political justice, and, out of this deliberation, reach some agreement on a set of shared targets and on the proper distribution of their consequent shared responsibilities. Indeed, as Daalder and Lindsay suggest, a concert of democracies of that sort can create a deeper sense of group identity amongst the democracies of the world, and thus to facilitate collective decision-making between them. As they put it (Daalder and Lindsay 2007, unnumbered): 'the simple truth about human experience is that group membership leads to group identity and to collective action' (cf. Lindsay 2009, p. 8).

The second way in which a League of Democracies could assist in promoting cosmopolitan aspirations is that it can increase democracies' *commitment* to a cosmopolitan agenda. After all, it is obvious that ambitious projects of the kind cosmopolitans envisage – from the solidification of human rights status across the globe, to changes in international trade law, to enhancing the UN's military force – require long-term commitment from states. An IGO which would generate policy decisions on those issues could increase democracies' commitment to implement them for three key reasons. First, as suggested by Pevehouse and Russett (2006, pp. 973–974), commitments that democracies make in IGOs tend to be more binding in the long term than policy decisions they make only at the domestic level (*inter alia*, because democratic governments feel more committed to keep agreements that were made by predecessors at the international level than at the domestic level). Second, like other IGOs, a League of Democracies could create mechanisms that would incentivize democracies not to default on their domestic or international promises, for example through litigation, sanctions, persuasion, and shaming (Moravcsik 1995, Abbott and Snidal 1998, pp. 26–27). Finally, participation in an international institution that is dedicated to the promotion of cosmopolitan ideals could 'socialize' its member states into accepting certain norms and behaviour, thus increasing domestic pressures on the government to comply with its cosmopolitan international and domestic commitments (Pevehouse and Russett 2006, pp. 978–980).[8]

I have suggested so far that an exclusive IGO for the democracies of the world, whose agenda would be to define and discharge democracies' international responsibilities, could perform important functions from a cosmopolitan point of view, serving as a decision-generating forum of deliberation, and enhancing democracies' commitment to cosmopolitan goals. If correct, these observations raise several follow-up questions about the nature and institutional design of such an organization.

First, what should this organization's membership criteria be? The starting point of the discussion here is that the League ought to be open to, and limited to, states whose 'democratic credentials are uncontroversial' (Buchanan and Keohane 2004 p. 18) and that, domestically, respect a standard set of democratic values such as individual rights, the rule of law, and government by the people (Slaughter and Ikenberry 2007, p. 26, Lindsay

2009, p. 6).[9] The justification for such restrictions is that they are necessary in order to create a solidified sense of common goals and unity between the League's members, and, as a result, to generate more effective decision-making. But there is room for developing clear, public and transparent membership criteria (Buchanan and Keohane 2004, p. 19). A second issue concerns the structure of the organization, and more specifically, whether it would take a formal structure, with a treaty, secretariat, headquarters and permanent staff, or whether it should take the form of an informal IGO, with clear membership criteria and regular meetings, but no other institutional characteristics.[10] A third issue concerns the structure of its decision-making and delegation: would it be an international organization, which 'facilitates the intergovernmental self-coordination of national decision-making units' (Rittberger, Zangl and Kruck 2006, p. 11), or would it be a supra-national entity, with a more hierarchical, centralized decision-making process, of the type we see, for example, in the EU? Finally, a fourth issue to consider is the type of obligations the League of Democracies would generate: would it generate 'hard law' obligations, which are legally binding, precise, and accompanied by clear mechanisms for interpretation and enforcement (Abbott and Snidal 2000, pp. 421–422)? Or would it generate 'soft law' obligations, which are not necessarily legally binding, and are more flexible and imprecise?[11]

The choices made on each of these parameters would generate functional advantages and disadvantages for the League. Indeed, bearing in mind the specific challenges I suggested the League of Democracies could help to address, it is likely that its design would constitute a trade-off between generating agreement and generating commitment. As Abbott and Snidal (2000) suggest, formal hard law generating organizations have the advantage of securing more credible commitments from their members, for example through sanctions, increased exit costs, constraining and domestic socialization mechanisms. However, such organizations have high set-up and sovereignty costs, and hence states are often less inclined to join them. Informal soft law organizations, on the other hand, are less successful in generating binding commitments, but their flexibility means that they can more easily generate compromise and long-term agreement, especially when there are high degrees of divergence of opinions and uncertainty about the risks that may follow the outcomes (Abbott and Snidal 2000, Vabulas and Snidal 2011). The decision on whether a League of Democracies should take the form of a formal, hard law institution, or an informal soft law organization must take these trade-offs into account, and raises questions that cannot be addressed within the scope of this paper. Indeed, it is quite likely that the answer to such questions would at least partly depend on the precise cosmopolitan vision one seeks to promote, and the specific challenges it raises, both in terms of potential agreement and commitment. For that reason, my goal here is not to provide a prescriptive account for the League of Democracies, but rather to suggest that if – as I have argued in the previous section – international democratic cooperation is an important element in the implementation of various cosmopolitan proposals, then more attention should be given, in the cosmopolitan literature, to the ways in which such cooperation ought to be organized and/or institutionalized.

4. Addressing critiques

In the previous sections I outlined a proposal for an exclusive IGO for the democracies of the world, the goal of which would be to facilitate the discharge of democracies' specific international responsibilities. In this section I turn to address what I take to be the two major challenges against this line of thought, drawing on critiques that were laid against a League of Democracies in the context of the American presidential debate.[12] The first critique is normative, and concerns the legitimacy of the League. It argues that a League of Democracies (in whatever institutional form it takes) would be an IGO with the capacity to deliberate and make major international policy decisions, but which, at the same time, would be open only to a portion of the world's states. As such, its decisions would not be accountable to all the world's citizens, and hence would lack universal legitimacy (Kupchan 2008, pp. 103–104, Mahbubani 2009, p. 23). The fact that the League lacks universal accountability also raises the concern that its decisions would end up being biased towards the interests of its participating members, who in most cases are already amongst the more rich and powerful states of the world, and against 'the interests of the world's worst-off people' (Buchanan and Keohane 2006, p. 416).

Obviously, proposals for a League of Democracies must take normative concerns about universal legitimacy and accountability into account. These issues should then be added to the aforementioned list of institutional considerations that such proposals ought to reflect upon. Importantly, a solution of an 'all-state-included' format (like that of the UN general assembly for example) would not be a satisfactory response to the legitimacy concern. After all, that format is partly comprised of states whose heads do not respect the interests and perspectives of the people they rule, and for that reason it too raises concerns about universal accountability (Daalder and Lindsay 2007). Briefly, there are two other routes that could be considered here: on the first route, the League's accountability range would be increased by the incorporation of non-state representative agents – for example, civil society groups and non-governmental organizations (NGOs). These can represent the interests of stakeholders in and across states, and thus increase the League's accountability to those who are not part of democratic states.[13] The second route takes into account the fact that including non-state NGOs and civil society groups may prove to be too difficult, too costly, or simply insufficient to generate universal accountability. The (not incompatible) alternative for resolving the League's legitimacy problem would acknowledge that universal accountability is infeasible in this context, and instead search for other standards that can ground its international legitimacy. A helpful starting point here is recent debates on standards of institutional legitimacy that are not tied to representation. It will be beyond the scope of this paper to investigate such standards in depth, but one helpful example which is worth mentioning is Buchanan and Keohane's (2006) 'complex standard of legitimacy', which is developed specifically for the context of global governance institutions. Buchanan and Keohane suggest that an international institution can be legitimate even if it is not universally accountable, so long as it fulfils certain criteria. One such criterion is that the institution in question enjoys the consent of democratic states (Buchanan and Keohane 2006, p. 417). Another criterion is that the institution respects the human rights of all those who are affected by it, including those who cannot be represented in it (pp. 419–422). These or similar standards can be a starting point for thinking about the proper design of the League, so that it would avoid the universal legitimacy trap.

The second major objection to the League I will address here is practical. At this level, it has been suggested that a League of Democracies would never materialize, simply because it will not serve the interests of democracies, its potential members. This is so especially in light of the fact that the interests of the various democracies across the globe often conflict, and they can hardly be persuaded to unite in a body that would generate joint policy decisions. For example, US foreign policy interests have been different from those of Europe in the Middle East (Carothers 2008) and there are frequent conflicts of policy between developing democracies such as India and Brazil, and developed democracies such as the United States and Europe (Kupchan 2008, pp. 102–103).[14]

One possible answer to this worry is that, as argued in section 2, the argument for a cosmopolitan league of democracies is not interest- but duty-based. It *may* be the case that the democracies of the world would fare better in a world that is more just. But regardless of that they have specific international *duties*, generated from their shared capacities and their domestic values. And yet, the 'feasibility objection' is unlikely to be appeased by this response. For what it essentially suggests is that, as a matter of fact, democracies are not motivated by normative considerations in their behaviour in the international arena, and hence would not be inclined to promote an institution which seeks to assist them in discharging their international responsibilities. This is a legitimate concern, as it is hard to deny that the actual behaviour of democracies in the world rarely meet cosmopolitan standards (Archibugi 2008).

In order to address this challenge, we need to distinguish between three different versions of the claim that international democratic cooperation in the service of normative goals generally, and the erection of a League of Democracies specifically, are infeasible. On the first version, democracies act on raw interests and not on normative grounds at the international level. Thus, if supporting a League of Democracies is something that democracies are morally required to do, rather than something that serves their interests, there is no reason to think they would do so (Mahbubani 2009, Kupchan 2008). This is the classic realist objection to international normative thinking, the best reply to which is simply that there may indeed be a gap between how agents (individuals or states) behave in the world and how they ought to behave. But the actual failure of agents in the world to act morally is not in itself a reason to abandon the project of developing action-guiding moral principles and proposals (such as the League).[15]

The second, and probably more interesting, version of the feasibility concern identifies a tension between cosmopolitan aspirations and democratic procedures. The idea here is that while core democratic values such as democratic autonomy and the equality of persons should indeed lead one to conclude that cosmopolitan reforms are morally required, at the same time, these values also ground decision-making procedures which make it hard for policymakers to act on these conclusions. Democratic governments are by definition accountable to their own publics. Democratic governments are therefore obliged to promote the interests and wishes of their publics, rather than act on the latter's global duties. According to this worry, then, the reason that democratic governments are unlikely to engage in cosmopolitan projects is not that normative concerns do not interest them as such, but rather that the democratic rationale dictates that they first and foremost cater for the wishes of their own citizens. Cosmopolitan thinkers sometimes express a worry of this type when they consider the implementability of their proposed reforms. For example, Archibugi (1995, p. 131) notes that democratic governments justify their disregard of international law by evoking their accountability to their own publics (cf. Buchanan 1999). Caney (2005, p. 169) warns that democracies are unlikely to adopt cosmopolitan recommendations, because the incentives of democratic officials is to cater for the wishes of their citizens. 'They will therefore serve cosmopolitan ideals only if their citizens happen to have strong cosmopolitan beliefs'.

The starting point for addressing that concern is the observation that the tension between democratic values and democratic procedures is not an unfamiliar one. Recall, for example, the tension between 'the tyranny of the majority' and individual liberties in democracies. Democracy literature abounds with discussions of the type of democratic models that are better suited to deal with this kind of tension. It may be the case that a similar tension exists between cosmopolitan values and democratic procedures, and that for that reason, democratic governments are unlikely to engage in cosmopolitan projects. But there may also be ways to address this tension from within cosmopolitan thinking. For example, cosmopolitans can point to the types of democratic procedures in which this tension is less likely to arise.[16] The claim that democratic procedures are likely to make governments act in light of their publics' interests rather than duties simply opens the door, then, to the observation that some models of democracy are *better* precisely in the sense that they narrow the gap between democratic procedures and the execution of democratic values at the global level. Moreover, it is worth noting that – to the extent that policymakers are motivated by cosmopolitan concerns but are constrained by their public's wishes – joining a League of Democracies could help to resolve that tension, if such an IGO is indeed able, as I suggested before, to 'socialize' the publics of its member states to recognize the global responsibilities that are entailed by their values.

Finally, the third version of the concern about the feasibility of international democratic cooperation and of the League of Democracies argues that the tension we find between cosmopolitans' prescriptions on how democracies should behave in the world, and the actual foreign policies of democracies, is not the result of a tension between democratic principles and procedures. Rather, this gap is the result of a tension between different democratic principles – for example, the principle of equal respect for the fundamental interests of all persons arguably grounds global redistributive schemes. But the equally important democratic value of collective self-determination limits the extent to which a political community should be subjected to international schemes of that nature.[17] If this is indeed the case, then democracies have a reason not to take part in efforts to promote cosmopolitan projects – not because such efforts do not serve their immediate interest, or that their publics are blind to moral demands, but rather because there is no clear cosmopolitan normative agenda that follows from the democratic core principles. Different democratic values pull in different directions, and hence democracies can be justified in opting for a non-cosmopolitan interpretation of their global responsibilities, one that, *inter alia*, does not commit them to create a cosmopolitan League of Democracies.

This final practical concern poses a deep challenge to the cosmopolitan agenda: it defies the claim I made earlier that democracies have a duty to promote cosmopolitan projects, by arguing that these projects are not necessarily compatible with entrenched democratic norms. It will be beyond the scope of this paper to provide a full response to this critique. But I do not think such a response is merited here. After all, my goal is not to defend cosmopolitanism as such, but rather, more modestly, to suggest that if one is on board with the cosmopolitan premises, then one may have reasons to look favourably on ways of promoting intentional democratic cooperation, such as the League of Democracies in some version. For the purposes of this paper then, it suffices to say that cosmopolitans must surely believe that the claim about a disparity between democratic values and the cosmopolitan conclusions is at least partly false. That is, that at some basic level there is a strong enough link between democracies' values and cosmopolitan visions. Although, at the same time, cosmopolitans can acknowledge that there is no single, simple answer to the question of what obligations democracies have at the global level. One can accept the claim that 'democratic values lead to cosmopolitan conclusions' but still argue about the precise nature of these conclusions. As I pointed out before, a League of Democracies could be an important means for generating collective action in the face of this plurality of normative views, by providing a forum for deliberation in an attempt to resolve, by democratic means, these kinds of disagreements. The point then remains that, so long as one accepts the normative recommendations of cosmopolitan theory – one can accept the claim that institutionalizing a League of Democracies can contribute to their enactment.

5. Conclusions

This paper assessed the role of international democratic cooperation from a cosmopolitan perspective. Advocates of that perspective are certain of the moral validity of the core moral cosmopolitan premise, and that this premise calls for extensive transformation of the current international order, in the direction of cosmopolitan justice and democracy. I proposed that there are good reasons for cosmopolitans to assign democratic states with the duty to lead the way in promoting such institutional transformation. First, in light of democracies' unique capacities to engage in the international cooperation that is necessary for the realization of cosmopolitan policy proposals. Second, in light of democracies' shared values and principles, which arguably lead to cosmopolitan conclusions. I then suggested that an IGO for the democracies of the world might be able to facilitate such successful international cooperation. First, it would give democracies the opportunity to deliberate over the specific tasks each of them ought to engage in, and reach agreement on the goals ahead. Second, it can help to generate long-term commitment to those goals. Anticipating critiques to this line of thought, I argued that a cosmopolitan League of Democracies could be designed in a way that addresses universal legitimacy shortfalls, by incorporating non-state representative agents from across the globe, and/or by following a sophisticated standard of legitimacy which does not depend on universal representation. Finally, I addressed the realist concern that international democratic cooperation in the service of ethical demands, and the League of Democracies as an expression of such cooperation, are infeasible and unrealistic pipe dreams. As I suggested, the fact that democracies do not always, or even rarely, act morally at the international level does not imply that there is no point in developing cosmopolitan arguments, in the hope that they would end up doing some convincing work in the real world. Moreover, it is possible that an IGO like a League of Democracies could help to close the gap between how democracies act and how they ought to act, by providing democratic governments and publics with a forum to reflect upon and articulate their global duties, and thus shape their cosmopolitan sensitivities.

As I noted in section 3, these conclusions leave open many questions about the recommended institutional design of the League. Such questions ought to be answered from particular cosmopolitan perspectives, taking into account the possibly conflicting goals of – on the one hand – reaching agreement on the desired end-state, and – on the other hand – generating credible commitment to these goals from the world's democracies. If my core observation that international democratic cooperation has a crucial role to play in executing global justice reforms is correct, then precisely these types of questions ought to receive more attention from those interested in such reforms.

Acknowledgements

I should like to thank Harry Bauer, Bob Goodin, Patti Tamara Lenard, Roland Meeks, Terry Macdonald, Karolina Milewicz, Miriam Ronzoni, Zofia Stemplowska and an anonymous referee for their insightful suggestions. This paper was written for the Global Political Justice workshop that took place in Prato 2010. I thank the participants for an illuminating and highly beneficial discussion.

Notes

1. For helpful review see Kleingeld and Brown (2011).
2. Of course, cosmopolitans do not argue that it is only states that act at the international level. In fact, much cosmopolitan thinking, especially at its early stages, strove to emphasize the role of civil society in mobilizing institutional changes at the international level; see review in Brown (2000). But for brevity's sake, I mention here only the role that democratic *states* should play in realizing cosmopolitan visions.
3. Wenar may not be a staunched 'cosmopolitan', but proposals in similar spirit, though in less detail, are advocated by self-proclaimed cosmopolitans (e.g. Pogge 2002).
4. As argued for example by Doyle (1986), Moravcsik (1997), Pevehouse and Russett (2006), Risse-Kappen (1995), Slaughter (1995).
5. The claim that a capacity to put a bad situation right can generate the duty to do so is advocated most clearly by utilitarian thinkers (e.g. Singer 1972, Goodin 1985). But others, such as David Miller, acknowledge its force albeit more cautiously (see especially Miller (2001, pp. 460–462)).
6. See direct references to this claim in Archibugi (2004, p. 441), in the context of lamenting democracies' failure to live up to their standards when it comes to foreign policy (cf. Linklater 1992, p. 38, Bonanate 1995).
7. For helpful discussions see Abbott and Snidal (1998, 2000), Rittberger and Zangl (2006).
8. It is probably worth mentioning that the supporters of the League of Democracies I mentioned before highlight additional advantages it may have in

world politics. For example, increasing democracies' domestic commitment to the democratic agenda (Slaughter and Ikenberry 2007) and incentivizing other states in the world to become democratic in order to join it (Buchanan and Keohane 2004, pp. 19–20, Daalder and Lindsey 2007). To the extent that these potential impacts are valuable from a cosmopolitan point of view, attention should be given to them in the process of further thinking about the institutional design of a League of Democracies. For brevity's sake, I focus here only on features that relate to the League's role in facilitating cooperation.

9. According Daalder and Lindsey (2007, unnumbered), currently there are roughly 60 states that would be eligible for membership.
10. For the various distinctions between formal and informal IGOs see Vabulas and Snidal (2011).
11. For a discussion of the various forms of 'soft law legalization' see Abbott and Snidal (2000).
12. It is worth mentioning that, perhaps in light of the critiques that were levelled against the League, it never materialized into a concrete policy proposal. However, notice that my concern here is not with the question of whether the United States should promote a League of Democracies. Rather, I am interested in the question of whether such an IGO could be recommended from a cosmopolitan perspective. I therefore focus here only on those critiques against the League that are relevant for its cosmopolitan version.
13. For an illuminating account of the potential role of NGOs as representative agents see Macdonald (2008).
14. Another objection that was raised against the League, and that is worth mentioning here, is that such an institution is likely to alienate non-democracies, reduce their willingness to cooperate with democracies at a global level and undermine security and peace (Kupchan 2008, p. 105, Schlesinger 2009, p. 14, Mahbubani 2009). This objection is based on empirical projections, which supporters of the League deny. Since further evidence is necessary in order to support either side of this argument, I put it to the side.
15. For further discussion of the tension between morality and interest, specifically in the context of international relations theory see Beitz (1979, pp. 55–59). Of course, ethical requirements may take costs into account: for example, it is commonly assumed that one is morally obligated be help others only at reasonable costs to herself; see discussion specifically with relation to the duty to aid the global poor in Miller (2004). But my point here is that the requirement to take part in a League is not generated from the fulfilment of interests. Rather, it is generated from duties, taking into account that fulfilling these duties should not entail unreasonable costs.
16. For example, advocates of deliberative democracy argue that deliberation makes people more truthful, reasonable and cooperative – e.g. Fishkin (1993). Perhaps it can be shown that deliberative democracy also makes citizens more aware of their global responsibilities.
17. David Miller (2009) argues along those lines, although he does not phrase the problem as a tension between democratic principles, but rather as a tension between different understandings of the value of democracy.

Note on contributor

Avia Pasternak is a lecturer in political theory at the government department, the University of Essex. She has published works on collective responsibility in democracies, on collective punishment, and on international economic sanctions.

She currently works on the relation between accounts of global justice and democratic theory.

References

Abbot, K.W. and Snidal, D., 1998. Why states act through formal interantional organizations. *The journal of conflict resolution*, 42 (1), 3–32.

Abbot, K.W. and Snidal, D., 2000. Hard and soft law in international governance. *International organizaton*, 54 (3), 421–456.

Archibugi, D., 1995. From the United Nations to cosmopolitan democracy. *In*: D. Archibugi and D. Held, eds. *Cosmopolitan democracy*. Cambridge: Polity Press, 121–162.

Archibugi, D., 2004. Cosmopolitan democracy and its critics. *European Journal of International Relations*, 10 (3), 437–473.

Archibugi, D., 2008. A league of democracies or a democratic United Nations [online]. *Harvard International Review*. Available from: http://www.danielearchibugi.org/downloads/papers/Archibugi_A_League_of_Democracies_or_a_Democratic_UN.pdf. [Accessed 12 May 2010].

Beitz, C.R., 1979. *Political theory and international relations*. Princeton, NJ: Princeton University Press.

Bonanate, L., 1995. Peace or democracy? *In*: D. Archibugi and D. Held, eds. *Cosmopolitan democracy*. Cambridge: Polity Press, 42–67.

Brown, C., 2000. Cosmopolitanism, world citizenship and global civil society. *Critical review of social and political philosphy*, 3 (1), 6–27.

Buchanan, A., 1999. The internal legitimacy of humanitarian intervention. *The journal of political philosophy*, 7 (1), 71–87.

Buchanan, A. and Keohane, R., 2004. The preventive use of force: a cosmopolitan institutional proposal. *Ethics and international affairs*, 18 (1), 1–22.

Buchanan, A. and Keohane, R., 2006. The legitimacy of global governance institutions. *Ethics and international affairs*, 20 (4), 405–437.

Caney, S., 2005. *Justice beyond borders: a global political theory*. Oxford: Oxford University Press.

Cabrera, L., 2004. *Political theory of global justice*. Oxford: Routledge.

Carothers, T., 2008. Is a league of democracies a good idea? [online] The Carnegie Endowment for International Peace. Available from: http://www.carnegieendowment.org/files/pb59_carothers_league_final.pdf. [Accessed 8 October 2012].

Daalder, I. and Lindsay, J., 2007. Democracies of the world, unite! *The American Interest*, January/Feburary Issue.

Doyle, M.W., 1986. Liberalism and world politics. *The American political science review*, 80 (4), 1151–1169.

Falk, R. and Strauss, A., 2001. Toward global parliament. *Foreign affairs*, 80, 212–220.

Fishkin, J., 1993. *Democracy and deliberation: new directions for democratic reform*. New Haven, CT: Yale University Press.

Goodin, R., 1985. *Protecting the vulnerable*. Chicago, IL: Chicago University Press.

Goodin, R., 2007. Enfranchising all affected interests, and its alternatives. *Philosophy and public affairs*, 35 (1), 40–68.

Held, D., 1995. *Democracy and the global order: from the modern state to cosmopolitan governance*. Cambridge: Polity Press.

Held, D., 1996. *Models of Democracy*. 2nd ed. Cambridge: Polity.

Kagan, R., 2007. End of dreams, return of history. [online] The Hoover Institution *Policy Review*, no. 144. Stanford University. Available at www.hoover.org/publications/policy-review/article/6136. [Accessed 8 October 2012].

Kleingeld, P. and Brown, E., 2011. Cosmopolitanism [online]. In: E.N. Zalta, ed. *The Stanford encyclopedia of philosophy.* available at http://plato.stanford.edu/archives/spr2011/entries/cosmopolitanism/. [Accessed 8 October 2012].

Kupchan, C., 2008. Minor league, major problems. *Foreign affairs*, 87, 96–110.

Lindsay, J., 2009. The case for a concert of democracies. *Ethics and international affairs*, 23 (1), 5–11.

Linklater, A., 1992. What is a good international citizen. *In*: P. Keal, ed. *Ethics and foreign policy.* Canbara: Allen & Unwin Press, 21–43.

Mahbubani, K., 2009. The dangers of democratic delusions. *Ethics and international affairs*, 23 (1), 19–25.

Macdonald, T., 2008. *Global stakeholder democracy.* Oxford: Oxford University Press.

Macdonald, T. and Ronzoni M., 2012. Introduction: the idea about global political justice. *Critical review of international social and political philosophy*, 15 (5) 521–533.

Miller, D., 2001. Distributing responsibilities. *Journal of political philosophy*, 9 (4), 453–471.

Miller, D., 2009. Democracy's domain. *Philosophy and public affairs*, 37 (3), 201–228.

Miller, R.W., 2004. Beneficence, duty and distance. *Philosophy and public affairs*, 32 (4), 357–383.

Moravcsik, A., 1995. Explaining international human rights regimes: liberal theory and Western Europe. *European journal of, international relations*, 1 (2), 157–189.

Moravcsik, A., 1997. Taking preferences seriously: a liberal theory of international politics. *International organization*, 51 (4), 513–553.

Pasternak, A., 2009. Sanctioning liberal democracies. *Political studies*, 57 (1), 54–74.

Pevehouse, J. and Russett, B., 2006. Democratic international governmental organizations promote peace. *International organization*, 60 (4), 969–1000.

Pogge, T., 2002. *World poverty and human rights: cosmopolitan responsibilities and reforms.* Cambridge: Polity Press.

Risse-Kappen, T., 1995. *Cooperation among democracies: the European influence on U.S. foreign policy.* Princeton, NJ: Princeton University Press.

Rittberger, V., Zangl, B., and Kruck, A., 2006. *International organization: polity, politics and policies.* Basingstoke: Palgrave Macmillan.

Singer, P., 1972. Famine, affluence and morality. *Philosophy and public affairs*, 1 (1), 229–243.

Slaughter, A.M., 1995. International law in a world of liberal states. *European journal of international relations*, 6 (3), 503–538.

Slaughter, A.M. and Ikenberry, J., 2007. *Forging a world of liberty under law: U.S national security in the 21st century [online].* Princeton, NJ: Woodrow Wilson School, Princeton University. Available from: www.princeton.edu/~ppns/report/FinalReport.pdf. [Accessed 8 October 2012].

Sleshinger, S., 2009. Why a league of democracies will not work. *Ethics and international affairs*, 23 (1), 13–18.

Strauss, A., 2005. Taking democracy global: assessing the benefits and challenges of a global parliamentary assembly [online]. One World Trust Pamphlet Series. Available from: http://tinyurl.com/8f8aqyh. [Accessed 8 October 2012].

Vabulas, F. and Snidal D., 2011. Informal intergovernmental organizations (IIGOs). APSA 2011 Annual Meeting Paper [online]. Available from: http://papers.ssrn.com/sol3/papers.cfm?abstract_id=1900274. [Accessed 8 October 2012].

Wenar, L., 2008. Property rights and the resource curse. *Philosophy and public affairs*, 36 (1), 2–32.

On the concept of climate debt: its moral and political value

Jonathan Pickering and Christian Barry

Centre for Moral, Social, and Political Theory, Research School of the Social Sciences, Australian National University, Canberra, Australia

A range of developing countries and international advocacy organizations have argued that wealthy countries, as a result of their greater historical contribution to human-induced climate change, owe a 'climate debt' to poor countries. Critics of this argument have claimed that it is incoherent or morally objectionable. In this essay we clarify the concept of climate debt and assess its value for conceptualizing responsibilities associated with global climate change and for guiding international climate negotiations. We conclude that the idea of a climate debt can be coherently formulated, and that while some understandings of the idea of climate debt could lead to morally objectionable conclusions, other accounts would not. However, we argue that climate debt nevertheless provides an unhelpful frame for advancing global justice through international climate negotiations – the only existing means of resolving political conflict over the collective action problems posed by human-induced climate change – due to its retrospective and potentially adversarial emphasis, and to problems of measurement.

Introduction

Do developed countries, as a result of their greater historical contribution to causing human-induced climate change, owe a 'climate debt' to poor countries? Numerous developing countries and international advocacy organizations have argued that they do. They assert this on the ground that these countries have used more than their fair share of the Earth's ability to absorb the greenhouse gas emissions that cause climate change. The resulting need to reduce emissions globally now constrains the ability of poorer countries to develop. Further, climate change is increasingly generating adverse impacts for poor countries, many of which are particularly vulnerable to a warming climate. This debt should be repaid, it is argued, through developed countries rapidly reducing their emissions and providing finance to help developing countries adopt low-emissions technologies and adjust to the adverse impacts of climate change. Many others, including senior officials of wealthy countries, on the other hand, have resisted these claims. They have done so principally by means of two arguments: that the idea of a climate debt makes no sense – we will call this *the incoherence argument*; or that employing climate debt as a frame for understanding climate related responsibilities will lead to morally objectionable conclusions – which we refer to as *the implausibility argument*.

Our aim in this essay is to clarify the idea of climate debt and assess its value for conceptualizing responsibilities associated with climate change and guiding international climate negotiations. There are various ways in which responsibilities relating to climate change could be distributed. Invoking climate debts is one way of providing a 'frame' for understanding how these responsibilities *should* be distributed. Frames represent 'interpretive storylines that set a specific train of thought in motion, communicating why an issue might be a problem, who or what might be responsible for it, and what should be done about it' (Nisbet 2009, p. 15). As such, they provide rationales for particular distributions of responsibilities, and involve distinctive forms of rhetoric. There may often be several possible frames in which complex policy issues can be encapsulated, and incompatibility among frames proposed by different actors may give rise to entrenched conflicts (Fischer 2003). The analysis of conceptual 'frames' for global policy debates is of significance to the broader question of global political justice insofar as such frames structure the interface between the moral arguments in which responsibilities of *distributive* justice are debated and determined, and the political conflicts and authoritative actions through which decisions are taken and executed as matters of *political* justice.

When assessing the value of particular frames, we can distinguish between ethical and political analyses. An ethical analysis of a frame examines whether the premises and line of reasoning it invokes are morally plausible. Political analysis of a frame seeks to determine whether it is likely to be a feasible and desirable means of advancing valuable goals.[1] While political analysis may indicate whether a particular frame is likely to further the interests of the individual party proposing it, here we focus on the question of whether the frame of climate debt helps to resolve a collective action problem – in this case a fair allocation of responsibilities to address human-induced climate change.

Accordingly, our article proceeds along two tracks. In the first part of the paper, we provide an ethical analysis of climate debt arguments. We begin by giving examples of how the idea of climate debt has been employed recently in discussions of climate policy and identify five core propositions that appear to underlie the use of this framing concept. We explicate each of the propositions and examine whether they are individually or jointly vulnerable to the incoherence or implausibility arguments. Against critics of the idea of climate debt, we shall argue that climate debt is indeed a coherent concept, and that while *some* understandings of this idea could indeed lead to morally objectionable or implausible conclusions, it need not do so. Indeed, the climate debt frame highlights considerations that must be given significant weight in any fair agreement on climate-related responsibilities. In the second part of the paper, we provide a political analysis of climate debt arguments. Against proponents of the idea of climate debt, we argue that it provides a largely unhelpful and potentially counterproductive frame for guiding future international climate negotiations. While this frame may have played a valuable role in giving voice to the claims of some developing countries, we argue that there are alternative frames that are more likely to foster reflective deliberation and eventually cooperation in the form of binding agreements.

The use of climate debt

The theoretical roots of the concept of climate debt can largely be traced back to broader themes such as the global distribution of ecological resources and the allocation of responsibilities for addressing environmental harms. Since the early 1990s, theorists – notably in Latin America but also more broadly – have developed variations on the concept of 'ecological debt' as a way of characterizing unsustainable patterns of resource use, encompassing not only climate change but also overuse of other resources such as forests and fisheries (see e.g. Smith 1991, Martinez-Alier 1993, Srinivasan *et al.* 2008, Simms 2009). These accounts in turn have built on earlier theorists' characterizations of global environmental issues as involving global commons or common pool resources (Hardin 1968, Ostrom 1990) as well as structuralist accounts of global economic relations (Roberts and Parks 2007, p. 165). Climate debt (or carbon debt as it also sometimes called[2]) is ordinarily viewed as a component of a broader ecological debt.[3] Such debts are commonly conceived as both *intergenerational* – accrued by current people and owed to future generations – and *international* – accrued by the populations of some countries and owed to the populations of other countries. Accounts of climate debt vary in their relative emphasis on each dimension (compare Hayward 2006, Botzen, Gowdy and Van Den Bergh 2008).

Although arguments asserting climate debt are not altogether new to international climate negotiations conducted under the United Nations Framework Convention on Climate Change (UNFCCC), they have recently come into increased currency, particularly since the lead-up to the UNFCCC conference in Copenhagen in 2009. Climate debt arguments have been raised in formal submissions (notably by Bolivia, the most vocal proponent of climate debt in the UNFCCC negotiations), draft negotiating texts, and arguments by activists and non-government organizations seeking to influence the negotiations (see, for example, Klein 2009).

While calls for repayment of climate debt have been highly visible in media reporting of recent climate change negotiations, they have been omitted from resulting agreements, with other principles for allocating responsibilities such as 'comparable effort' or equity gaining far more traction. However, minority discourses often garner significant attention in negotiations due to the consensus-based nature of decision-making under the UNFCCC. Although Bolivia's attempt to block consensus single-handedly at the 2010 Cancún conference was neutralized by a procedural workaround, such tactics may not always be available in future, and it remains important to engage substantively with claims about climate debt.

Core elements of the climate debt idea

While arguments for climate debt vary in some respects, the focus in negotiations has been mainly on international rather than intergenerational aspects of climate debt, and our essay will accordingly focus on arguments for this type of debt.[4] We interpret common arguments for climate debt as having the following features:

A1. Moral responsibilities. Countries that have emitted more than their fair share of the Earth's capacity to safely absorb emissions have moral responsibilities towards low-emitting countries and those vulnerable to the impacts of climate change.

A2. Characterization of these responsibilities as debts. The stringency of these moral responsibilities is such that they constitute a debt that is claimable as a matter of right by the agents to whom the debt is owed.

A3. The content of the responsibility. A primary factor in calculating the extent of each country's debt is the magnitude of its share of global cumulative emissions since the Industrial Revolution.

A4. Identity of debtors and creditors. The debt is owed specifically by developed countries towards developing countries.

A5. Form of repayment required. Climate debt must be repaid by (i) distributing emissions rights in ways that effectively compensate developing countries for historical overuse and allow developing countries' emissions to rise in order to accommodate their development needs (repayment of 'emissions debt'); and (ii) compensating developing countries for the adverse effects of climate change (repayment of 'adaptation debt').[5]

We discuss these elements in turn, examining as we go whether they involve propositions that are vulnerable to the incoherence or implausibility arguments. We focus primarily on arguments A2 and A3, which we see as representing the core issues that are specifically contested in the context of climate debt, while briefly discussing the other arguments.

Ethical analysis

Threshold issues: causal and moral responsibilities associated with climate change

The first premise of the argument (A1) involves both factual and moral claims. The factual claims are relatively uncontroversial. It is now increasingly accepted that the Earth has a finite capacity over the very long term to absorb emissions (Allen *et al.* 2009). Developed countries[6] have emitted the larger proportion of cumulative emissions since the Industrial Revolution and their per capita emissions are higher than those of developing countries, even though developing countries' current aggregate annual emissions now exceed those of developed countries, largely due to the rapid growth of populous countries such as China and India (World Bank 2010). There is also widespread agreement that poorer countries are particularly vulnerable to climate change. Not only do the impacts of climate change affect access to goods such as health protection, food, water and shelter, but constraints on emissions may (in the absence of support for costly low-emitting technologies) have adverse impacts on the livelihoods of poor people (Caney 2006, 2010).

The moral claims in A1 are somewhat more contentious, but some possible theoretical bases for climate debt rely on accounts of responsibilities relating to natural resource use that are very widely held. The idea that the atmosphere is a global commons has been argued for or simply assumed by philosophers and economists of different temperaments and political stripes (see, for example, Nordhaus 1994, Gardiner 2001). Similarly, there is considerable support for the idea that commons – whether conceived as originally owned by humankind in general or as unowned – give rise to certain moral responsibilities relating to fair use (see e.g. Hayward 2006, Vanderheiden 2008). The best-known account of such responsibilities is John Locke's proviso that the use of natural resources be constrained by the requirement to leave 'enough, and as good' for others (Locke 1988, pp. 288–289). A related and more recent formulation that has gained currency among both researchers and negotiators is that of the equitable distribution of 'ecological space' (see, for example, Page 2007, Hayward 2007, Bolivia 2009).

Given the Earth's limited capacity to absorb emissions safely, most people generally accept that global emissions should be subject to *some* criterion of fair use. Variants on Locke's proviso, for example, have been employed by a number of authors in support of arguments for roughly equal per capita allocations of emissions rights (see e.g. Singer 2002, Vanderheiden 2008). Whether fair-use criteria require equality or sufficiency in the allocation of emissions remains subject to dispute (Bovens 2011). But developed countries seem to have used more than their fair share on any plausible understanding of this notion. We conclude that the propositions in A1 are defensible against both the incoherence and implausibility arguments.

Guiltless responsibility, excusable ignorance and the intergenerational objection

One fundamental objection to the idea of climate debt is that even if excessive emissions result in some kind of moral obligation, this falls short of being an obligation of 'debt', as asserted in A2.

This type of argument was made, for example, at the Copenhagen conference by the United States' chief climate negotiator Todd Stern:

> I actually completely reject the notion of a debt or reparations or anything of the like. ... Let's just be mindful of the fact for most of the 200 years since the Industrial Revolution, people were blissfully ignorant of the fact that emissions cause the greenhouse effect. It's a relatively recent phenomenon. It's the wrong way to look at this. We absolutely recognize our historical role in putting emissions in the atmosphere that are there now. But the sense of guilt or culpability or reparations, I categorically reject that.[7]

These objections are also typically advanced against premise A3 – the claim that responsibility for debt should be apportioned largely according to a country's cumulative emissions. We consider in turn three interconnected objections to climate debt that may be distinguished in Stern's statement.

Guiltless responsibility

The objection from guiltless responsibility asserts that it only makes sense to speak of debt where there is culpability or a responsibility to provide reparations, but it does not follow from the fact that wealthy countries are responsible for having caused emissions that they were *culpable* for having done so. But surely, as Bolivia's ambassador to the United Nations pointed out in his response to Stern's statement, the point of discussing climate debt need not be to assign guilt, but merely *responsibility* for bearing cost (Climate Justice Now 2009).[8] As a general matter, liability for debt does not imply guilt or direct culpability. We can become indebted by bad luck, even when we have acted prudently. Consider, for example, ordinary contractual debts, which are acquired through reciprocal arrangements freely entered into, and are frequently associated with legal obligations. It is true that contractual debtors are thought to be responsible or liable for repaying their debts, but this is quite distinct from responsibility that carries connotations of blameworthiness (although *failure* to service these debts may of course carry such connotations).

So too with respect to non-contractual debts (Martinez-Alier 2002, p. 228). While we may speak coherently of non-contractual debts that result from deliberate wrongdoing (resulting, for example, in a figurative 'debt to society') or negligent harm under tort law, debts may also arise in circumstances involving neither voluntary bargaining nor culpable harm. One such circumstance, which seems particularly pertinent to claims of climate debt, is unjust enrichment. If you receive a mistaken payment, for example, you are by law strictly liable to repay it, even if you were unaware that you were not entitled to it (Birks 2003, pp. 6–9). The same applies to cases in which you appropriate (however innocently) that which you are not entitled to appropriate.

The fact that overuse of the earth's emissions absorptive capacity was neither the subject of a contractual resource-sharing arrangement nor clearly the result of a deliberate intent to appropriate that capacity does not provide a convincing objection to the idea that there are climate debts.

Excusable ignorance

The objection from excusable ignorance asserts that because countries were reasonably ignorant of the harmful effects of emissions until relatively recently, they should not be held morally responsible for those emissions or their effects.[9] Since there is no moral responsibility, there is no debt involved.

Although reasonable ignorance may ordinarily be a legitimate defence to claims of negligence in tort law, it may not be sufficient in all circumstances to provide relief from liability to bear cost when damage has occurred. Bolivia's response to the United States' statement suggests some parallels – albeit using examples that do not involve common pool resources – where responsibility for inadvertent harm may arise:

> Admitting responsibility for the climate crisis without taking necessary actions to address it is like someone burning your house and then refusing to pay for it. Even if the fire was not started on purpose, the industrialised countries, through their inaction, have continued to add fuel to the fire. As a result they have used up two thirds of the atmospheric space, depriving us of the necessary space for our development and provoking a climate crisis of huge proportions. … We are not assigning guilt, merely responsibility. As they say in the US, if you break it, you buy it. (Climate Justice Now 2009)

Are these analogies and arguments cogent? The second ('shop breakage') example in Bolivia's response is a common example of a strict liability rule. However, it is not particularly apt for thinking about climate debt, since in such cases strict liability is generally assumed only after the agent is taken to have accepted the terms and conditions of entry analogous to a contractual arrangement.

What about the first ('burning house') analogy? Should the neighbour be held responsible if they unintentionally (and excusably) allow a fire on her property to escape to a neighbouring property? Our willingness to attribute liability to bear cost in such cases will surely depend in some measure upon whether some element of fault (such as recklessness or negligence) can be identified – the more reckless or negligent the conduct, the more it seems appropriate to allocate most or all of the cost to the agent causing harm. But how should we allocate costs in the absence of any fault whatsoever?

As a matter of international law, the answer to this question is not entirely clear. In cases of transboundary pollution, states are not usually held liable for 'harm resulting from risks of which the state concerned was not and could not have been objectively aware' (Birnie, Boyle and Redgwell 2009, p. 217). While strict liability may apply to certain instances of harm from ultra-hazardous activities (Kiss and Shelton 2007), it is widely considered that state liability for climate-induced damage would require a failure of due diligence by a state to regulate greenhouse gas emissions (Faure and Nollkaemper 2007, Voigt 2008).

As a moral matter it is ordinarily preposterous to leave innocent victims to bear the entire cost of accidents that have been caused faultlessly by others.[10] If a fire is started innocently and burns down a house, we are faced with a choice of how distribute the cost of the ensuing harm between these two innocent people and uninvolved third parties (compare Vanderheiden 2011). Cost sharing between those who are causally responsible for the damage, those who suffer its damages, and third parties may be a more appropriate solution, particularly where others have much deeper pockets than the victim (Calabresi 1970). Some have argued on these grounds that the current international law of transboundary harm fails to protect adequately the victims of such harm and thus stands in need of substantial reform (Sachs 2008).

Even if excusable ignorance were to provide exemption from liability for climate debt, states may nevertheless subsequently acquire responsibility for taking on additional cost to address the harm through subsequent acts or inaction undertaken after the country acquired knowledge of the harmful effects of the earlier act. Importantly, we will attribute greater responsibility to an actor for exacerbating actions (such as adding fuel to a fire, or continuing to emit at unsustainable levels), and for failing to assist those at risk when they could do so at very low cost (Barry and Øverland 2011).

The objection from excusable ignorance would no longer apply once the risks associated with greenhouse gas emissions became widely recognized internationally. For this reason, a number of authors have proposed that liability for emissions could begin at a point such as 1990, when the first report of the Intergovernmental Panel on Climate Change was published (Vanderheiden 2008, p. 190). And it could plausibly be argued that liability should begin significantly earlier than this.[11] The argument from excusable ignorance would therefore not show that the idea of climate debt is incoherent or implausible, but only that we should in some circumstances *discount* the amount owing.

The intergenerational objection

The intergenerational objection claims that it is implausible to hold countries responsible now for conduct that was undertaken before anyone living in them was alive. Objections to the intergenerational transmission of debts have a long pedigree (Thompson 2009, p. 120). However, while individuals generally do not inherit personal debts from one generation to the next, this is not the case for sovereign debt, which can remain owed by a country over successive generations. *Pacta sunt servanda*, or 'agreements must be kept', is the basic norm that underlies the present treatment of sovereign debt contracts, so that when a sovereign borrower defaults it is treated as being in breach of contract and under obligation to repay the loan (Barry and Tomitova 2007). Unless a creditor decides to 'forgive' (or cancel) a debt, the creditor retains full rights to claim it.

There are good incentive-based reasons to uphold intergenerational responsibilities of this sort. Since intergenerational transmission of sovereign debts facilitates borrowing by boosting lenders' assurance of ultimate repayment, it is ordinarily justified as facilitating a beneficial practice. Intergenerational transmission may also be justified in the case of non-contractual international debts. Intergenerational transmission of non-contractual debts could serve a number of important functions, not least by providing incentives for countries to take a more cautious approach when engaging in activities that may pose long-term risks to the populations of other countries.

This is not to say that the transmission of debts should not in some ways be limited by consideration of the circumstances under which the debt was initially acquired. With respect to contractual sovereign debt, for example, there are precedents for the cancellation of 'odious debt' acquired by illegitimate heads of state (Khalfan, King and Thomas 2003, Shafter 2007). Non-contractual debts (such as reparative debts) may also be subject to limitation over time, for example as structures of expectation form around resources that were originally appropriated unjustly, or if the background distribution of economic and social resources among agents and victims changes (Waldron 1992).

Insofar as developed countries owe a climate debt to developing countries, it is hard to argue that such debts are odious. Indeed, the great wealth of many developed countries is in large measure dependent on their having made use of the global commons in excess of their fair share. While an uneven global pattern of emissions commenced when the Earth's ability to absorb emissions was plentiful, that capacity is now scarce, making the responsibility to account for the emissions debt of past generations correspondingly greater (compare Waldron 1992, pp. 24–25).

One could also argue that current generations should be held responsible for historical emissions because they have *benefited from* those emissions in the form of the higher standards of living produced by industrialization (Meyer and Roser 2010, p. 234). Do agents have responsibilities to service debts that were incurred by them without their knowledge? There are certainly cases in which it seems that they do. Suppose, for example, you discover that something you possess has come to you as a result of wrongdoing, and that you benefit at the expense of those to whom wrongdoing has been done. You learn that a car that your mother gave you as a gift was stolen. What are your responsibilities in this case? In the first instance it seems you have a duty to relinquish the benefits of the wrongdoing and return the property to its rightful owner.[12] But a similar principle seems to apply in cases where direct restitution – giving a discrete and wrongfully appropriate 'thing' back – is not possible.[13] The crucial point, as David Miller (2007, p. 154) points out, is 'that a claim to inherit must depend on the bequeathers having a valid title to the assets they are bequeathing'.

Some deny that there is a direct link between a unique, identifiable beneficiary and a unique, identifiable victim of unfair resource usage. However, in the case of climate change, both the benefits and costs of climate change have been transferred across generations through individuals' participation in ongoing economic structures (Shue 1999, pp. 536–537). While some developing countries have acquired some benefits (and great benefits in some cases) from industrialization (in the form of technology, physical and human capital, and public goods), it seems hard to argue that they have by and large enjoyed a fair share of them (Shue 1999, p. 534).

Identity of debtors and creditors

Proponents of climate debt generally argue that climate debt is owed by 'developed countries' towards 'developing countries' (A4; Bolivia 2009, p.46). This claim may seem to provide a broad-brush approximation of who owes debts to whom based on trends in global emissions, but it is problematic. A range of countries now reasonably argue that the categories of 'developed' and 'developing' countries as defined by the UNFCCC – which have remained largely static since its inception – may not neatly map objective differences in wealth and emissions (Depledge 2009, Pickering, Vanderheiden and Miller forthcoming). Moreover, a number of countries currently classed as developing would likely also have exceeded their fair share or will soon do so (Pan and Chen 2010, p. 20). There are also now a large number of wealthy individuals in otherwise low-income countries whose per capita emissions are comparable to average per capita emissions of wealthy countries (Chakravarty *et al.* 2009).

In order to be plausible, climate debt arguments will need to move away from a from a rigid emphasis on developed and developing countries as the only categories of analysis and identify debtors as those individuals or groups that have used more than their fair share of the Earth's emissions absorptive capacity, however fair shares are defined.

Forms of repayment

The distinction between emissions debt and adaptation debt (A5) may provide a useful way of delineating climate-related responsibilities and associated forms of repayment. The specific distinction has not been elaborated, to our knowledge, in academic literature,[14] but other authors have highlighted the distinct ethical responsibilities associated with mitigation and adaptation (Jagers and Duus-Otterström 2008, Vanderheiden 2011).

Climate debt proposals generally place strong emphasis on the idea that emissions debt should be discharged primarily by the reallocation of future emissions rights to offset past overuse. However, once we acknowledge that climate debt could be repaid in more than one currency, we could envisage the possibility of other forms of repayment, provided that they are agreed to and yield equivalent benefits for creditors (compare Caney 2009, p. 137). One alternative could be to allocate prospective emissions entitlements on an equal per capita basis, but to compensate for retrospective overuse by imposing additional responsibilities on high-emitting countries for *financing* any reductions needed in other countries to meet their per capita entitlements. Thus financing could address both the retrospective element of emissions debt as well as servicing adaptation debt.

Political analysis

Even if we accept that the idea of climate debt is coherent and morally plausible, this does not mean that it must necessarily be useful for informing climate negotiations. In this section we provide a political analysis of climate debt arguments, and conclude that that their future political value is likely to be quite minimal.

Measurement problems

When compared with harms to poorer countries resulting from other historical acts (such as slavery and colonialism), the prospect of quantifying responsibilities for climate-related harms seems at first glance to be much easier. However, while relatively sound country-level emissions data is available for recent decades, its coverage becomes progressively limited for decades preceding 1990, and there are a number of other methodological choices that add further complexity to the accounting task (Posner and Weisbach 2010, Höhne *et al.* 2011). As noted above, since the idea of climate debt itself does not necessarily imply debt for all historical emissions, this is not a decisive objection to the application of the concept. However, it does suggest that those arguing in favour of an expansive notion of liability for historical emissions should take into account the very real problems of quantifying pre-1990 emissions, as well as the ethical complexity – for reasons rehearsed above – of allocating responsibility for such emissions. If problems of quantification proved insuperable, there may be other ways of taking a broader notion of historical responsibility into consideration. For example, it could shift the burden of proof onto developed countries to demonstrate why they should not take on a greater share of the costs of adaptation and mitigation than they otherwise would on the basis of their current emissions alone (compare Barry 2005). The problem, however, is that unless reasonably accurate estimates of climate debt can be produced, assertions of climate debt are likely to be interpreted more as aggrieved political rhetoric than as considered policy proposals. As such, these arguments are more likely to undermine reflective deliberation than to foster it, and consequently reduce the prospects for binding agreements on climate-related responsibilities.

Rhetorical emphasis

Climate debt represents one of several possible frames for characterizing the responsibilities to address climate change outlined so far in our article. Identifying frames that resonate with others is an important component in the emergence of norms of international cooperation (Finnemore and Sikkink 1998). However, frames may serve a broader range of political purposes by virtue of their rhetorical emphasis. In a related context John Dryzek (2010) usefully distinguishes between 'bonding rhetoric', which aims to motivate people who are already similarly disposed, and 'bridging rhetoric' that aims to reach (and persuade) an audience whose dispositions are different. Both forms of rhetoric, Dryzek (2010, pp. 330–332) points out, can have value and can play an important role in public deliberation about political issues. Bridging rhetoric is frequently preferable as a means of facilitating reflective deliberation and cooperation. However, bonding rhetoric can help to mobilize dispossessed groups and bring wider public attention to their political concerns. Just which form of rhetoric is of greatest value depends highly on context, and it is also actor-specific: reflective public deliberation may be best promoted overall if some actors employ bonding rhetoric while others employ bridging rhetoric.

Climate debt is best characterized as a form of bonding rhetoric. It is notable for its adversarial emphasis on dividing the world into debtors and creditors, where the former group is comprised of poorer countries and the latter group richer countries. In this sense, the rhetoric of climate debt is consistent with and expressive of the oppositional tactics used by some of its main advocates, the Latin American ALBA group.[15] At first glimpse the rhetoric of climate debt may seem to exemplify the commonly observed technique of seeking to establish a new norm by grafting it onto an existing one (namely the obligation to repay conventional debts; compare Finnemore and Sikkink 1998, p. 908). However, the appeal of the idea to constituencies in developing countries and international advocacy communities arguably derives more from the fact that it inverts the prevailing narrative according to which poorer countries are economically indebted to wealthy ones (compare Simms 2009, p.13).

Regardless of its value as a bonding mechanism, it could be argued that the adversarial approach implied by climate debt has significant value for the broader system of climate governance by holding richer countries to account. Indeed the use of climate debt has likely helped to attract attention to the concerns of countries and civil society groups that typically have little influence in climate negotiations. However, given the nature of the collective action problem involved in addressing climate change, a multilateral framework freely accepted by a consensus or near-consensus of the 195 parties to the UNFCCC is required to address climate change effectively. Overcoming the mistrust that has plagued climate negotiations since their inception will require serious efforts on the part of both developed and developing countries to adopt mutually acceptable frames for collective action. In this context, bridging rhetoric has a greater prospect of facilitating a meaningful and reasonably fair agreement. The bonding rhetoric of climate debt may at best serve to challenge the intransigence of countries that have failed so far to take sufficiently strong action to curb climate change. But it is highly unlikely to provide the foundation for a specific policy framework for allocating responsibilities among countries. At worst the idea of climate debt may be perceived therefore as a mere slogan, in the process tarring the idea of climate justice (which is frequently also voiced by the same actors) with the same brush. Understandably then, many developing countries (including highly vulnerable small island states) have themselves eschewed the rhetoric of climate debt in favour of other strategies for boosting collective responsibilities to address climate change.

Furthermore, as Stern's statement suggests, many developed countries link the idea of debt with that of reparations, which bears associations with uncomfortable and politically contentious issues such as reparations for slavery and colonial injustices. If the climate debt arguments are sound, then the fact that some countries associate it with other notions of obligation that they reject does not of course justify discarding the concept. But it may make it less feasible to employ this concept in support of a meaningful and reasonably fair agreement on climate-related responsibilities.

Addressing the problem of climate change requires not only taking account of past patterns of emissions, but also working out a fair distribution of rights and responsibilities for the future (Vanderheiden 2011). Developing countries' emissions are growing rapidly, and will eventually exceed those of developed countries even in cumulative terms. Thus some countries that were previous creditors may ultimately become debtors, and vice versa (Botzen, Gowdy and Van Den Bergh 2008). The idea of climate debt is capable in principle of representing future as well as present liabilities, and it does not seem to be inherently incompatible with incorporating distributional considerations (including a country's capacity to pay) as well. Nevertheless, use of the term as a frame for characterizing climate-related responsibilities poses the risk of overemphasizing retrospective liability at the expense of future distributive concerns.

These objections to climate debt as a rhetorical frame are by no means decisive, but they do give us good reason to explore other formulations that could provide a more constructive approach – emphasizing bridging over bonding rhetoric – to framing and distributing responsibilities in a morally defensible manner. Considerations of space preclude a detailed discussion of alternatives, but we note one example briefly. The concept of a global 'carbon budget' is being used increasingly in scientific and policy analysis for quantifying the maximum level of cumulative global emissions that is permissible over time to avoid dangerous climate change.[16] The concept of a carbon budget may encompass both forward-looking and backward-looking considerations. As such, while the carbon budget concept is compatible with recognition of the existence of climate debt, the former does not depend on positing the latter. Although some of the terminology associated with a budget may appear similar to that of climate debt (e.g. some countries' budgets may be in 'deficit' while others are in 'surplus'), the carbon budget idea does not highlight a divisive two-way relationship between debtors and creditors. Instead, it suggests that all countries participate in a broader common (though of course contentious) enterprise of 'balancing the budget'.

Conclusion

In this essay we have argued that climate debt is a coherent idea that can potentially be used to express a plausible account of moral responsibilities related to climate change provided that its scope is clearly circumscribed. We have also argued, however, that climate debt has at best a limited role to play in negotiations, and that other frames are likely to present more promising means for promoting a reasonably fair distribution of climate change related responsibilities. Given the mistrust among parties currently impeding effective coordinated action on climate change, parties concerned about climate justice may be more likely to present a workable basis for advancing this aim by proposing frames that seek to bridge rather than exacerbate existing divides.

The example of climate debt may yield broader implications for the relationship between theory and policy. The rhetorical elements that accompany the use of certain normative concepts can impact significantly the degree to which arguments invoking them will foster more reflective public deliberation and help resolve collective action problems. For this reason, even if we find that a normative concept may have some plausibility in theory, we need to assess at the very least its feasibility and rhetorical implications before assuming it has merit as a specific device for advancing global justice.

Acknowledgements

Earlier versions of this essay were presented to the Marie Curie Training Course on the Human Dimension of Global Environmental Change (Berlin 2010), the workshop on Climate Change and Philosophy at the Victoria University of Wellington, and the Ethics and International Public Policy Reading Group at the Australian National University. The authors would like to thank participants in those seminars for their valuable feedback, and Christian Baatz, Garrett Cullity, Simon Keller, Holly Lawford-Smith and Hayley Stevenson for helpful advice and comments. We are particularly grateful for extensive written comments on an earlier draft provided by Lucas Kengmana, Terry Macdonald, Miriam Ronzoni, and an anonymous referee. Christian Barry acknowledges support from the Australian Research Council (DP110100175 'Benefitting from Injustice').

Notes

1. Emphasizing the ethical aspects of a particular problem may itself represent a political strategy – as in the case of successful efforts by activists to reframe debt relief for developing countries as a moral and religious issue rather than as a purely economic concern (Roberts and Parks 2007, p. 240) – but this is consistent with the distinction between forms of analysis drawn here.
2. Carbon being a component of major greenhouse gases emitted through human activity (including carbon dioxide and methane).
3. See e.g. Hayward (2006), Page (2007). Simms (2009) uses ecological debt in a narrow sense to refer primarily to climate debt.
4. Of course the idea of international climate debt has an intergenerational element, since responsibilities are being attributed to the present populations of developed countries for 'debts' acquired largely by their ancestors.
5. This distinction has been highlighted in Bolivia (2009) and Climate-Justice. Info (2010).
6. While noting some complexities about the precise categorization of parties to the UNFCCC, for simplicity we will generally use 'developed' countries to refer to parties listed in Annex I of the UNFCCC, and 'developing' countries to refer to non-Annex I parties.
7. Samuelsohn (2009); see also Walsh (2009).
8. Compare also Shue (1999, p. 535) and Vanderheiden (2008, p. 174).
9. This argument is generally extended both to emissions of previous generations and emissions of the present generation before the point at which excusable ignorance no longer applied.

10. Not always, because it may well be plausible to allocate costs in this way if the agent who has suffered the damage has very deep pockets and those who non-culpably caused it has very shallow ones.
11. In morality (if not always in law), the recognition that one's conduct may carry risk of doing severe harm gives one a relatively stringent (though of course defeasible) reason not to engage in it until its effects are further understood, and to compensate victims in case these risks ripen into injuries (Cranor 1990, Barry 2005).
12. It does not seem important that the person making the bequest was your mother – your duty to disgorge the benefit would hold even if it were given to you by a stranger. Nor does it seem to matter whether your mother knew or should have known of these abuses. What matters in the first instance is that you have been unjustly enriched (see, e.g. Birks 2003, Smith 1997).
13. If you discover, for example, that your father's bequest to you upon his death is the result of profits from a mining company that he owns whose extraction practices inflict serious human rights violations on its workers, you should disgorge this benefit. And you should redistribute these gains to those who have been disadvantaged by the wrongdoing that was materially involved in producing them insofar as this is possible (cf. Goodin and Barry 2011).
14. Although Neumayer (2000, p. 186) has proposed a formula for quantifying countries' 'Historical Emission Debt'.
15. ALBA translates in full as 'Bolivarian Alliance for the Peoples of Our America'. The main countries negotiating as part of the group in UNFCCC negotiations are Venezuela, Bolivia, Cuba, Ecuador and Nicaragua (Stevenson 2011, p. 8).
16. See for example Allen *et al.* (2009), TERI (2009), WBGU (2009). Another possible frame referred to above is the idea of 'ecological space' (or similar terms such as 'atmospheric space' or 'development space').

Notes on contributors

Jonathan Pickering is a PhD candidate in philosophy in the Research School of the Social Sciences, Australian National University.

Christian Barry is the Director of the Centre for Moral, Social, and Political Theory in the Research School of the Social Sciences, Australian National University.

References

Allen, M.R., *et al.*, 2009. Warming caused by cumulative carbon emissions towards the trillionth tonne. *Nature*, 458, 1163–1166.

Barry, C., 2005. Applying the contribution principle. *Metaphilosophy*, 36 (1–2), 210–227.

Barry, C. and Øverland, G., 2011. On the implications of failing to assist. Unpublished manuscript.

Barry, C. and Tomitova, L., 2007. Fairness in sovereign debt. *Ethics & international affairs*, 21 (S1), 41–79.

Birks, P., 2003. *Unjust enrichment*. Oxford: Oxford University Press.

Birnie, P., Boyle, A., and Redgwell, C., 2009. *International law and the environment*. 3rd ed. Oxford: Oxford University Press.

Bolivia, 2009. Commitments for Annex I parties under paragraph 1(b)(i) of the Bali Action Plan: evaluating developed countries' historical climate debt to developing countries, 25 April. Bonn: UNFCCC, 44–51.

Botzen, W.J.W., Gowdy, J.M., and Van Den Bergh, J.C.J.M., 2008. Cumulative CO_2 emissions: shifting international responsibilities for climate debt. *Climate policy*, 8 (6), 569–576.
Bovens, L., 2011. A Lockean defense of grandfathering emission rights. *In*: D.G. Arnold, ed. *The ethics of global climate change*. Cambridge: Cambridge University Press, 124–144.
Calabresi, G., 1970. *The cost of accidents: a legal and economic analysis*. New Haven, CT: Yale University Press.
Caney, S., 2006. Cosmopolitan justice, rights and global climate change. *Canadian journal of law and jurisprudence*, 19 (2), 255–278.
Caney, S., 2009. Justice and the distribution of greenhouse gas emissions. *Journal of global ethics*, 5 (2), 125–146.
Caney, S., 2010. Climate change, human rights and moral thresholds. *In*: S. Humphreys, ed. *Human rights and climate change*. Cambridge: Cambridge University Press, 69–90.
Chakravarty, S. *et al.*, 2009. Sharing global CO_2 emission reductions among one billion high emitters. *Proceedings of the National Academy of Sciences USA*, 106, 11884–11888.
Climate Justice Info, 2010. *World people's conference on climate change and the rights of Mother Earth, Cochabamba, Bolivia (19–20 April 2010): Outcome on climate debt* [online]. http://climate-justice.info/2010/04/world-peoples-conference-outcome-on-climate-debt/ [Accessed 8 October 2012].
Climate Justice Now, 2009. *Bolivia responds to U.S. On climate debt: 'If you break it, you buy it'* [online]. http://www.climate-justice-now.org/bolivia-responds-to-us-on-climate-debt-if-you-break-it-you-buy-it/ [Accessed 8 October 2012].
Cranor, C., 1990. Some moral issues in risk assessment. *Ethics*, 101 (1), 123–143.
Depledge, J., 2009. The road less travelled: difficulties in moving between annexes in the climate change regime. *Climate policy*, 9, 273–287.
Dryzek, J.S., 2010. Rhetoric in democracy: a systemic appreciation. *Political theory*, 38 (3), 319–339.
Faure, M.G. and Nollkaemper, A., 2007. International liability as an instrument to prevent and compensate for climate change. *Stanford journal of international law*, 43, 123–179.
Finnemore, M. and Sikkink, K., 1998. International norm dynamics and political change. *International organization*, 52 (4), 887–917.
Fischer, F., 2003. *Reframing public policy*. Oxford: Oxford University Press.
Gardiner, S.M., 2001. The real tragedy of the commons. *Philosophy & public affairs*, 30 (4), 387–416.
Goodin, R.E. and Barry, C., 2011. Benefitting from other people's wrongdoing. Unpublished working paper.
Hardin, G., 1968. The tragedy of the commons. *Science*, 162 (3859), 1243–1248.
Hayward, T., 2006. Global justice and the distribution of natural resources. *Political studies*, 54 (2), 349–369.
Hayward, T., 2007. Human rights versus emissions rights: climate justice and the equitable distribution of ecological space. *Ethics & international affairs*, 21 (4), 431–450.
Höhne, N. *et al.*, 2011. Contributions of individual countries' emissions to climate change and their uncertainty. *Climatic change*, 106 (3), 359–391.
Jagers, S.C. and Duus-Otterström, G., 2008. Dual climate change responsibility: on moral divergences between mitigation and adaptation. *Environmental politics*, 17 (4), 576–591.

Khalfan, A., King, J., and Thomas, B., 2003. *Advancing the odious debt doctrine.* Centre for International Sustainable Development Law working paper. Montreal: McGill University.

Kiss, A. and Shelton, D.L., 2007. Strict liability in international environmental law. *In*: T.M. Ndiaye and R. Wolfrum, eds. *Law of the sea, environmental law and settlement of disputes: liber amicorum Judge Thomas A. Mensah*. Leiden: Brill Academic Publishers, 1131–1151.

Klein, N., 2009. Climate rage. *Rolling Stone*. 11 November.

Locke, J., 1988 [1690]. *Two treatises of government*. Cambridge: Cambridge University Press.

Martinez-Alier, J., 1993. Distributional obstacles to international environmental policy: the failures at Rio and prospects after Rio. *Environmental values*, 2, 97–124.

Martinez-Alier, J., 2002. *The environmentalism of the poor: a study of ecological conflicts and valuation*. Cheltenham; Northhampton, MA: Edward Elgar.

Meyer, L.H. and Roser, D., 2010. Climate justice and historical emissions. *Critical review of international social and political philosophy*, 13 (1), 229–253.

Miller, D., 2007. *National responsibility and global justice*. Oxford: Oxford University Press.

Neumayer, E., 2000. In defence of historical accountability for greenhouse gas emissions. *Ecological economics*, 33 (2), 185–192.

Nisbet, M.C., 2009. Communicating climate change: why frames matter for public engagement. *Environment: science and policy for sustainable development*, 51 (2), 12–23.

Nordhaus, W.D., 1994. *Managing the global commons: the economics of climate change*. Cambridge, MA: MIT Press.

Ostrom, E., 1990. *Governing the commons: the evolution of institutions for collective action*. Cambridge; New York: Cambridge University Press.

Page, E.A., 2007. Intergenerational justice of what: welfare, resources or capabilities? *Environmental politics*, 16 (3), 453–469.

Pan, J. and Chen, Y., 2010. Carbon budget proposal: a framework for an equitable and sustainable international climate regime. *Social sciences in China*, 31 (1), 5–34.

Pickering, J., Vanderheiden, S., and Miller, S., Forthcoming. "If equity's in, we're out": scope for fairness in the next global climate agreement. *Ethics and International Affairs*.

Posner, E.A. and Weisbach, D., 2010. *Climate change justice*. Princeton, NJ: Princeton University Press.

Roberts, J.T. and Parks, B.C., 2007. *A climate of injustice. global inequality, north–south politics, and climate policy*. Cambridge, MA: MIT Press.

Sachs, N., 2008. Beyond the liability wall: strengthening tort remedies in international environmental law. *UCLA law review*, 55 (4), 837–904.

Samuelsohn, D., 2009. No 'pass' for developing countries in next climate treaty, says U.S. envoy. *New York Times*, 9 December.

Shafter, J., 2007. The due diligence model: a new approach to the problem of odious debts. *Ethics & international affairs*, 20 (1), 49–67.

Shue, H., 1999. Global environment and international inequality. *International affairs*, 75 (3), 531–545.

Simms, A., 2009. *Ecological debt: global warming and the wealth of nations*. 2nd ed. London: Pluto Press.

Singer, P., 2002. *One world: the ethics of globalisation*. Melbourne: Text.

Smith, K.R., 1991. Allocating responsibility for global warming: the natural debt index. *Ambio*, 20 (2), 95–96.

Smith, L.D., 1997. *The law of tracing*. Oxford: Clarendon Press.

Srinivasan, U.T., *et al.*, 2008. The debt of nations and the distribution of ecological impacts from human activities. *Proceedings of the National Academy of Sciences USA*, 105 (5), 1768–1773.

Stevenson, H., 2011. *Representing 'the peoples'? Post-neoliberal states in the international climate negotiations* [online]. Working Paper 2011/1. Canberra: Centre for Deliberative Democracy and Global Governance, The Australian National University. Available from: http://deliberativedemocracy.anu.edu.au/sites/default/files/documents/working_papers/STEVENSON%20Hayley%202011-1.pdf [Accessed 8 October 2012].

TERI, 2009. *Right to sustainable development: an ethical approach to climate change*. New Delhi: The Energy and Resources Institute (TERI).

Thompson, J., 2009. *Intergenerational justice. rights and responsibilities in an intergenerational polity*. New York: Routledge.

Vanderheiden, S., 2008. *Atmospheric justice. a political theory of climate change*. New York: Oxford University Press.

Vanderheiden, S., 2011. Globalizing responsibility for climate change. *Ethics & international affairs*, 25 (1), 65–84.

Voigt, C., 2008. State responsibility for climate change damages. *Nordic journal of international law*, 77 (1–2), 1–22.

Waldron, J., 1992. Superseding historic injustice. *Ethics*, 103 (1), 4–28.

Walsh, B., 2009. Do rich nations owe poor ones a climate debt? *Time*, 10 December.

WBGU, 2009. *Solving the climate dilemma: the budget approach* [online]. Berlin: German Advisory Council on Global Change (WBGU). Available from: http://www.wbgu.de/en/special-reports/sr-2009-budget-approach/ [Accessed 8 October 2012].

World Bank, 2010. *Development and climate change* [online]. World Development Report 2010. Washington, DC: World Bank. Available from: http://siteresources.worldbank.org/INTWDR2010/Resources/5287678-1226014527953/WDR10-Full-Text.pdf [Accessed 8 October 2012].

Index

Page numbers followed by 'n' refer to notes